Windows Vista™

maranGraphics®

&

THOMSON

COURSE TECHNOLOGY

Professional ■ Technical ■ Reference

MARAN ILLUSTRATED™ Windows Vista™

Distributed in the U.S. and Canada by Thomson Course Technology PTR. For enquiries about Maran Illustrated™ books outside the U.S. and Canada, please contact maranGraphics at international@maran.com

For U.S. orders and customer service, please contact Thomson Course Technology at 1-800-354-9706. For Canadian orders, please contact Thomson Course Technology at 1-800-268-2222 or 416-752-9448.

ISBN-13: 978-1-59863-319-1
ISBN-10: 1-59863-319-8

Library of Congress Catalog Card Number: 2006908262

Printed in the United States of America

06 07 08 09 10 BU 10 9 8 7 6 5 4 3 2 1

APR 11 2007

Trademarks

maranGraphics is a registered trademark of maranGraphics Inc. Maran Illustrated, the Maran Illustrated logos and any trade dress related to or associated with the contents or cover of this book are trademarks of maranGraphics Inc. and may not be used without written permission.

The Thomson Course Technology PTR logo is a trademark of Course Technology and may not be used without written permission.

Windows Vista is a trademark of Microsoft Corporation.

All other trademarks are the property of their respective owners.

Important

maranGraphics and Thomson Course Technology PTR have attempted throughout this book to distinguish proprietary trademarks by following the capitalization style used by the source. However, we cannot attest to the accuracy of the style, and the use of a word or term in this book is not intended to affect the validity of any trademark.

Permissions

CBS SportsLine: Copyright © 2006-2007 SportsLine USA, Inc., http://www.sportsline.com All rights reserved. **Golf:** Copyright © 2006-2007, golf.com LLC. **Smithsonian Institution:** Copyright © 2006-2007 Smithsonian Institution. **Wal-Mart:** Copyright © 2006-2007 Wal-Mart Stores, Inc., **MSN.com:** Copyright © 2006-2007 Microsoft Corporation. All rights reserved. **YAHOO!:** Text and artwork copyright © 2006-2007 by Yahoo! Inc. All rights reserved. YAHOO! and the YAHOO! logo are trademarks of YAHOO!, Inc. **Other Permissions Granted:** Discovery Channel Online, Google, and Sunkist.

THOMSON
COURSE TECHNOLOGY
Professional ■ Technical ■ Reference

Thomson Course Technology PTR, a division of Thomson Course Technology
25 Thomson Place ■ Boston, MA 02210 ■ http://www.courseptr.com

Copies

Educational facilities, companies, and organizations located in the U.S. and Canada that are interested in multiple copies of this book should contact Thomson Course Technology PTR for quantity discount information. Training manuals, CD-ROMs, and portions of this book are also available individually or can be tailored for specific needs.

maranGraphics®

maranGraphics Inc.
5755 Coopers Avenue
Mississauga, Ontario
L4Z 1R9
www.maran.com

maranGraphics is a family-run business.

At **maranGraphics**, we believe in producing great books—one book at a time.

Each maranGraphics book uses the award-winning communication process that we have been developing over the last 30 years. Using this process, we organize screen shots, text and illustrations in a way that makes it easy for you to learn new concepts and tasks.

We spend hours deciding the best way to perform each task, so you don't have to! Our clear, easy-to-follow screen shots and instructions walk you through each task from beginning to end.

We want to thank you for purchasing what we feel are the best books money can buy. We hope you enjoy using this book as much as we enjoyed creating it!

Sincerely,

The Maran Family

We would love to hear from you! Send your comments and feedback about our books to family@maran.com

To sign up for sneak peeks and news about our upcoming books, send an e-mail to newbooks@maran.com

Please visit us on the Web at:
www.maran.com

CREDITS

Authors:
Ruth Maran
Kelleigh Johnson

**Technical Consultant
& Post Production:**
Robert Maran

Project Manager:
Judy Maran-Tarnowski

Editor:
Dana Grimaldi

Layout Design & Illustrations:
Mark Porter
Sam Lee
Sarah Kim

Indexer:
Kelleigh Johnson

**Publisher and General Manager,
Thomson Course Technology PTR:**
Stacy L. Hiquet

**Associate Director of Marketing,
Thomson Course Technology PTR:**
Sarah O'Donnell

**Manager of Editorial Services,
Thomson Course Technology PTR:**
Heather Talbot

ACKNOWLEDGMENTS

Thanks to the dedicated staff of maranGraphics, including
Dana Grimaldi, Kelleigh Johnson, Sam Lee, Jill Maran Dutfield,
Judy Maran-Tarnowski, Robert Maran, Ruth Maran and Mark Porter.

Finally, to Richard Maran who originated the easy-to-use graphic
format of this guide. Thank you for your inspiration and guidance.

TABLE OF CONTENTS

Chapter 1

WINDOWS BASICS

Chapter 2

WORKING WITH FILES

Chapter 3

Chapter 4

Chapter 5

TABLE OF CONTENTS

Chapter 6

CREATE MOVIES

Chapter 7

USING WINDOWS MEDIA CENTER

Chapter 8

CUSTOMIZE WINDOWS

Chapter 9

SHARE YOUR COMPUTER

Chapter 10

BROWSE THE WEB

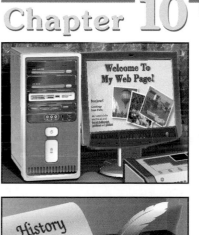

TABLE OF CONTENTS

Chapter 11

EXCHANGE E-MAIL

Chapter 12

WORK ON A NETWORK

Chapter 13

OPTIMIZE COMPUTER PERFORMANCE

Chapter 14

GET HELP AND FIX PROBLEMS

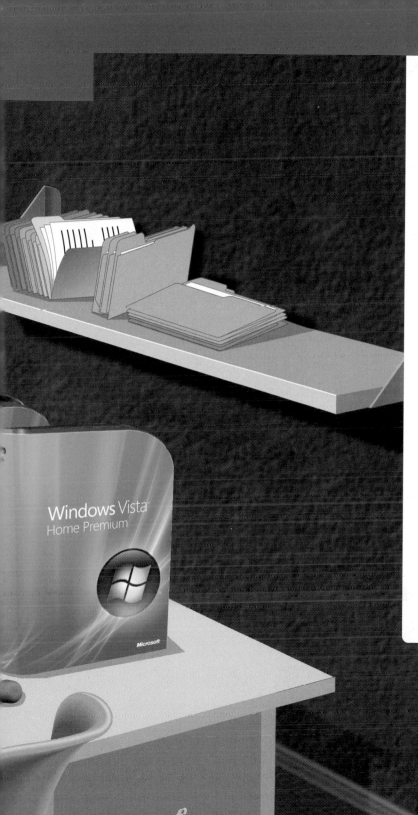

Windows Basics

INTRODUCTION TO WINDOWS

Microsoft® Windows Vista™ is a program that controls the overall activity of your computer.

Windows Vista is available in several different editions. The Windows Vista edition installed on your computer determines the programs and features available to you.

Windows Vista provides visual effects, such as see-through windows and animations, known as Windows Aero. Your computer must meet certain hardware requirements and run the Windows Home Premium, Business, Enterprise or Ultimate edition to experience Windows Aero.

WINDOWS VISTA EDITIONS

Windows Vista Home Editions

Windows Vista is available in two editions for the typical home computer user—Home Basic and Home Premium. The Home Basic edition allows you to perform basic computer tasks, such as working with documents and browsing the Web. The Home Premium edition also lets you perform everyday tasks, including working with photos and videos and playing games.

Windows Vista Business Editions

Windows Vista is available in two editions designed for business computer users—Business and Enterprise. These editions have robust security and networking features, but do not include some of the multimedia and entertainment features of the Home Premium edition. While the Business edition can meet the needs of small and large businesses, the Enterprise edition is better suited to complex, worldwide organizations.

Windows Vista Ultimate Edition

Windows Vista Ultimate edition contains all the features and programs of both the Home Premium and Business editions. Windows Vista Ultimate edition is ideal for computer users who want to be able to use their computer for both work and play.

WINDOWS VISTA FEATURES

Work with Documents, Pictures, Sounds and Videos

Windows lets you open, print, delete and search for files, organize and play sound and video files and copy songs from your computer to an MP3 player. You can also transfer pictures from a digital camera and transfer home movies from a video camera to your computer.

Customize and Optimize Windows

Windows offers many ways that you can customize your computer to suit your preferences. You can also use the many tools that Windows provides to optimize your computer's performance.

Keep Your Computer Secure

Windows provides security features to help protect your computer, such as firewall software to prevent unauthorized people or unwanted programs from accessing your computer through the Internet or a network. Windows also comes with an antispyware program which actively protects your computer from potentially harmful programs which can collect information about you or change your computer's settings.

Share Your Computer

If you share your computer with other people, you can create user accounts to keep the personal files and settings for each person separate. You can assign a password to each user account and easily share files with other users.

Work on a Network

Windows allows you to share information and equipment, such as a printer, with other people on a network. Windows allows you to access a wired network as well as a wireless network, which allows computers to communicate without using cables.

Access the Internet

Windows allows you to browse through the information on the Web and search for Web pages of interest. You can also use Windows to exchange electronic mail with people around the world.

USING THE START MENU

You can use the Start menu to start programs, open files, change computer settings, get help with Windows and more.

The programs available on the Start menu depend on the software installed on your computer.

USING THE START MENU

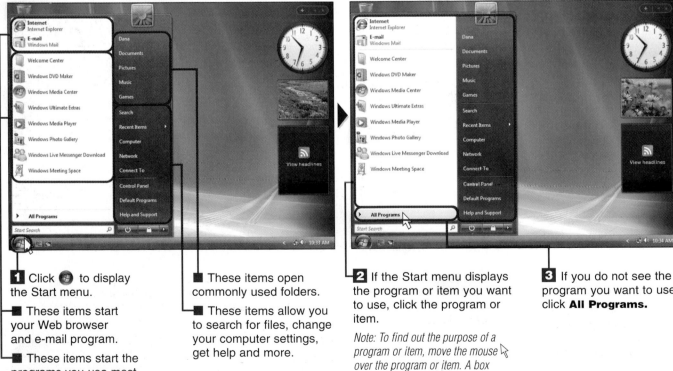

1 Click 🟦 to display the Start menu.

■ These items start your Web browser and e-mail program.

■ These items start the programs you use most frequently.

■ These items open commonly used folders.

■ These items allow you to search for files, change your computer settings, get help and more.

2 If the Start menu displays the program or item you want to use, click the program or item.

Note: To find out the purpose of a program or item, move the mouse over the program or item. A box appears, displaying a description of the program or item.

3 If you do not see the program you want to use, click **All Programs.**

Tip

Which programs does Windows provide?

Windows comes with many useful programs. Here are some examples.

Internet Explorer Browse through information on the Web.	**Windows Movie Maker** Make your own movies.
Windows Mail Send and receive e-mail messages.	**Windows Calendar** Manage your appointments and tasks.
Windows Media Player Play music, videos, CDs and DVDs.	**Windows DVD Maker** Make DVDs that include photos and videos from your computer.
Windows Photo Gallery View, edit and manage your photos and videos.	**Windows Fax and Scan** Send and receive faxes and scan documents.

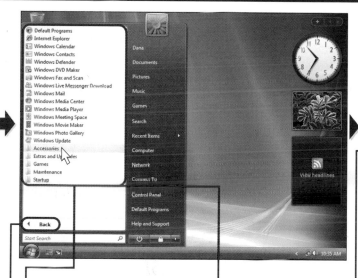

■ A list of the programs on your computer appears.

■ If you want to once again display the programs listed when you first opened the Start menu, click **Back**.

4 Click the program you want to use or click a folder ( ) to display its contents.

Note: To close the Start menu without selecting a program, click outside the menu.

■ If you selected a folder in step **4**, a list of the programs in the folder appears.

5 Click the program you want to use.

Note: You may need to click another folder ( ) before you can select the program you want to use.

■ The program opens. In this example, the Calculator program opens.

6 When you finish working with the program, click to close the program.

SCROLL THROUGH A WINDOW

You can use a scroll bar to browse through the information in a window. Scrolling is useful when a window is not large enough to display all the information it contains.

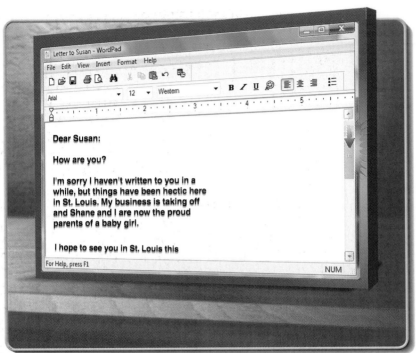

If your mouse has a wheel, you can use the wheel to scroll through a window. To scroll down, roll the wheel toward you. To scroll up, roll the wheel away from you.

SCROLL THROUGH A WINDOW

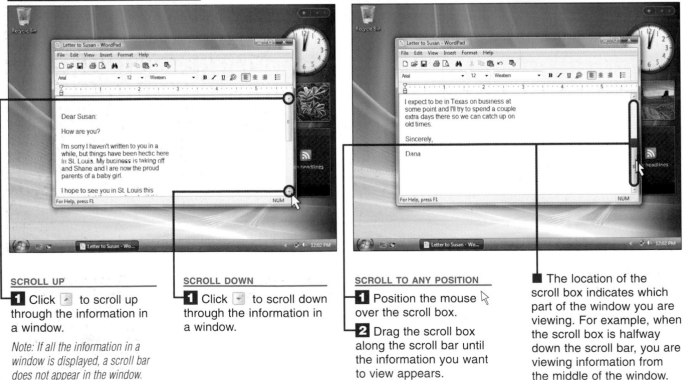

SCROLL UP

1 Click ▲ to scroll up through the information in a window.

Note: If all the information in a window is displayed, a scroll bar does not appear in the window.

SCROLL DOWN

1 Click ▼ to scroll down through the information in a window.

SCROLL TO ANY POSITION

1 Position the mouse over the scroll box.

2 Drag the scroll box along the scroll bar until the information you want to view appears.

■ The location of the scroll box indicates which part of the window you are viewing. For example, when the scroll box is halfway down the scroll bar, you are viewing information from the middle of the window.

CLOSE A WINDOW

When you finish working with a window, you can close the window to remove it from your screen.

CLOSE A WINDOW

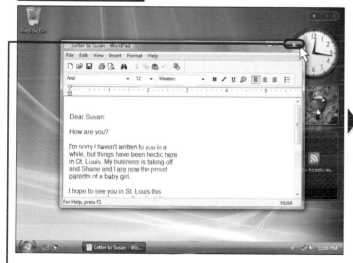 

1 Click ☒ in the window you want to close.

■ The window disappears from your screen.

■ The button for the window disappears from the taskbar.

Note: If you close a document without saving your changes, a message will appear, allowing you to save your changes.

MOVE A WINDOW

If a window covers items on your screen, you can move the window to a different location.

You may also want to move windows so you can see the contents of multiple windows at once.

MOVE A WINDOW

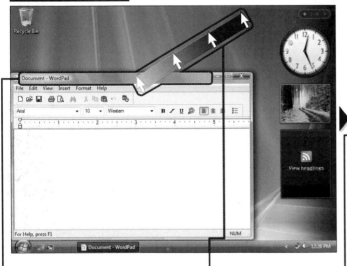

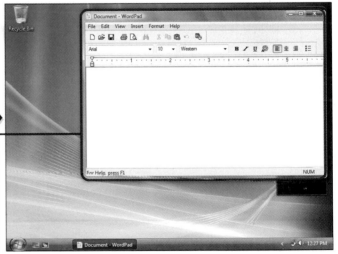

1 Position the mouse Ⓡ over the title bar of the window you want to move.

2 Drag the mouse Ⓡ to where you want to place the window.

■ The window moves to the new location.

Note: You cannot move a maximized window. For information on maximizing a window, see page 22.

You can easily change the size of a window displayed on your screen.

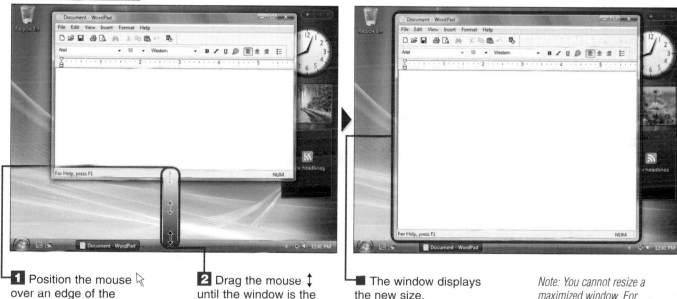

Increasing the size of a window allows you to view more information in the window. Decreasing the size of a window allows you to view items covered by the window.

RESIZE A WINDOW

1 Position the mouse ⊠ over an edge of the window you want to resize (⊠ changes to ↕, ↔, ↖ or ↗).

2 Drag the mouse ↕ until the window is the size you want.

▪ The window displays the new size.

Note: You cannot resize a maximized window. For information on maximizing a window, see page 22.

MAXIMIZE A WINDOW

You can maximize a
window to fill your
entire screen. This
allows you to view
more of the window's
contents.

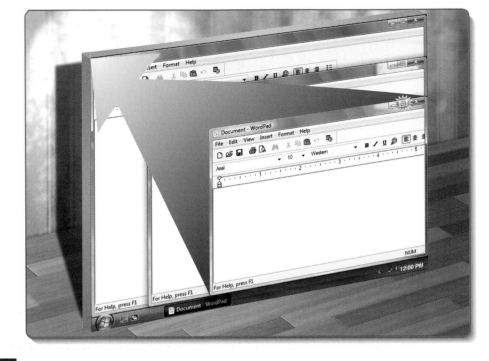

MAXIMIZE A WINDOW

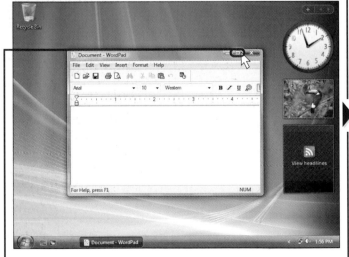

1 Click 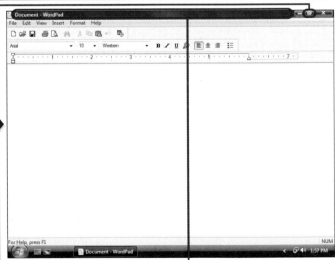 in the window
you want to maximize.

■ The window fills your
entire screen.

■ To return the window to
its previous size, click 🗗.

■ You can also double-click
the title bar of a window to
maximize the window.

MINIMIZE A WINDOW

If you are not using a window, you can minimize the window to temporarily remove it from your screen. You can redisplay the window at any time.

Minimizing a window allows you to temporarily put a window aside so you can work on other tasks.

MINIMIZE A WINDOW

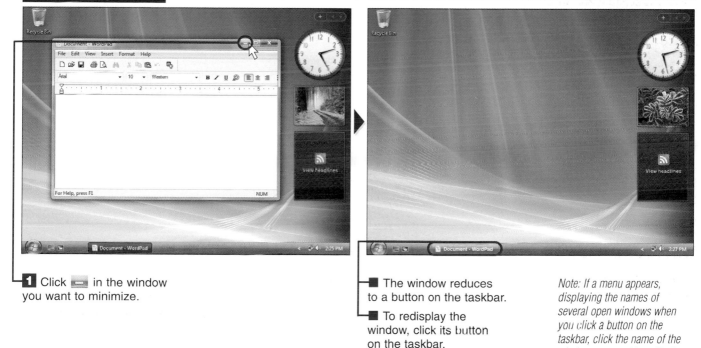

1 Click 🗕 in the window you want to minimize.

■ The window reduces to a button on the taskbar.

■ To redisplay the window, click its button on the taskbar.

Note: If a menu appears, displaying the names of several open windows when you click a button on the taskbar, click the name of the window you want to redisplay.

SWITCH BETWEEN WINDOWS

If you have more than one window open on your screen, you can easily switch between the windows.

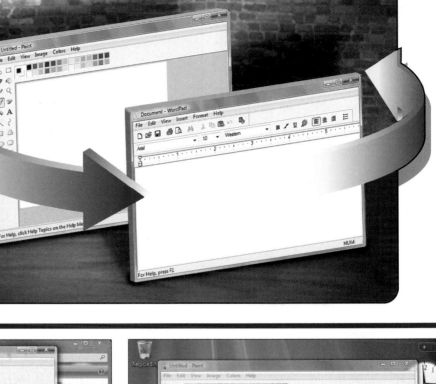

Each window is like a separate piece of paper. Switching between windows is like placing a different piece of paper at the top of the pile.

USING THE TASKBAR

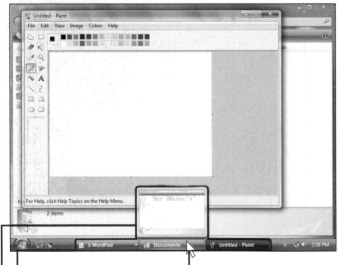

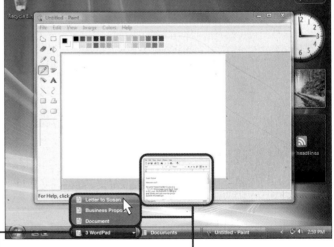

■ The taskbar displays a button for each open window.

1 When you position the mouse ⟑ over a button, a miniature version of the window appears.

2 To display the window you want to work with, click its button on the taskbar.

■ The window will appear in front of all other windows so you can clearly view the contents of the window.

Note: You can also click anywhere inside a window to display the window in front of all other windows.

MANY OPEN WINDOWS

■ If you have many windows open, all the buttons for a program may appear as a single button on the taskbar.

1 When you click the button on the taskbar, a menu will appear, displaying the name of each open window in the program.

2 When you position the mouse ⟑ over the name of a window, a miniature version of the window appears.

3 To display a window, click the name of the window.

Tip

Why can't I perform some of the tasks below to switch between windows?

You cannot use the taskbar to view miniature versions of your open windows or use the Flip 3D feature if your computer does not meet certain hardware requirements or you are using the Windows Vista Home Basic edition of Windows.

Tip

Is there another way to switch between windows?

Yes. To switch between windows, press and hold down the `Alt` key and then press the `Tab` key. A box appears, displaying each open window. Still holding down the `Alt` key, press the `Tab` key until the window you want to work with is highlighted. Then release the `Alt` key. This method is especially useful if you cannot use the Flip 3D feature to flip through your open windows.

USING FLIP 3D

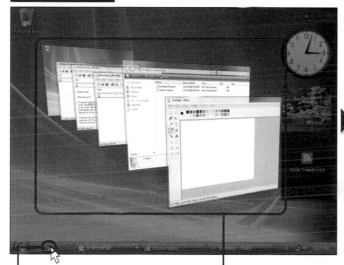

1 Click 🔲 to view all the windows you have open in a three-dimensional stack.

■ Each window you have open will appear in a three-dimensional stack on your screen.

2 To quickly flip through the open windows, press the `Tab` key or roll the wheel on your mouse.

3 When the window you want to work with appears in front of all other windows, press the `Enter` key.

■ The window will appear in front of all other windows.

SHOW THE DESKTOP

You can instantly minimize all your open windows to temporarily remove them from your screen. This allows you to clearly view the desktop.

SHOW THE DESKTOP

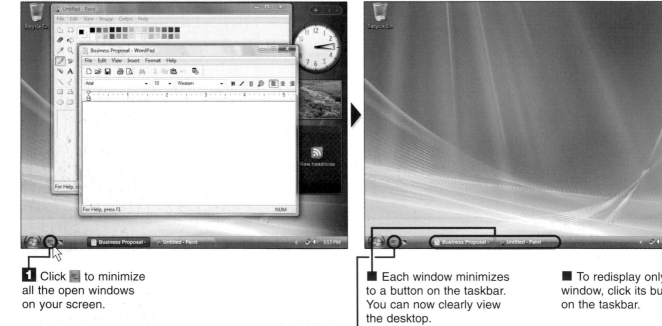

1 Click 🖳 to minimize all the open windows on your screen.

■ Each window minimizes to a button on the taskbar. You can now clearly view the desktop.

■ You can click 🖳 again to redisplay all the windows.

■ To redisplay only one window, click its button on the taskbar.

LOCK YOUR COMPUTER

If you will temporarily be away from your computer and want to protect your computer from unauthorized access, you can instantly lock your computer.

If you want to prevent a colleague or family member from seeing the contents of your computer screen, you can also lock your computer to instantly hide the information on your screen.

To make your computer secure, you should assign a password to your user account. To assign a password to a user account, see page 188.

LOCK YOUR COMPUTER

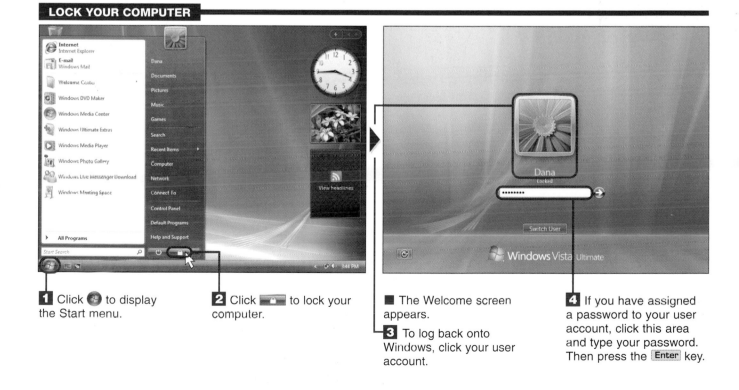

1 Click 🪟 to display the Start menu.

2 Click ⬛ to lock your computer.

■ The Welcome screen appears.

3 To log back onto Windows, click your user account.

4 If you have assigned a password to your user account, click this area and type your password. Then press the `Enter` key.

PUT YOUR COMPUTER TO SLEEP

When you finish using your computer, you can put your computer into a power-saving state known as sleep. When you wake your computer, you will be able to resume working almost immediately.

When sleeping, a computer uses about 90 to 99 percent less power.

By default, if you do not use your computer for one hour, your computer will automatically go to sleep. If your notebook computer is running on battery power, your computer will automatically go to sleep after 15 minutes.

PUT YOUR COMPUTER TO SLEEP

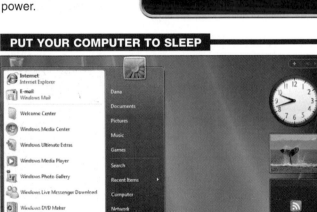

■ When putting your computer to sleep, you can leave your files and programs open. Windows will automatically save your work for you. When you later wake your computer, your screen will look exactly the same.

1 Click  to display the Start menu.

2 Click ⏻ to put your computer to sleep.

Note: You can also put a notebook computer to sleep by closing its lid.

WAKE YOUR COMPUTER

1 To wake your computer, quickly press the power button on your computer. Do not press and hold down the power button since this will restart your computer.

■ If you are using a notebook computer, you can also wake your computer by opening the computer's lid.

Note: You may also be able to move your mouse or press a key on your keyboard to wake your computer.

SHUT DOWN WINDOWS

You should shut down Windows when you need to turn off the power to your computer.

For example, shut down Windows before installing new hardware inside your computer, such as memory, a disk drive, a sound card or a video card, or before changing a notebook computer's battery.

When you finish using your computer, put your computer to sleep instead of shutting down Windows. To put your computer to sleep, see page 28.

SHUT DOWN WINDOWS

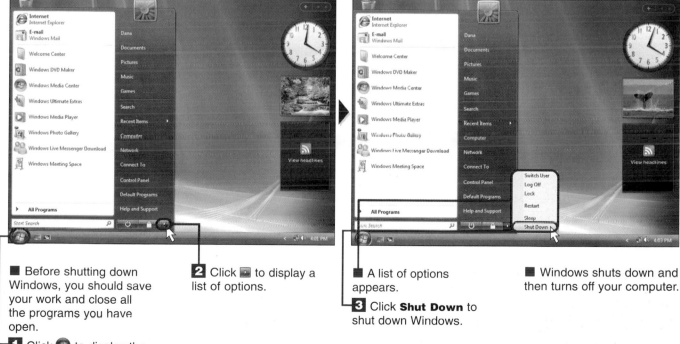

■ Before shutting down Windows, you should save your work and close all the programs you have open.

1 Click 🌐 to display the Start menu.

2 Click 🔲 to display a list of options.

■ A list of options appears.

3 Click **Shut Down** to shut down Windows.

■ Windows shuts down and then turns off your computer.

PLAY GAMES

Windows includes several games that you can play on your computer.

Some examples of games that you can play include Chess Titans, Minesweeper and Solitaire.

PLAY GAMES

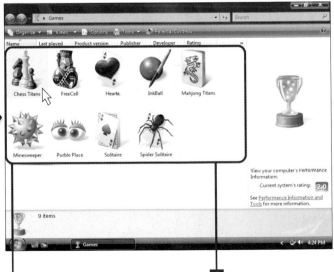

1 Click  to display the Start menu.

2 Click **Games** to display the Games window.

Note: Windows games are not automatically installed in the Windows Vista Business and Windows Vista Enterprise editions of Windows.

■ The Games window appears, displaying the games available on your computer.

■ The Games window is the central location for all the games on your computer. Games that come with Windows as well as most games you install will appear in the Games window.

3 Double-click the game you want to play.

Tip

How do I learn to play a game?

You can get help information for a game you want to play. After opening a game, press the F1 key to display help information for the game.

Tip

Where can I get more games?

There are thousands of games available for you to play on your computer. Many free games as well as games that you can purchase are available on the Internet from Web sites such as msngames.com. A wide range of computer games are also available at computer stores.

■ A window appears, displaying the game. In this example, the Chess Titans window appears.

Note: The first time you open Chess Titans, a dialog box appears, asking you to select a difficulty level. Click the difficulty level you want to play.

4 To make a move in Chess Titans, click a piece and then click the square where you want the piece to move. Squares where you can move the piece will appear blue.

5 When you finish playing a game, click ✕ to close the window.

■ If you leave a game in progress, a dialog box will appear, asking if you want to save the game.

6 Click **Save** to save the game.

■ If you do not want to save the game, click **Don't save**.

Note: If you chose to save a game, Windows will ask if you want to continue with your saved game the next time you open the game.

USING WINDOWS CALENDAR

You can use Windows Calendar to keep track of your appointments, such as business meetings and lunch dates.

Windows Calendar uses the date and time set in your computer to determine today's date. To change the date and time set in your computer, see the top of page 169.

USING WINDOWS CALENDAR

1 Click 🌐 to display the Start menu.

2 Click **All Programs** to view a list of the programs on your computer.

3 Click **Windows Calendar**.

■ The Windows Calendar window appears.

Tip

Can I create more than one calendar to keep track of appointments?

By default, Windows Calendar creates one calendar for you. You can create additional calendars to keep track of specific types of activities. For example, you may have one calendar to keep track of your business meetings and another calendar to keep track of your child's school events. The appointments you add to each calendar display a different color. To create a new calendar, click **File** and then click **New Calendar** in the menu that appears.

Tip

How can I change the number of days displayed in the calendar at one time?

To view appointments for more than one day at a time, click █ beside **View**. In the menu that appears, click an option to view one day, one work week, one week or one month at a time. A check mark (✓) appears beside the current option.

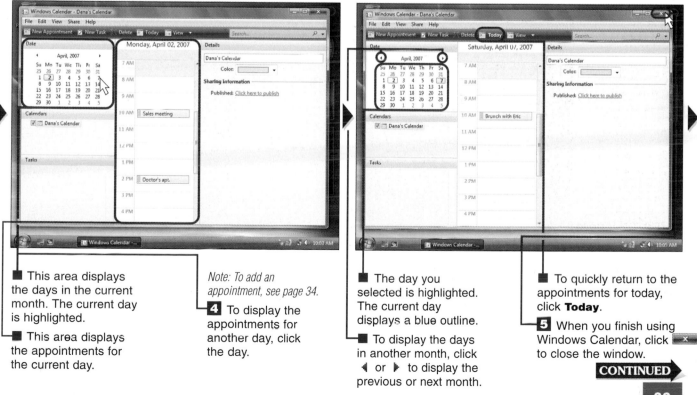

■ This area displays the days in the current month. The current day is highlighted.

■ This area displays the appointments for the current day.

Note: To add an appointment, see page 34.

4 To display the appointments for another day, click the day.

■ The day you selected is highlighted. The current day displays a blue outline.

■ To display the days in another month, click ◀ or ▶ to display the previous or next month.

■ To quickly return to the appointments for today, click **Today**.

5 When you finish using Windows Calendar, click ▬ to close the window.

CONTINUED

USING WINDOWS CALENDAR

You can add an appointment to Windows Calendar to remind you of an activity, such as a seminar or a doctor's appointment.

When scheduling an appointment, you can have Windows Calendar display a reminder dialog box on your screen several minutes, hours, days or weeks before the appointment.

USING WINDOWS CALENDAR (CONTINUED)

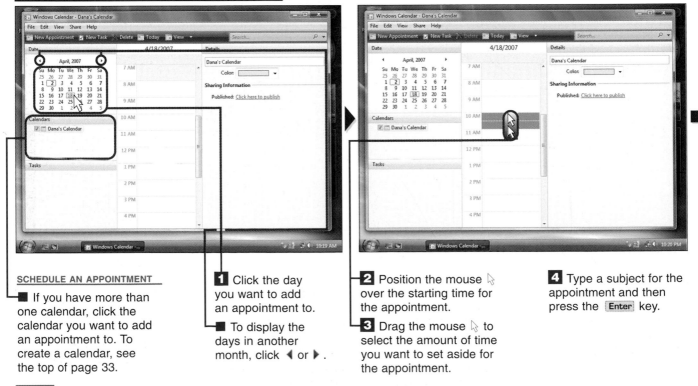

SCHEDULE AN APPOINTMENT

■ If you have more than one calendar, click the calendar you want to add an appointment to. To create a calendar, see the top of page 33.

1 Click the day you want to add an appointment to.

■ To display the days in another month, click ◀ or ▶ .

2 Position the mouse over the starting time for the appointment.

3 Drag the mouse to select the amount of time you want to set aside for the appointment.

4 Type a subject for the appointment and then press the Enter key.

Tip

Can I schedule an appointment to repeat on a regular basis?

You can schedule an appointment to repeat at the same time every day or on the same day every week, month or year. Perform steps **1** to **6** below to schedule an appointment. In the Details pane, click ▼ beside **Recurrence**. In the menu that appears, click an option to specify how often you want the appointment to repeat.

Tip

How do I set up an all-day appointment?

Perform steps **1** to **6** below to schedule an appointment. In the Details pane, click ☐ beside **All-day appointment** (☐ changes to ☑) to set the appointment as an all-day appointment.

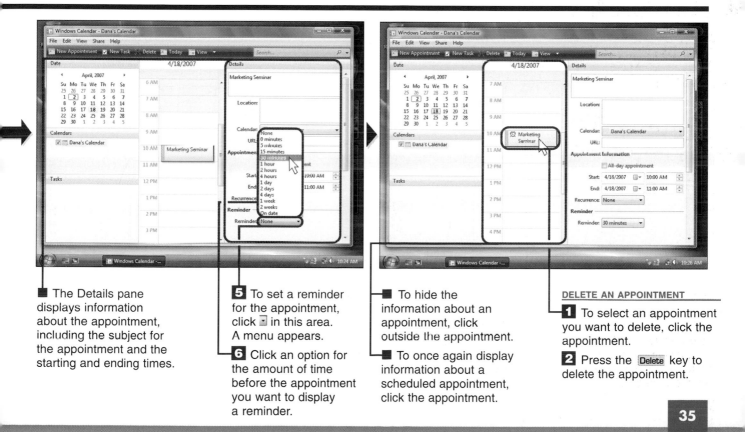

■ The Details pane displays information about the appointment, including the subject for the appointment and the starting and ending times.

5 To set a reminder for the appointment, click ▣ in this area. A menu appears.

6 Click an option for the amount of time before the appointment you want to display a reminder.

■ To hide the information about an appointment, click outside the appointment.

■ To once again display information about a scheduled appointment, click the appointment.

DELETE AN APPOINTMENT

1 To select an appointment you want to delete, click the appointment.

2 Press the Delete key to delete the appointment.

Working With Files

VIEW YOUR PERSONAL FOLDERS

Windows provides personal folders that offer convenient places for you to store and manage your files. You can view the contents of your personal folders at any time.

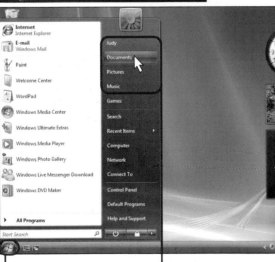

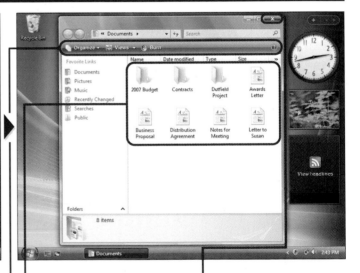

1 Click ⊕ to display the Start menu.

2 Click the type of files you want to view.

Note: The first item in the list, which displays the name you use to log on to your computer, allows you to view all of your personal files.

■ In this example, the Documents window appears, displaying your documents.

■ This area displays options you can select to work with the files in the window.

Note: More options appear when you click a file in the window.

3 When you finish viewing the contents of the window, click ▬X▬ to close the window.

YOUR PERSONAL FOLDERS

User Folder

The User folder displays all of your personal folders, including the Documents, Pictures, Music and Videos folders, in one location. The name of the User folder is the same as the name you use to log on to your computer.

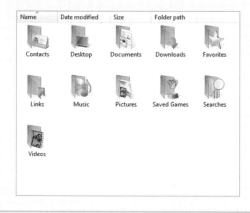

Documents

The Documents folder provides a convenient location to store letters, reports, notes, presentations, spreadsheets and other types of documents. Many programs will automatically save documents you create in the Documents folder.

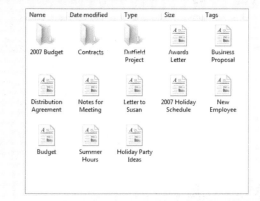

Pictures

The Pictures folder provides a convenient location to store photographs, images and graphics files. Many programs will automatically save pictures you create or edit in this folder. When you transfer pictures from a digital camera to your computer, Windows will automatically save the pictures in the Pictures folder.

Music

The Music folder provides a convenient location to store music and other sound files. When you copy songs from a music CD to your computer or download music from the Internet, the music is often automatically saved in the Music folder.

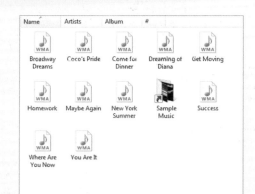

ACCESS DRIVES ON YOUR COMPUTER

You can easily access your hard drive, CD drive, DVD drive and any other storage devices that are connected to your computer.

ACCESS DRIVES ON YOUR COMPUTER

1 Click 🟦 to display the Start menu.

2 Click **Computer** to view the drives and other storage devices that are connected to your computer.

■ The Computer window appears.

■ This area displays an icon for your hard drive, which is the primary storage location for all the programs and files on your computer.

Note: Some computers may display an icon for more than one hard drive.

■ Windows displays the amount of free space and the total amount of space that is available on your hard drive in gigabytes (GB).

Note: Checking the available free space on your hard drive allows you to ensure that your computer is not running out of space.

Tip

What is a USB flash drive?

A USB flash drive is a small, lightweight storage device that plugs into a USB port on your computer. You can use a USB flash drive to easily transfer information between computers. USB flash drives are also known as memory keys, pen drives, thumb drives and key drives.

What is a memory card reader?

Most new computers come with a memory card reader, which is a device that reads and records information on memory cards. Memory cards are most commonly used to transfer information between a computer and an external device such as a digital camera or MP3 player.

A memory card reader typically has several slots that allow the reader to accept memory cards from different manufacturers and devices.

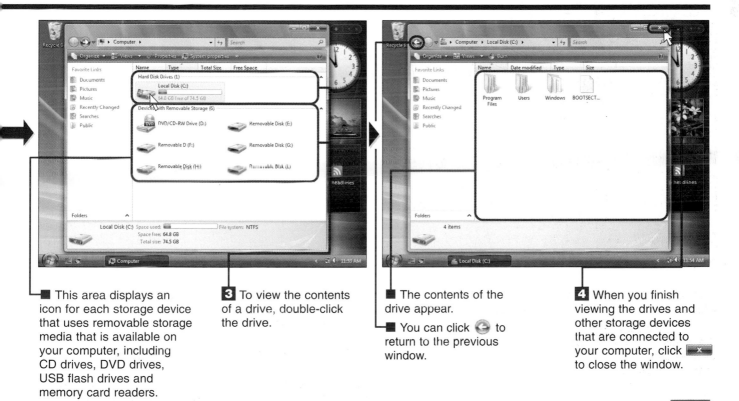

■ This area displays an icon for each storage device that uses removable storage media that is available on your computer, including CD drives, DVD drives, USB flash drives and memory card readers.

3 To view the contents of a drive, double-click the drive.

■ The contents of the drive appear.

■ You can click ◀ to return to the previous window.

4 When you finish viewing the drives and other storage devices that are connected to your computer, click ✖ to close the window.

CHANGE VIEW OF FILES

You can change the view of files and folders in a window. The view you select determines the way files and folders will appear in the window.

CHANGE VIEW OF FILES

1 Click ⌄ beside **Views** to change the view of the files and folders in a window.

■ A list of the available views appears.

2 Click the way you want to view the files and folders in the window.

Note: You can also drag the slider (⬜) to select the way you want to view the files and folders in the window.

■ In this example, the files and folders appear in the Details view.

■ To sort the files and folders in the Details view, click the heading for the column you want to use to sort the files and folders. Click the column heading again to sort the files and folders in the reverse order.

■ To quickly switch between the views, click **Views** until the files and folders appear the way you want.

THE VIEWS

Extra Large Icons

The Extra Large Icons view displays files and folders as extra large icons.

Large Icons

The Large Icons view displays files and folders as large icons.

Medium Icons

The Medium Icons view displays files and folders as medium-sized icons.

Small Icons

The Small Icons view displays files and folders as small icons.

List

The List view displays files and folders as small icons arranged in a list.

Details

The Details view displays files and folders as small icons and provides detailed information about each file and folder.

Tiles

The Tiles view displays files and folders as medium-sized icons and provides the file type and size of each file and folder.

SELECT FILES

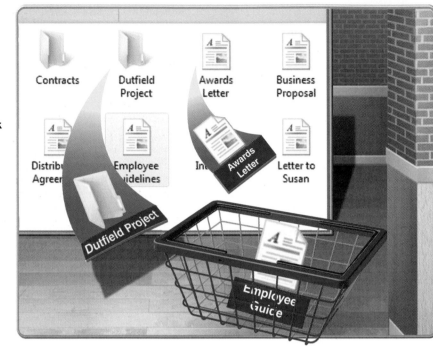

Before working with files, you often need to select the files you want to work with. Selected files appear highlighted on your screen.

You can select folders the same way you select files. Selecting a folder will select all the files in the folder.

SELECT FILES

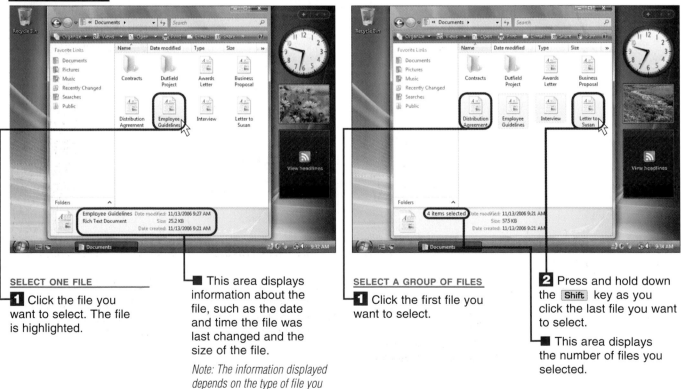

SELECT ONE FILE

1 Click the file you want to select. The file is highlighted.

■ This area displays information about the file, such as the date and time the file was last changed and the size of the file.

Note: The information displayed depends on the type of file you selected.

SELECT A GROUP OF FILES

1 Click the first file you want to select.

2 Press and hold down the **Shift** key as you click the last file you want to select.

■ This area displays the number of files you selected.

Tip

How do I deselect files?

To deselect all the files in a window, click a blank area in the window.

To deselect one file from a group of selected files, press and hold down the Ctrl key as you click the file you want to deselect.

Tip

Can I select a group of files without using the keyboard?

Yes. To select a group of files without using your keyboard, position the mouse slightly above and to the left of the first file you want to select. Then drag the mouse diagonally across the files. While you drag the mouse, a box appears around the files that will be selected. Release the mouse when you finish selecting the files.

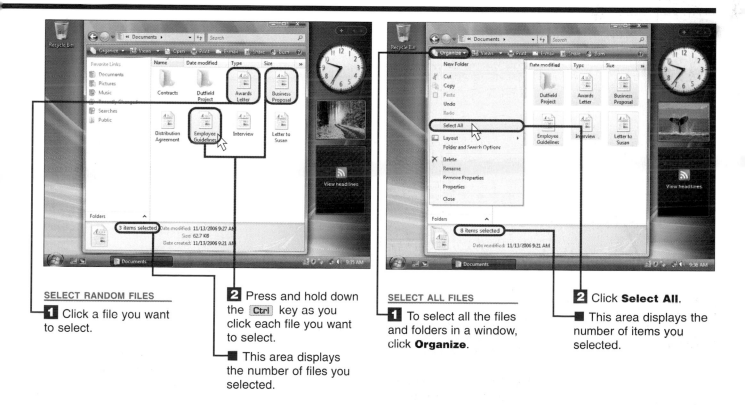

SELECT RANDOM FILES

1 Click a file you want to select.

2 Press and hold down the Ctrl key as you click each file you want to select.

■ This area displays the number of files you selected.

SELECT ALL FILES

1 To select all the files and folders in a window, click **Organize**.

2 Click **Select All**.

■ This area displays the number of items you selected.

OPEN A FILE

You can open a file to display its contents on your screen. Opening a file allows you to review and make changes to the file.

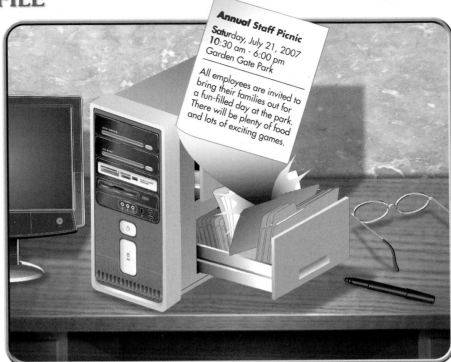

You can open folders the same way you open files.

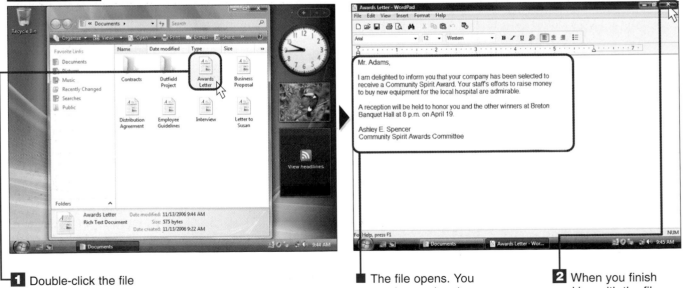

1 Double-click the file you want to open.

■ The file opens. You can review and make changes to the file.

2 When you finish working with the file, click to close the file.

46

RENAME A FILE

You can rename a file to better describe the contents of the file. Renaming a file can help you more quickly locate the file in the future.

You can rename folders the same way you rename files.

RENAME A FILE

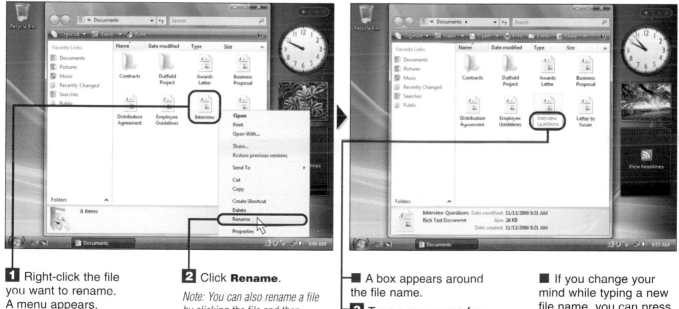

1 Right-click the file you want to rename. A menu appears.

2 Click **Rename**.

Note: You can also rename a file by clicking the file and then pressing the F2 *key.*

■ A box appears around the file name.

3 Type a new name for the file and then press the Enter key.

*Note: A file name cannot contain the \ / : * ? " < > or | characters.*

■ If you change your mind while typing a new file name, you can press the Esc key to return to the original file name.

CREATE A NEW FILE

You can instantly create, name and store a new file in the location you want without starting any programs.

Creating a new file without starting any programs allows you to focus on the organization of your files rather than the programs you need to accomplish your tasks.

CREATE A NEW FILE

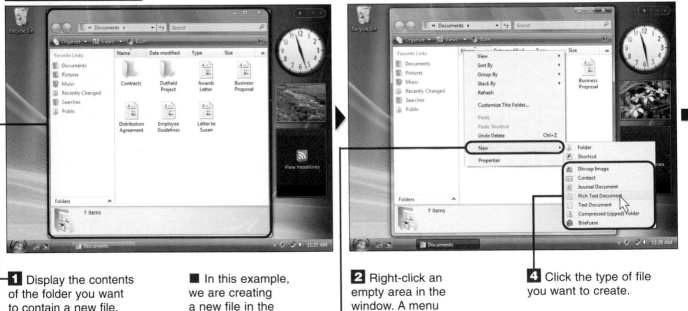

1 Display the contents of the folder you want to contain a new file.

■ In this example, we are creating a new file in the Documents folder.

2 Right-click an empty area in the window. A menu appears.

3 Click **New**.

4 Click the type of file you want to create.

What types of files can I create?

The types of files you can create depend on the programs installed on your computer. By default, Windows allows you to create the following types of files.

File Type	Description
Bitmap Image	Creates an image file.
Contact	Creates a contact, which allows you to store a collection of information about a person, such as a person's e-mail address, phone number and street address.
Journal Document	Creates a note you can record in your own handwriting.
Rich Text Document	Creates a document that can contain formatting, such as bold text and colors.
Text Document	Creates a document that cannot contain formatting.
Compressed (zipped) Folder	Creates a folder that reduces the size of the files it contains to save storage space.
Briefcase	Stores copies of files that you want to keep synchronized between two computers, such as your work and home computers.

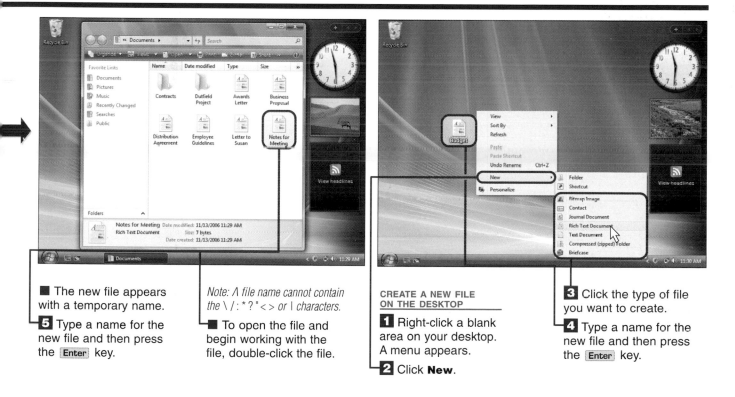

■ The new file appears with a temporary name.

5 Type a name for the new file and then press the Enter key.

*Note: A file name cannot contain the \ / : * ? " < > or | characters.*

■ To open the file and begin working with the file, double-click the file.

CREATE A NEW FILE ON THE DESKTOP

1 Right-click a blank area on your desktop. A menu appears.

2 Click **New**.

3 Click the type of file you want to create.

4 Type a name for the new file and then press the Enter key.

CREATE A NEW FOLDER

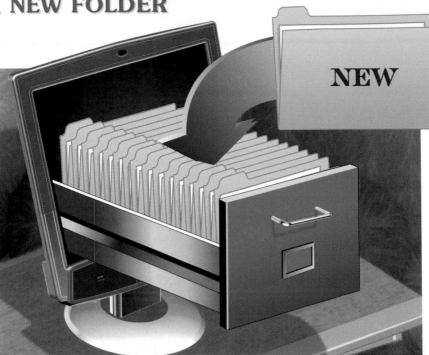

You can create a new folder to help you organize the files stored on your computer.

Creating a new folder is useful when you want to keep related files together, such as the files for a particular project.

Creating a new folder is like placing a new folder in a filing cabinet.

CREATE A NEW FOLDER

1 Right-click an empty area in the window you want to contain a new folder. A menu appears.

■ To create a new folder on your desktop, right-click an empty area on the desktop. A menu appears.

2 Click **New**.

3 Click **Folder**.

■ The new folder appears, displaying a temporary name.

4 Type a name for the new folder and then press the Enter key.

*Note: A folder name cannot contain the \ / : * ? " < > or | characters.*

You can delete a file you no longer need. The Recycle Bin stores all the files you delete.

Before you delete a file, make sure you will no longer need the file.

You can delete a folder the same way you delete a file. When you delete a folder, all the files in the folder are also deleted.

DELETE A FILE

1 Right-click the file you want to delete. A menu appears.

■ To delete more than one file, select all the files you want to delete and then right-click one of the files. To select multiple files, see page 44.

2 Click **Delete**.

Note: You can also delete a file by clicking the file and then pressing the Delete *key.*

■ The Delete File dialog box appears.

3 Click **Yes** to delete the file.

■ The file disappears.

■ Windows places the file in the Recycle Bin in case you later want to restore the file.

Note: To restore a file from the Recycle Bin, see page 52.

RESTORE A DELETED FILE

The Recycle Bin stores all the files you have deleted. You can easily restore any file in the Recycle Bin to its original location on your computer.

You can restore folders the same way you restore files. When you restore a folder, Windows restores all the files in the folder.

You can empty the Recycle Bin to create more free space on your computer. When you empty the Recycle Bin, the files are removed and cannot be restored.

RESTORE A DELETED FILE

1 Double-click **Recycle Bin**.

■ The Recycle Bin window appears, displaying all the files you have deleted.

2 Click the file you want to restore.

■ To restore more than one file, select all the files you want to restore. To select multiple files, see page 44.

3 Click **Restore this item**.

Note: If you selected multiple files, click ***Restore the selected items*** *in step* ***3***.

■ The file will disappear from the Recycle Bin window and return to its original location on your computer.

4 Click ▬✕▬ to close the Recycle Bin window.

EMPTY THE RECYCLE BIN

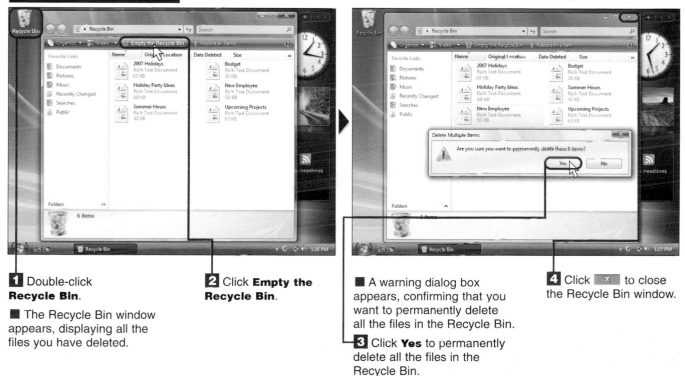

1 Double-click **Recycle Bin**.

■ The Recycle Bin window appears, displaying all the files you have deleted.

2 Click **Empty the Recycle Bin**.

■ A warning dialog box appears, confirming that you want to permanently delete all the files in the Recycle Bin.

3 Click **Yes** to permanently delete all the files in the Recycle Bin.

4 Click x to close the Recycle Bin window.

PRINT A FILE

You can produce a paper copy of a file stored on your computer.

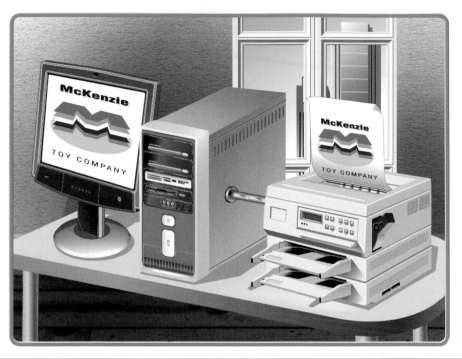

Before printing a file, make sure your printer is turned on and contains paper.

1 Click the file you want to print.

■ To print more than one file, select all the files you want to print. To select multiple files, see page 44.

2 Click **Print**.

Note: If you selected a picture, the Print Pictures dialog box appears. For information on printing pictures, see page 80.

■ Windows quickly opens, prints and then closes the file.

■ When you print a file, a printer icon (🖶) appears in this area. The printer icon disappears when the file has finished printing.

Tip

How can I stop a file from printing?

You may want to stop a file from printing if you accidentally selected the wrong file or if you want to make last-minute changes to the file.

Samsung ML-2250 Series PCL6

Printer   Document   View

Document Name	Status	Owner	Pages	Size	Sub
Updates	Printing	Emily	1/18	55.9 KB/512 KB	2:4

1 document(s) in que

Printers

Are you sure you want to cancel the document?

Yes   No

1 When viewing the files waiting to print, click the file you no longer want to print and then press the Delete key.

2 A confirmation dialog box will appear. You can click **Yes** to stop the file from printing.

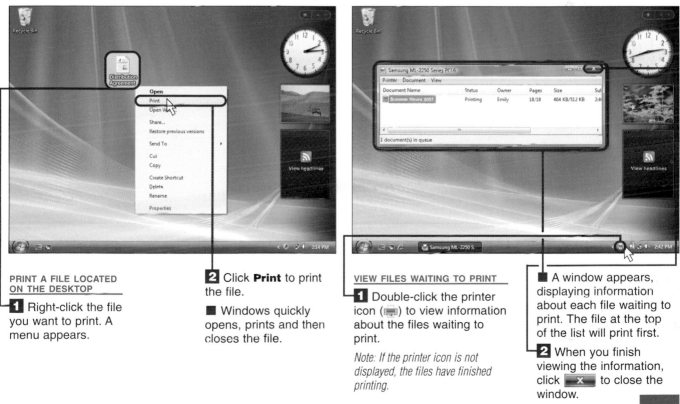

PRINT A FILE LOCATED ON THE DESKTOP

1 Right-click the file you want to print. A menu appears.

2 Click **Print** to print the file.

■ Windows quickly opens, prints and then closes the file.

VIEW FILES WAITING TO PRINT

1 Double-click the printer icon (🖨) to view information about the files waiting to print.

Note: If the printer icon is not displayed, the files have finished printing.

■ A window appears, displaying information about each file waiting to print. The file at the top of the list will print first.

2 When you finish viewing the information, click ❌ to close the window.

MOVE OR COPY A FILE

You can move or copy a file to a new location on your computer.

When you move a file, the file will disappear from its original location and appear in the new location.

When you copy a file, the file appears in both the original and new locations.

You can move or copy a folder the same way you move or copy a file. When you move or copy a folder, all the files in the folder are also moved or copied.

MOVE A FILE

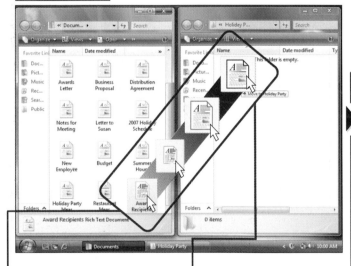

■ Before moving a file, make sure you can clearly see the location where you want to move the file.

1 Position the mouse over the file you want to move.

■ To move more than one file at once, select all the files you want to move. Then position the mouse over one of the files. To select multiple files, see page 44.

2 Drag the file to a new location.

■ The file moves to the new location.

■ The file disappears from its original location.

Why would I want to move or copy a file?

You may want to move a file to a different folder to keep files of the same type in one location. For example, you can move your documents to the Documents folder provided by Windows. Windows also includes the Pictures and Music folders that you can use to store your pictures and music files. To open one of these folders, see page 38. You may want to copy a file before you make major changes to the file. This will give you two copies of the file—the original file and a file that you can change.

Is there another way to move or copy a file?

Yes. To move or copy a file, right-click the file you want to move or copy. On the menu that appears, click **Cut** to move the file or **Copy** to copy the file. Open the folder where you want to place the file and then right-click a blank area in the folder. On the menu that appears, click **Paste** to move or copy the file. This method is ideal when you need to move or copy a file but you cannot clearly see the location where you want to place the file.

COPY A FILE

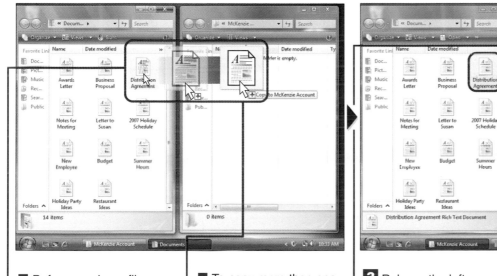

■ Before copying a file, make sure you can clearly see the location where you want to copy the file.

1 Position the mouse ⟍ over the file you want to copy.

■ To copy more than one file at once, select all the files you want to copy. Then position the mouse ⟍ over one of the files. To select multiple files, see page 44.

2 Press and hold down the **Ctrl** key as you drag the file to a new location.

3 Release the left mouse button and then the **Ctrl** key.

■ A copy of the file appears in the new location.

■ The original file remains in the original location.

More Working With Files

VIEW

OPEN A RECENTLY USED FILE

Windows keeps track of the files you have recently used. You can quickly open any of these files.

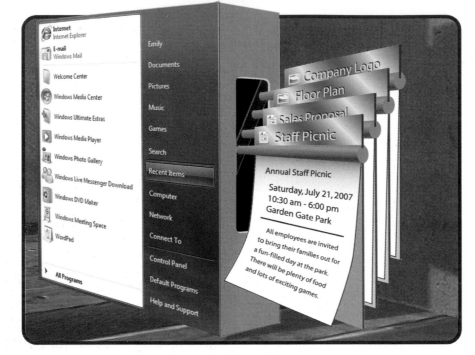

OPEN A RECENTLY USED FILE

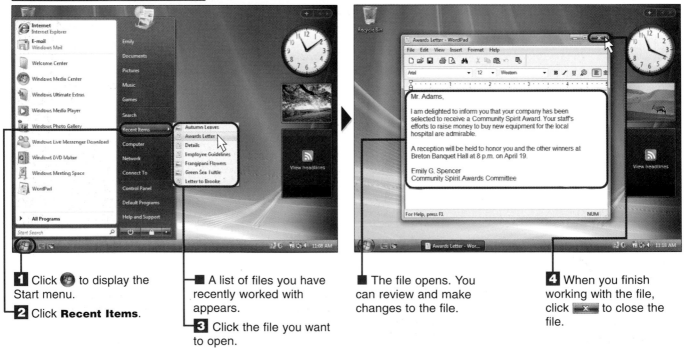

1 Click ⊞ to display the Start menu.

2 Click **Recent Items**.

■ A list of files you have recently worked with appears.

3 Click the file you want to open.

■ The file opens. You can review and make changes to the file.

4 When you finish working with the file, click ✕ to close the file.

You can choose the
program you want
to use to open a file.

For example, you
can choose to open
a picture in an image
editing program or in
Windows Photo Gallery.

OPEN A FILE IN A SPECIFIC PROGRAM

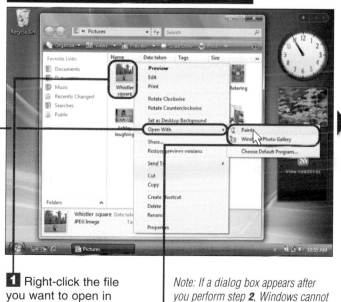

1 Right-click the file
you want to open in
a specific program.
A menu appears.

2 Click **Open With**.

*Note: If a dialog box appears after
you perform step 2, Windows cannot
recommend more than one program
to open the file. Click OK to open the
file in the recommended program.*

3 Click the program you
want to use to open the file.

■ Windows opens the
file in the program you
selected.

4 When you finish
working with the file,
click ▄▄▄ to close the
file.

You can e-mail a file to a friend, colleague or family member. You must have an e-mail account set up to be able to e-mail a file.

You can e-mail many types of files, including documents, pictures, music and videos. The computer receiving the file must have the necessary hardware and software installed to display or play the file.

E-MAIL A FILE

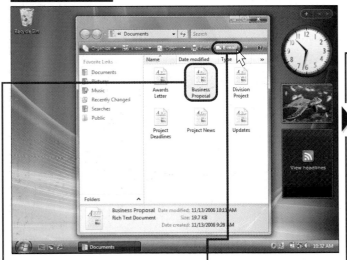

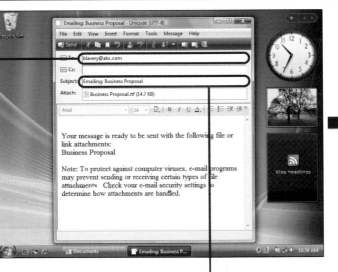

1 Click the file you want to send in an e-mail message.

■ To send more than one file in an e-mail message, select all the files you want to send. To select multiple files, see page 44.

2 Click **E-mail**.

■ A window appears that allows you to compose a message.

3 Type the e-mail address of the person you want to receive the message.

Note: To send the message to more than one person, separate each e-mail address with a semicolon (;).

4 Windows uses the name of the file as the subject. To specify a different subject, drag the mouse I over the subject and then type a new subject.

Tip

Why does a dialog box appear when I try to e-mail a picture?

Windows can change the file size and dimensions of a picture you are sending in an e-mail message so the picture will transfer faster over the Internet and fit better on a recipient's computer screen. Reducing the file size of a picture is useful when you are e-mailing a large picture or many pictures at once, since most companies that provide e-mail accounts do not allow you to send messages larger than 10 MB. Changing the size of pictures you are e-mailing will not change the size or quality of the original pictures on your computer.

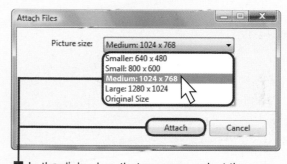

■ In the dialog box that appears, select the picture size you want to use and then click **Attach** to continue.

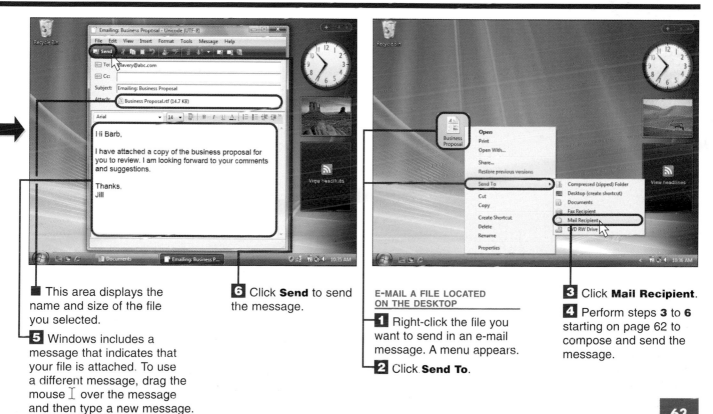

■ This area displays the name and size of the file you selected.

5 Windows includes a message that indicates that your file is attached. To use a different message, drag the mouse I over the message and then type a new message.

6 Click **Send** to send the message.

E-MAIL A FILE LOCATED ON THE DESKTOP

1 Right-click the file you want to send in an e-mail message. A menu appears.

2 Click **Send To**.

3 Click **Mail Recipient**.

4 Perform steps **3** to **6** starting on page 62 to compose and send the message.

SEARCH FOR FILES

If you do not remember where you stored a file on your computer, you can have Windows search for the file.

As you create files on your computer, Windows updates an index to keep track of your files. The index is similar to an index you would find at the back of a book.

When you want to find a file on your computer, Windows scans the index instead of searching your entire computer. This allows Windows to perform very fast searches.

SEARCH FOR FILES USING THE SEARCH FOLDER

1 Click 🟦 to display the Start menu.

2 Click **Search** to search for a file, such as a document, music file, picture or e-mail message.

■ The Search Results window appears.

3 Click the type of file you want to search for.

4 Click this area and type the word or part of the word you want to search for.

■ For example, you can type all or part of the file name you are searching for or type a word or phrase that appears within the file.

What types of files can Windows search for?

When you use the Search folder to search for files, Windows will search your personal folders, including the Documents, Pictures and Music folders, as well as the files on your desktop, your e-mail messages and your list of favorite Web pages. When you use the Start menu to search for files, Windows will also find matching programs as well as Web pages you have recently viewed.

Can I search for files in a particular folder?

Yes. Searching for files in a particular folder is useful when a folder contains numerous files. In the folder you want to search, click the Search box at the top-right corner of the window and type the word or part of the word you want to search for. As you type, the window immediately displays the matching files that Windows finds. You will find the Search box in every folder on your computer.

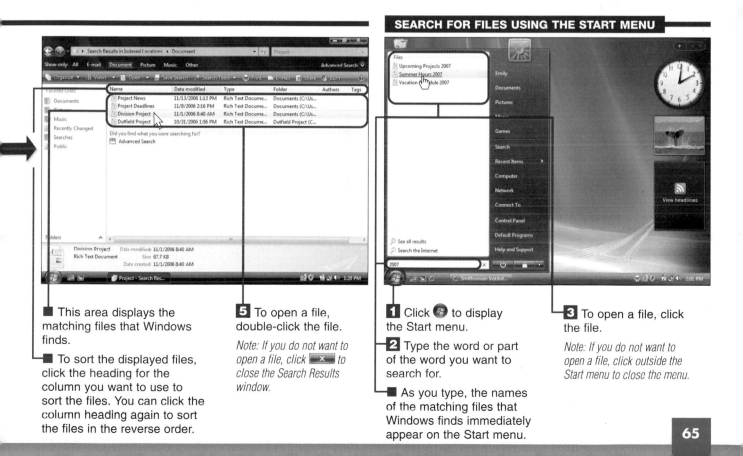

SEARCH FOR FILES USING THE START MENU

■ This area displays the matching files that Windows finds.

■ To sort the displayed files, click the heading for the column you want to use to sort the files. You can click the column heading again to sort the files in the reverse order.

5 To open a file, double-click the file.

Note: If you do not want to open a file, click ▬✗▬ to close the Search Results window.

1 Click 🟦 to display the Start menu.

2 Type the word or part of the word you want to search for.

■ As you type, the names of the matching files that Windows finds immediately appear on the Start menu.

3 To open a file, click the file.

Note: If you do not want to open a file, click outside the Start menu to close the menu.

ADD A SHORTCUT TO THE DESKTOP

You can add a shortcut to the desktop to provide a quick way of opening a file you regularly use.

ADD A SHORTCUT TO THE DESKTOP

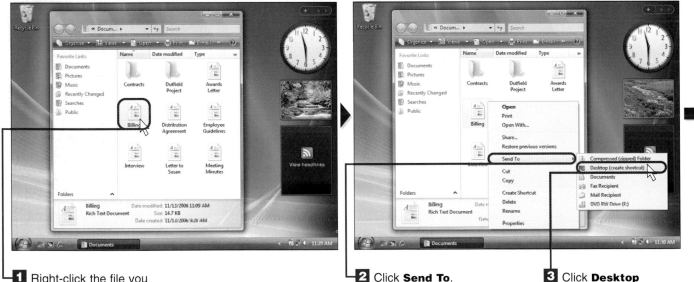

1 Right-click the file you want to create a shortcut to. A menu appears.

2 Click **Send To**.

3 Click **Desktop (create shortcut)**.

Tip

How do I rename or delete a shortcut?

You can rename or delete a shortcut the same way you would rename or delete any file. Renaming or deleting a shortcut will not affect the original file. To rename a file, see page 47. To delete a file, see page 51.

Tip

Can I move a shortcut to a different location?

Yes. If you do not want a shortcut to appear on your desktop, you can move the shortcut to a different location on your computer. You can move a shortcut the same way you would move any file. To move a file, see page 56.

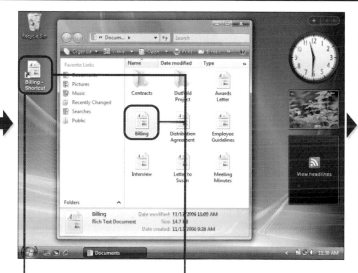

■ The shortcut appears on your desktop.

■ You can tell the difference between the shortcut and the original file because the shortcut icon displays an arrow ( ).

■ You can double-click the shortcut to open the file at any time.

Note: You can create a shortcut to a folder the same way you create a shortcut to a file. Creating a shortcut to a folder will give you quick access to all the files in the folder.

COPY FILES TO A USB FLASH DRIVE

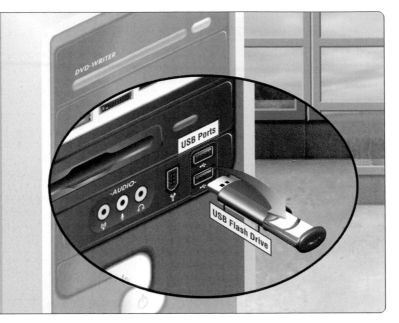

You can copy files stored on your computer to a USB flash drive.

Copying files to a USB flash drive is useful when you want to transfer files between computers. For example, you may want to transfer files between your home and work computers or give a copy of a file to a friend, family member or colleague.

A USB flash drive is a small, lightweight storage device that plugs into a USB port on your computer. A USB flash drive is also known as a memory key, pen drive, thumb drive or key drive.

COPY FILES TO A USB FLASH DRIVE

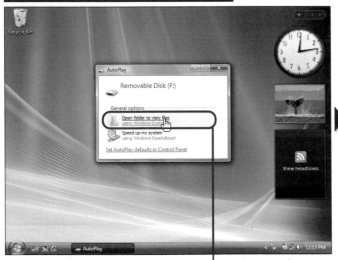

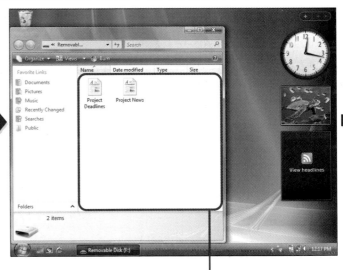

1 Insert a USB flash drive into your computer's USB port.

■ The AutoPlay window appears, listing options that you can select.

2 Click **Open folder to view files** to view the files stored on the USB flash drive.

■ A window appears, displaying the contents of the USB flash drive.

■ This area displays the folders and files currently stored on the USB flash drive.

Is there another way to display the contents of a USB flash drive?

Yes. After you insert a USB flash drive into your computer, you can use the Computer window to view the contents of the drive. The Computer window allows you to view the contents of a USB flash drive as well as any other storage devices that are connected to your computer. To view the Computer window, see page 40.

How can I safely remove a USB flash drive from my computer?

Before you remove a USB flash drive from your computer, you should ensure that your computer has finished saving information to the drive. After you insert a USB flash drive into your computer, the Safely Remove Hardware icon ( ) appears at the bottom-right corner of your screen. When you want to safely remove a USB flash drive, click the icon and then click the device from the list of devices that appears. A dialog box will appear, indicating whether or not you can safely remove the device. Click **OK** to close the dialog box.

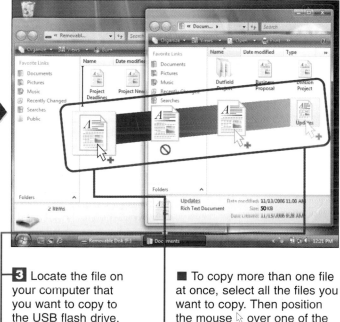

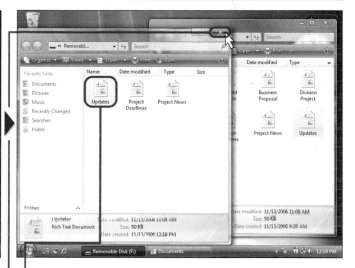

3 Locate the file on your computer that you want to copy to the USB flash drive.

4 Position the mouse ⌖ over the file.

■ To copy more than one file at once, select all the files you want to copy. Then position the mouse ⌖ over one of the files. To select multiple files, see page 44.

5 Drag the file to the window displaying the contents of the USB flash drive.

■ Windows places a copy of the file on the USB flash drive.

6 Click ✕ to close the window displaying the contents of the USB flash drive.

7 Remove the USB flash drive from your computer.

■ You can now use the USB flash drive to transfer the file to another computer.

SCAN A DOCUMENT

You can scan paper documents into your computer.

You can scan documents such as photographs, drawings, reports, newsletters, newspaper articles and forms into your computer.

You need a scanner or a device with scanning capabilities connected and installed on your computer to scan a document.

1 Place the document you want to scan in your scanner.

2 Click ⊞ to display the Start menu.

3 Click **All Programs** to view a list of the programs on your computer.

4 Click **Windows Fax and Scan**.

■ The Windows Fax and Scan window appears on your screen.

Tip

**What should I do if Windows Fax and
Scan does not appear on the Start menu?**

Windows Fax and Scan is only available
in the Business, Enterprise and Ultimate
editions of Windows Vista.

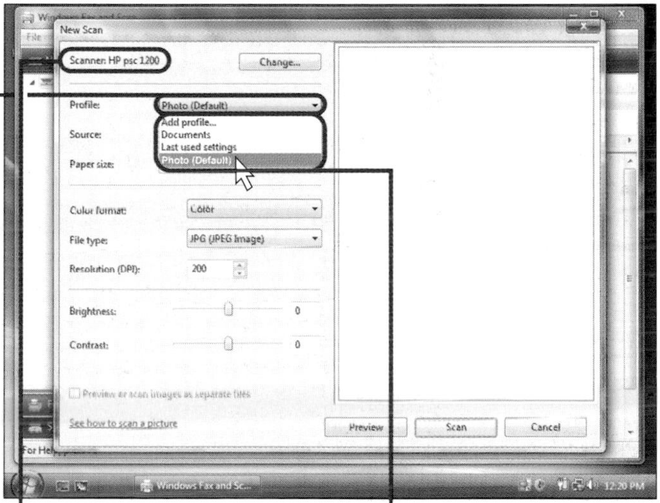

5 Click **Scan** to scan a
document.

6 Click **New Scan**.

■ The New Scan dialog
box appears.

■ This area displays
the name of the scanner
installed on your computer.

7 Click this area to select
the type of document you
are scanning. A menu
appears.

8 Click the type of
document you are
scanning.

*Note: You can select **Last used
settings** to automatically use the
selections you made the last
time you scanned a document.*

CONTINUED

SCAN A DOCUMENT

You can specify the color format you want to use to scan a document.

Color Grayscale Black & White

You can scan a color, grayscale or black and white document. For example, if you are scanning a document that contains only shades of gray, select the grayscale option.

SCAN A DOCUMENT (CONTINUED)

■ This area displays the color format that Windows will use to scan the document. You can click this area to select a different color format, such as color, grayscale or black and white.

9 Click this area to list the available file formats that Windows can use to save the document.

10 Click the file format you want to use.

■ This area displays the resolution Windows will use to scan the document, measured in Dots Per Inch (DPI). You can click ▲ or ▼ to increase or decrease the resolution.

11 Click **Preview** to view how the scanned document will appear with the settings you selected.

Tip 💡 **Which file format should I select for my scanned document?**

The file format you should select depends on how you plan to use the scanned document. The Bitmap Image and TIFF Image file formats are useful for producing high-quality pictures. The JPEG Image and PNG Image file formats are useful for pictures you plan to publish to the Web.

Tip 💡 **How can I later access and work with my scanned documents?**

To view and work with documents you have scanned, display the contents of your Documents folder (see page 38). Then double-click the Scanned Documents folder to display the contents of the folder. You can double-click a document you have scanned to rename, edit and work with the document in the Windows Photo Gallery window. For information on Windows Photo Gallery, see page 76.

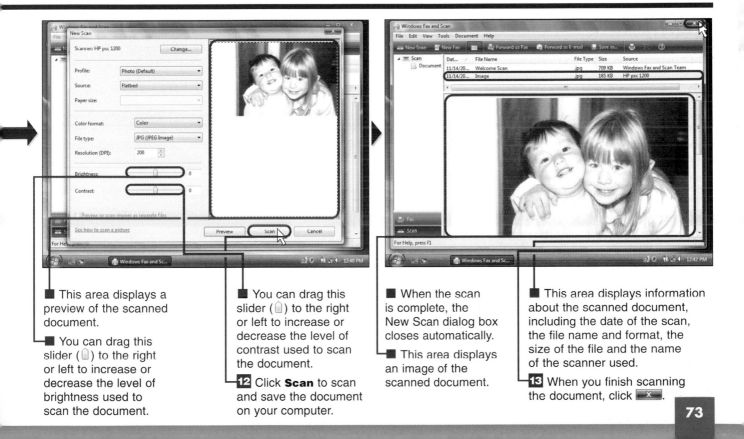

■ This area displays a preview of the scanned document.

■ You can drag this slider (🔲) to the right or left to increase or decrease the level of brightness used to scan the document.

■ You can drag this slider (🔲) to the right or left to increase or decrease the level of contrast used to scan the document.

12 Click **Scan** to scan and save the document on your computer.

■ When the scan is complete, the New Scan dialog box closes automatically.

■ This area displays an image of the scanned document.

■ This area displays information about the scanned document, including the date of the scan, the file name and format, the size of the file and the name of the scanner used.

13 When you finish scanning the document, click ❎.

CHAPTER 4

Working With Pictures

VIEW PICTURES IN WINDOWS PHOTO GALLERY

You can use Windows Photo Gallery to view, organize and find the pictures and videos on your computer.

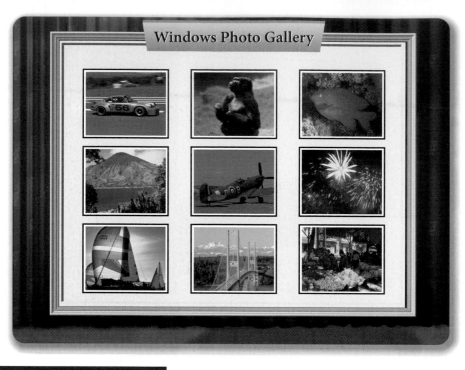

Windows Photo Gallery displays the pictures and videos stored in the Pictures and Videos folders on your computer.

VIEW PICTURES IN WINDOWS PHOTO GALLERY

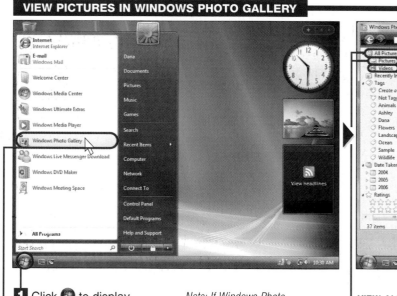

1 Click 🔵 to display the Start menu.

2 Click **Windows Photo Gallery**.

*Note: If Windows Photo Gallery does not appear on the Start menu, click **All Programs** on the Start menu and then click **Windows Photo Gallery**.*

■ The Windows Photo Gallery window appears.

VIEW ALL PICTURES

1 To view all of your pictures and videos, click **All Pictures and Videos**.

■ To view only your pictures, click **Pictures**.

■ To view only your videos, click **Videos**.

■ This area displays your pictures and videos.

Tip

After copying pictures from my digital camera to my computer, how can I quickly find the pictures in Windows Photo Gallery?

In Windows Photo Gallery, click the **Recently Imported** category on the left side of the window. You will instantly see all of the pictures and videos you have recently imported, including pictures you have copied from a digital camera to your computer.

Tip

How can I change the rating of a picture?

To change the rating of a picture or video, click the picture or video and then click the **Info** button to display the Info pane. In the Info pane, click a star (☆) to assign a rating to the picture or video. You can assign one, two, three, four or five stars to your pictures and videos.

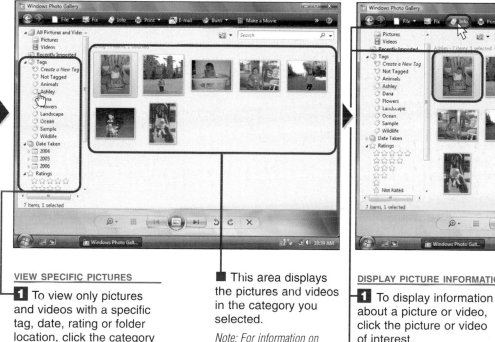

VIEW SPECIFIC PICTURES

1 To view only pictures and videos with a specific tag, date, rating or folder location, click the category of interest.

Note: To hide or display the options in a category, click ◢ or ▷ beside the category name.

■ This area displays the pictures and videos in the category you selected.

Note: For information on tags, see page 88. For information on picture and video ratings, see the top of this page.

DISPLAY PICTURE INFORMATION

1 To display information about a picture or video, click the picture or video of interest.

2 Click **Info** to display the Info pane.

■ The Info pane appears, displaying information about the picture or video, including the file name, rating and tags attached to the picture or video.

Note: To close the Info pane, click ✕.

CONTINUED

VIEW PICTURES IN WINDOWS PHOTO GALLERY

You can easily work with the pictures and videos in Windows Photo Gallery.

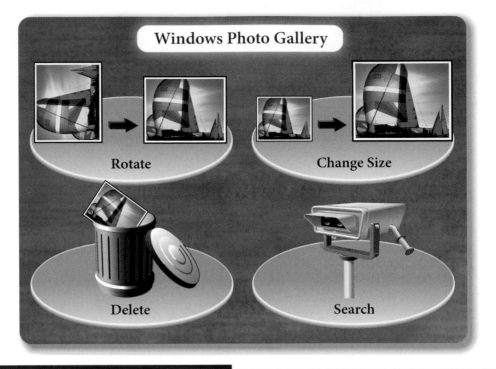

For example, you can rotate pictures, change the size of the displayed pictures, delete pictures or videos you no longer need and search for pictures and videos.

VIEW PICTURES IN WINDOWS PHOTO GALLERY (CONTINUED)

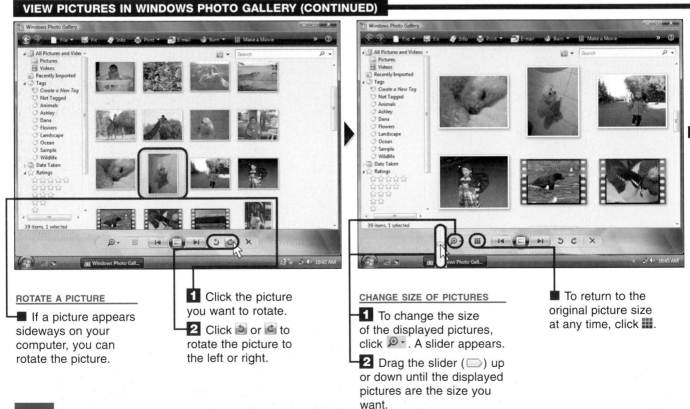

ROTATE A PICTURE

■ If a picture appears sideways on your computer, you can rotate the picture.

1 Click the picture you want to rotate.

2 Click 🔄 or 🔄 to rotate the picture to the left or right.

CHANGE SIZE OF PICTURES

1 To change the size of the displayed pictures, click 🔍▾. A slider appears.

2 Drag the slider (⬜) up or down until the displayed pictures are the size you want.

■ To return to the original picture size at any time, click ▦.

Tip

Can I see a picture in a larger view?

Yes. To see a picture in a larger view, position the mouse ⬉ over the picture in the Windows Photo Gallery. After a moment, a larger view of the picture appears, along with information about the picture. To see a picture in a much larger view, double-click the picture. A larger view of the picture appears. To return to all of your pictures, click the **Back To Gallery** button at the top-left corner of the window.

Tip

How can I change the name of a picture?

To change the file name of a picture or video, right-click the picture or video in the Windows Photo Gallery and then select **Rename** from the menu that appears. In the Info pane on the right side of the window, type a new name for the picture or video and then press the **Enter** key.

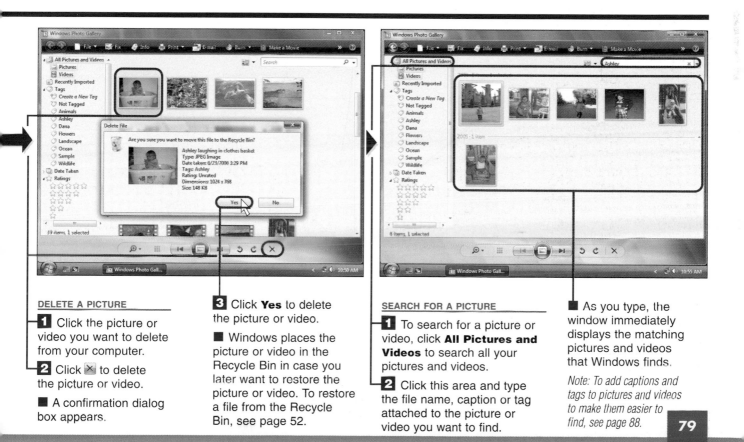

DELETE A PICTURE

1 Click the picture or video you want to delete from your computer.

2 Click ✕ to delete the picture or video.

■ A confirmation dialog box appears.

3 Click **Yes** to delete the picture or video.

■ Windows places the picture or video in the Recycle Bin in case you later want to restore the picture or video. To restore a file from the Recycle Bin, see page 52.

SEARCH FOR A PICTURE

1 To search for a picture or video, click **All Pictures and Videos** to search all your pictures and videos.

2 Click this area and type the file name, caption or tag attached to the picture or video you want to find.

■ As you type, the window immediately displays the matching pictures and videos that Windows finds.

Note: To add captions and tags to pictures and videos to make them easier to find, see page 88.

PRINT PICTURES

You can print the pictures stored on your computer.

Printing pictures is especially useful when you want to print photographs you transferred from a digital camera to your computer.

PRINT PICTURES

1 Click the picture you want to print.

■ To print more than one picture, select all the pictures you want to print. To select multiple pictures, see page 44.

2 Click **Print** to print the pictures.

3 If you are printing pictures shown in the Windows Photo Gallery window, click **Print** in the menu that appears.

■ The Print Pictures dialog box appears.

■ This area displays a preview of how the first printed page of your pictures will appear.

4 Click the layout you want to use to print your pictures. You can choose to print one picture on each page or many pictures on each page.

Note: You can use the scroll bar to browse through the available layout options.

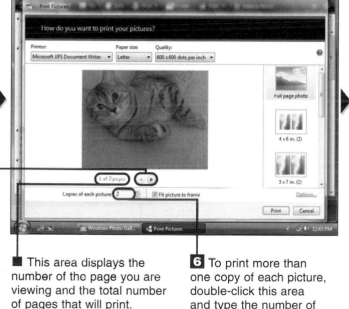

■ This area displays the number of the page you are viewing and the total number of pages that will print.

5 If you are printing more than one page, you can click ◀ and ▶ to browse through the pages that will print.

6 To print more than one copy of each picture, double-click this area and type the number of copies of each picture that you want to print.

7 This option enlarges the pictures to remove the blank border that may appear around the printed pictures. If this option is on, the edges of the pictures may be cut off. You can click this option to turn the option off (▢) or on (☑).

Note: Windows offers this option because digital pictures usually do not match standard print proportions.

8 To print the pictures, click **Print**.

DISPLAY PICTURES AS A SLIDE SHOW

You can display your pictures as a full-screen slide show.

During a slide show, you can select a theme to specify how you want to present your pictures. For example, the Fade theme slowly fades one picture into the next.

Displaying pictures in a slide show is a great way to view photos you have copied to your computer from a digital camera.

To view your slide show with high-quality graphics, including themes, you need a video card that is powerful enough to display these graphics. Some editions of Windows do not come with slide show themes.

DISPLAY PICTURES AS A SLIDE SHOW

START A SLIDE SHOW

1 Select the pictures you want to appear in your slide show. To select multiple pictures, see page 44.

Note: To include all of the displayed pictures in your slide show, click a blank area in the window.

2 Click 🖼 to start the slide show.

*Note: If you are not using Windows Photo Gallery to view your pictures, click the **Slide Show** button in the window to start the slide show.*

■ The slide show begins. Windows automatically moves from one picture to the next.

DISPLAY CONTROLS

3 To display the slide show controls, move the mouse on your desk. The slide show controls appear.

Note: When you stop moving your mouse, the slide show controls will automatically disappear.

Tip

Can I change the speed of the slide show?

Yes. When a slide show is running, move the mouse on your desk to display the slide show controls and then click the ⚙▾ slide show control. On the menu that appears, select **Slow**, **Medium** or **Fast** to select the speed at which you want the slide show to play.

Tip

The slide show controls do not appear on my screen. How can I control the slide show?

If the slide show controls do not appear on your screen, press the right button on your mouse while a slide show is running. A menu will appear, displaying a list of options for controlling the slide show. You can click an option to play the slide show, pause the slide show, display the next or previous picture, select a slide show speed or exit the slide show.

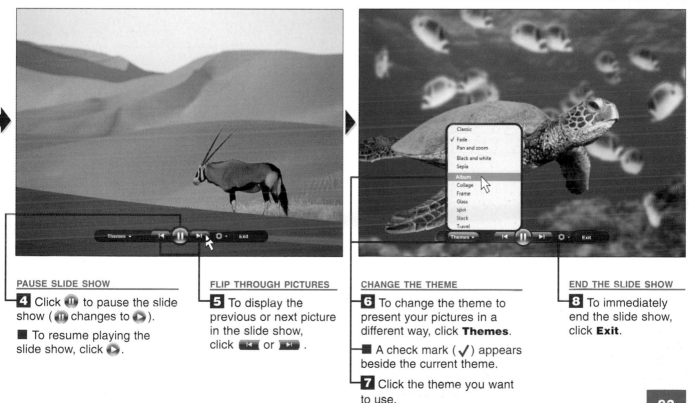

PAUSE SLIDE SHOW

4 Click ⏸ to pause the slide show (⏸ changes to ▶).

■ To resume playing the slide show, click ▶ .

FLIP THROUGH PICTURES

5 To display the previous or next picture in the slide show, click ⏮ or ⏭ .

CHANGE THE THEME

6 To change the theme to present your pictures in a different way, click **Themes**.

■ A check mark (✓) appears beside the current theme.

7 Click the theme you want to use.

END THE SLIDE SHOW

8 To immediately end the slide show, click **Exit**.

EDIT PICTURES

You can use Windows Photo Gallery to make changes to your pictures. For example, you can adjust the exposure and colors in a picture.

1 Click to display the Start menu.

2 Click **Windows Photo Gallery**.

*Note: If Windows Photo Gallery does not appear on the Start menu, click **All Programs** on the Start menu and then click **Windows Photo Gallery**.*

■ The Windows Photo Gallery window appears.

3 Click the picture you want to edit.

4 Click **Fix** to make changes to the picture.

Tip

Can I adjust a picture's exposure and colors myself?

Yes. While editing a picture in the Windows Photo Gallery, you can adjust a picture's exposure and colors yourself. To adjust a picture's exposure, click **Adjust Exposure** and then drag the sliders ( ) to adjust the brightness and contrast in the picture. To adjust a picture's color, click **Adjust Color** and then drag the sliders ( ) to adjust the color temperature, tint and saturation in the picture. The picture will immediately display the changes you make.

Tip

How can I make a picture black and white?

While editing a picture in the Windows Photo Gallery, click **Adjust Color** and then move the Saturation slider ( ) all the way to the left. The picture becomes a black and white picture.

■ A large version of the picture appears.

■ This area displays options you can select to make changes to the picture.

■ Although you can make changes to the picture in any order, you will end up with a higher-quality picture if you make changes in the order shown, starting with adjusting the picture's exposure and ending with fixing red eye.

AUTO ADJUST EXPOSURE AND COLORS

1 To have Windows automatically adjust the exposure and colors in the picture, click **Auto Adjust**.

■ Windows automatically corrects the exposure and colors in the picture.

■ After you make a change, Windows displays a check mark (✓) beside the option you adjusted.

CONTINUED

When editing a picture in the Windows Photo Gallery, you can crop the picture to remove parts of the picture you do not want to show or zoom in on certain parts of the picture. You can also fix red eye.

Crop Picture
Fix Red Eye

ADJUSTING...

EDIT PICTURES (CONTINUED)

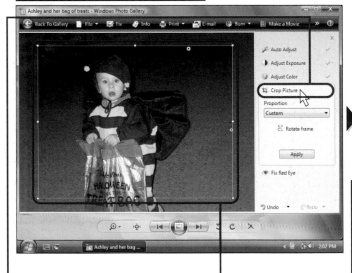

CROP A PICTURE

1 To remove parts of a picture you do not want to show or zoom in on certain parts of a picture, click **Crop Picture**.

■ A frame appears around the picture. Windows will remove the part of the picture that appears outside of the frame.

2 To change the size of the frame, position the mouse over a box (□) on the frame (changes to).

3 Drag the mouse until the frame includes the part of the picture you want to keep.

4 You can repeat steps **2** and **3** until the frame includes the part of the picture you want to keep.

5 Click **Apply** to remove the part of the picture that appears outside of the frame.

Tip

Can I crop a picture to fit in a standard print size?

Yes. While editing a picture in the Windows Photo Gallery, you can crop the picture to fit in a standard print size, such as 5 x 7. Click **Crop Picture** and then click the area below **Proportion** to select the print size you plan to use. If you want to rotate the frame so the frame is tall rather than wide, click **Rotate frame**.

Tip

Can I undo changes I made to a picture?

Yes. When editing a picture, you can click **Undo** at the bottom of the Windows Photo Gallery window to undo your last change. You can click **Undo** more than once to undo each change you have made, one at a time. If you later want to undo all of the changes you have made to a picture, click the picture in Windows Photo Gallery, click **Fix** and then click **Revert** to return to the original picture.

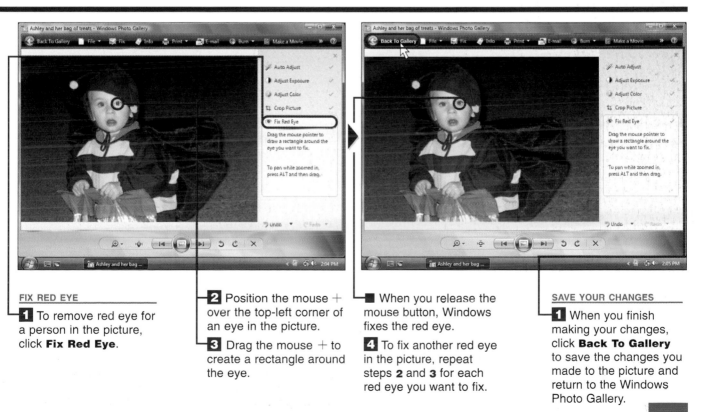

FIX RED EYE

1 To remove red eye for a person in the picture, click **Fix Red Eye**.

2 Position the mouse + over the top-left corner of an eye in the picture.

3 Drag the mouse + to create a rectangle around the eye.

■ When you release the mouse button, Windows fixes the red eye.

4 To fix another red eye in the picture, repeat steps **2** and **3** for each red eye you want to fix.

SAVE YOUR CHANGES

1 When you finish making your changes, click **Back To Gallery** to save the changes you made to the picture and return to the Windows Photo Gallery.

87

MAKE PICTURES EASIER TO FIND

You can add tags to your pictures to make your pictures easier to find and organize.

A tag is a meaningful word or phrase that you attach to pictures to help you categorize your pictures. For example, you can use tags to describe the location, people or event shown in your pictures.

When you copy pictures from a digital camera to your computer, Windows allows you to enter a tag that it will attach to every picture. For more information, see page 90. You can add more tags to the pictures at any time.

MAKE PICTURES EASIER TO FIND

■ In Windows Photo Gallery, this area displays the tags that come with Windows. You can also create your own tags, which will also appear in this area.

Note: To open Windows Photo Gallery, see page 76.

1 Click the picture you want to add a tag to.

2 Click **Info** to display the Info pane.

■ The Info pane appears, displaying information about the picture.

Note: You can close the Info pane at any time by clicking ✕ at the top of the Info pane.

■ This area displays the tags that are currently attached to the picture you selected.

3 To add a new tag to the picture, click **Add Tags**.

Tip

Is there a faster way to add tags to pictures?

Yes. To quickly add an existing tag to a picture, position the mouse ↖ over the picture in Windows Photo Gallery. Then drag the picture over the tag you want to add to the picture on the left side of the window.

You can also instantly add the same tag to many pictures at once. For example, you could add a "graduation" tag to 20 pictures of a graduation ceremony. In Windows Photo Gallery, select each picture you want to add a tag to (see page 44 to select multiple pictures). Then perform steps **3** and **4** below to add the same tag to all of the pictures.

Tip

Can I remove a tag I added to a picture?

Yes. When viewing information about a picture in Windows Photo Gallery, right-click the tag you want to remove in the Info pane. On the menu that appears, click **Remove Tag**.

4 Type the tag you want to attach to the picture and then press the Enter key. You can type an existing tag name or a new tag name.

■ The tag is added to the picture.

■ The tag appears in this area.

■ To add additional tags to the picture, repeat steps **3** and **4** for each tag you want to add. You can add as many tags as you want to a picture.

5 To add a caption to a picture, which allows you to provide a description of the picture and can also help you later find the picture, click this area and type a caption. Then press the Enter key.

Note: To use tags and captions to find pictures, see page 79.

COPY PICTURES FROM A DIGITAL CAMERA

You can copy pictures stored on a digital camera to your computer.

If your camera has a memory card that is compatible with a memory card reader in your computer, you can use the memory card to easily transfer the pictures to your computer.

After copying pictures to your computer, you can work with the pictures as you would any pictures on your computer. For example, you can edit, print or e-mail the pictures.

COPY PICTURES FROM A DIGITAL CAMERA

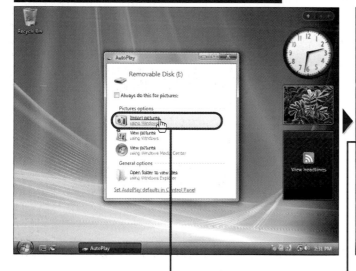

1 Remove the memory card from your digital camera.

Note: A memory card is a small card that stores pictures. Most digital cameras include a memory card.

2 Insert the memory card into your computer's memory card reader.

■ The AutoPlay dialog box appears, allowing you to select what you want to do.

3 Click this option to copy the pictures from the memory card to your computer.

■ The Importing Pictures and Videos dialog box appears.

4 To help categorize your pictures, click this area and then type a tag for the pictures.

Note: A tag is a meaningful word or phrase that you use to help categorize your pictures. For example, you can use a tag to describe the location, people or event shown in your pictures.

5 Click **Import** to copy the pictures.

Tip

The AutoPlay dialog box does not appear when I insert the memory card into my computer's memory card reader. What can I do?

Click 🎯 to display the Start menu and then click **Windows Photo Gallery**. In the Windows Photo Gallery window, click **File** and then click **Import from Camera or Scanner**. Click the drive for your memory card in the Import Pictures and Videos dialog box and then click **Import** to import the pictures from your memory card.

Tip

Can I connect my digital camera directly to my computer instead of using a memory card?

Yes. You can connect your digital camera to your computer using a cable and then copy pictures directly from the camera to your computer. To copy pictures, the camera must be installed on your computer and turned on. You may also need to set your camera to a specific mode. For more information, check the documentation that came with your camera. After connecting the camera to your computer, perform steps **3** to **6** below to copy the pictures to your computer.

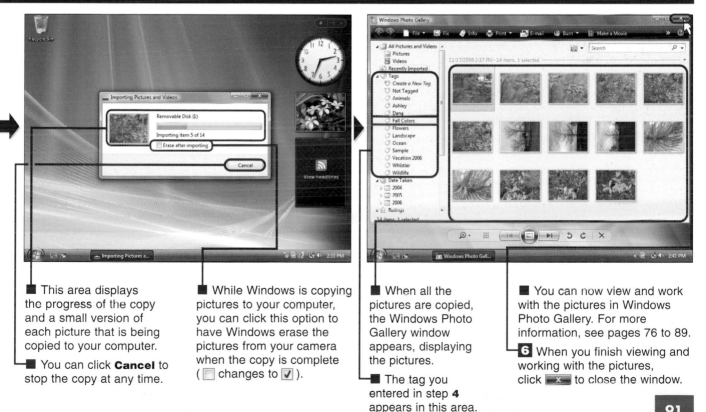

■ This area displays the progress of the copy and a small version of each picture that is being copied to your computer.

■ You can click **Cancel** to stop the copy at any time.

■ While Windows is copying pictures to your computer, you can click this option to have Windows erase the pictures from your camera when the copy is complete (☐ changes to ☑).

■ When all the pictures are copied, the Windows Photo Gallery window appears, displaying the pictures.

■ The tag you entered in step **4** appears in this area.

■ You can now view and work with the pictures in Windows Photo Gallery. For more information, see pages 76 to 89.

6 When you finish viewing and working with the pictures, click ✖ to close the window.

COPY PICTURES AND VIDEOS TO A DVD

You can use Windows DVD Maker to quickly and easily create DVDs that can include videos, pictures and music.

You can use Windows DVD Maker to show your home movies and create slide shows of your favorite pictures. You can even include projects you created in Windows Movie Maker on your DVDs.

After you create a DVD, you can play the DVD in a DVD player and watch the DVD on a television.

Windows DVD Maker is only available in the Home Premium and Ultimate editions of Windows Vista.

COPY PICTURES AND VIDEOS TO A DVD

COPY PICTURES AND VIDEOS TO A DVD

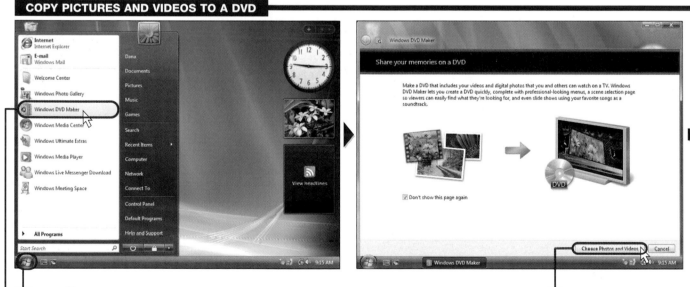

1 Click 🪟 to display the Start menu.

2 Click **Windows DVD Maker**.

*Note: If Windows DVD Maker does not appear on the Start menu, click **All Programs** on the Start menu and then click **Windows DVD Maker**.*

■ The Windows DVD Maker window appears.

■ The first time you start Windows DVD Maker, the window displays information about making DVDs.

3 Click **Choose Photos and Videos** to select the pictures and videos that you want to include on the DVD.

Tip

Can I add more than one picture or video at a time?

Yes. In the Add Items to DVD dialog box, press and hold down the Ctrl key as you click each picture or video you want to add. Then click **Add** to add all of the pictures or videos you selected.

Tip

How do I remove a video or picture I added?

If you no longer want to include a video on your DVD, click the video in the Windows DVD Maker window and then click **Remove items**. To remove a picture, double-click the Slide show folder to display all the pictures in the folder. Then click the picture you want to remove and click **Remove items**. To once again display the Slide show folder, click 🔼.

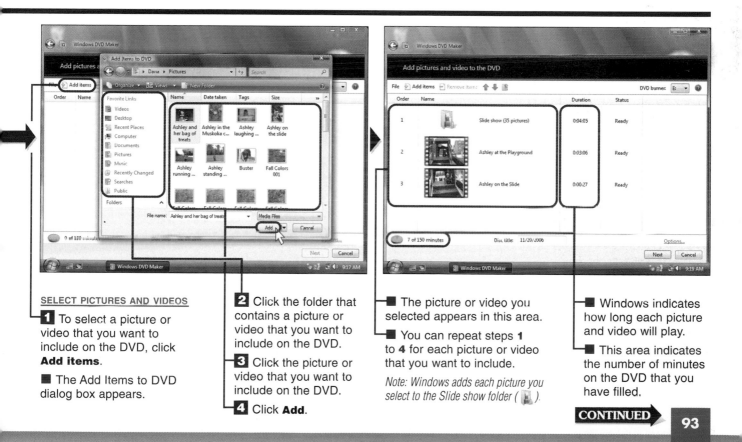

SELECT PICTURES AND VIDEOS

1 To select a picture or video that you want to include on the DVD, click **Add items**.

■ The Add Items to DVD dialog box appears.

2 Click the folder that contains a picture or video that you want to include on the DVD.

3 Click the picture or video that you want to include on the DVD.

4 Click **Add**.

■ The picture or video you selected appears in this area.

■ You can repeat steps **1** to **4** for each picture or video that you want to include.

Note: Windows adds each picture you select to the Slide show folder (   ).

■ Windows indicates how long each picture and video will play.

■ This area indicates the number of minutes on the DVD that you have filled.

CONTINUED

93

COPY PICTURES AND VIDEOS TO A DVD

When making your DVD, you can change the order of the videos and pictures on the DVD.

You can also specify a title for the DVD that will appear on the DVD's main menu and the style of main menu that you want to use.

COPY PICTURES AND VIDEOS TO A DVD (CONTINUED)

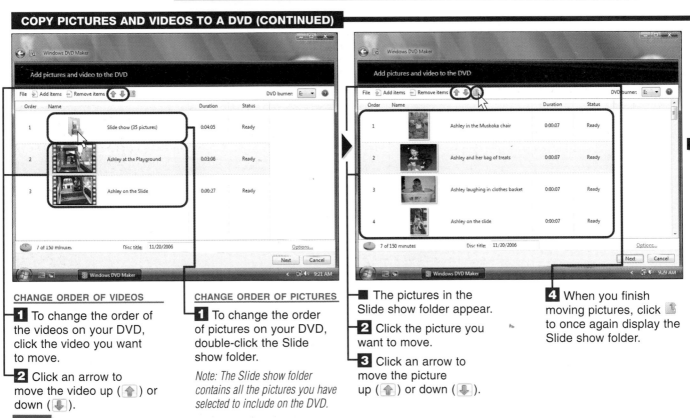

CHANGE ORDER OF VIDEOS

1 To change the order of the videos on your DVD, click the video you want to move.

2 Click an arrow to move the video up (⬆) or down (⬇).

CHANGE ORDER OF PICTURES

1 To change the order of pictures on your DVD, double-click the Slide show folder.

Note: The Slide show folder contains all the pictures you have selected to include on the DVD.

■ The pictures in the Slide show folder appear.

2 Click the picture you want to move.

3 Click an arrow to move the picture up (⬆) or down (⬇).

4 When you finish moving pictures, click 📁 to once again display the Slide show folder.

Tip

Can I customize the text that appears on the DVD's main menu?

Yes. While creating a DVD, click **Menu text** to customize the DVD's main menu text. You can select a font for the menu text, type a new title for the DVD and type different labels for the Play and Scenes buttons. You can also type notes that viewers can view when they click a Notes button. Changes you make are immediately previewed on the right side of the window. After you finish customizing the text, click **Change Text** to make the changes.

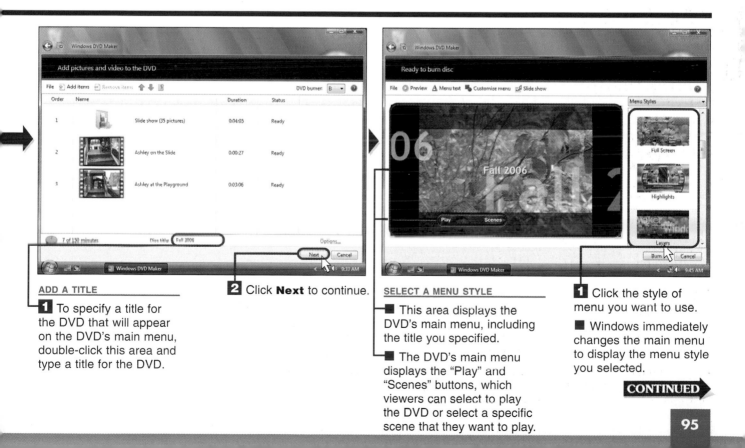

ADD A TITLE

1 To specify a title for the DVD that will appear on the DVD's main menu, double-click this area and type a title for the DVD.

2 Click **Next** to continue.

SELECT A MENU STYLE

■ This area displays the DVD's main menu, including the title you specified.

■ The DVD's main menu displays the "Play" and "Scenes" buttons, which viewers can select to play the DVD or select a specific scene that they want to play.

1 Click the style of menu you want to use.

■ Windows immediately changes the main menu to display the menu style you selected.

CONTINUED

COPY PICTURES AND VIDEOS TO A DVD

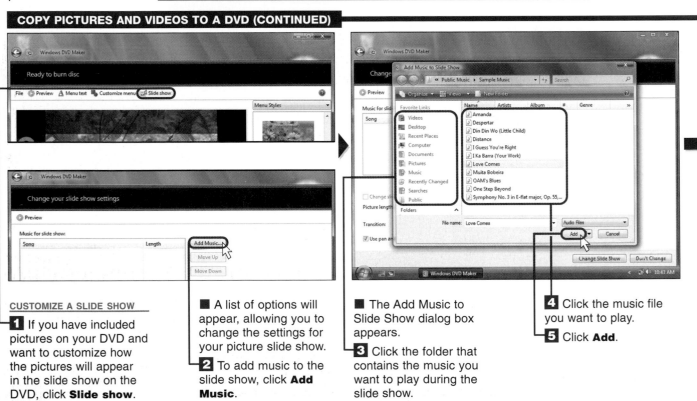

If you have included pictures on your DVD, you can customize how the pictures will appear in the slide show on the DVD.

You can add music to the slide show and select a transition to specify how you want the slide show to move from one picture to the next.

COPY PICTURES AND VIDEOS TO A DVD (CONTINUED)

CUSTOMIZE A SLIDE SHOW

1 If you have included pictures on your DVD and want to customize how the pictures will appear in the slide show on the DVD, click **Slide show**.

■ A list of options will appear, allowing you to change the settings for your picture slide show.

2 To add music to the slide show, click **Add Music**.

■ The Add Music to Slide Show dialog box appears.

3 Click the folder that contains the music you want to play during the slide show.

4 Click the music file you want to play.

5 Click **Add**.

Tip

Can I customize the style of the DVD's main menu?

Yes. While creating a DVD, click **Customize menu** to customize the style of the DVD's main menu. You can select a font for the menu text, select a picture or video you want to appear in the foreground and background of the menu, select music to play while the menu is displayed and select a shape for the Scenes button. Changes you make are immediately previewed on the right side of the window. After you finish customizing the main menu, click **Change Style** to make the changes.

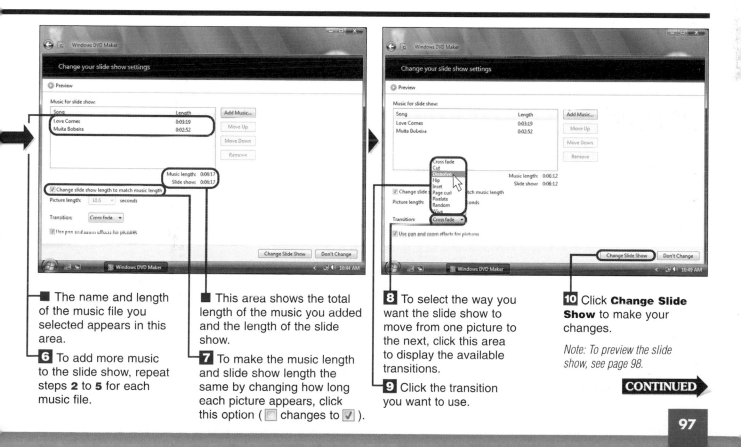

■ The name and length of the music file you selected appears in this area.

6 To add more music to the slide show, repeat steps **2** to **5** for each music file.

■ This area shows the total length of the music you added and the length of the slide show.

7 To make the music length and slide show length the same by changing how long each picture appears, click this option (☐ changes to ☑).

8 To select the way you want the slide show to move from one picture to the next, click this area to display the available transitions.

9 Click the transition you want to use.

10 Click **Change Slide Show** to make your changes.

Note: To preview the slide show, see page 98.

CONTINUED

COPY PICTURES AND VIDEOS TO A DVD

Before burning a DVD, you can preview how the DVD will play. Previewing a DVD allows you to determine if you need to make any changes to the DVD before burning the DVD.

COPY PICTURES AND VIDEOS TO A DVD (CONTINUED)

PREVIEW A DVD

1 To preview how the DVD will play, click **Preview**.

■ The preview of the DVD appears.

2 While previewing the DVD, you can click one of the following options.

▶ Play

❚❚ Pause

◄◄ , ►► Skip to previous or next chapter

▣ Display the main menu

3 To move through the menu options, click an arrow to move left (◄), right (►), up (▲) or down (▼). Then click ↩ to select the option.

4 When you finish previewing, click **OK**.

BURN A DVD

■ When you finish creating your DVD, you can burn the videos, pictures and music you selected to a DVD disc.

1 Insert a recordable DVD disc into your recordable DVD drive.

2 Click **Burn** to burn the DVD disc.

■ A dialog box will appear, showing the progress of the copy.

■ When Windows has successfully burned the DVD disc, a dialog box appears, indicating that the disc is ready.

■ If you want to make another copy of the DVD disc, remove the completed DVD disc, insert a new recordable DVD disc and then click **Make another copy of this disc**.

3 To close the dialog box, click **Close**.

CHAPTER 5

Working With Songs and Videos

PLAY A VIDEO OR SOUND

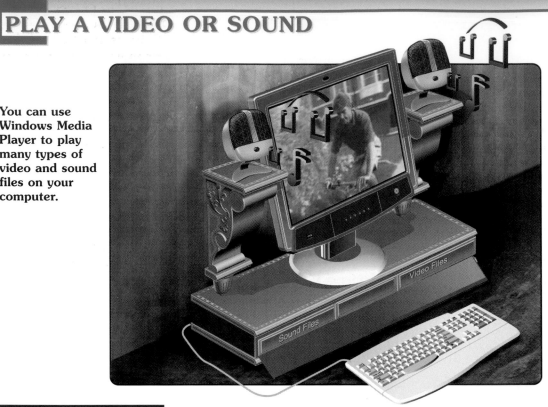

You can use Windows Media Player to play many types of video and sound files on your computer.

You can obtain video and sound files on the Internet or from friends, family members or colleagues in e-mail messages you receive.

PLAY A VIDEO OR SOUND

1 Double-click the video or sound file you want to play.

■ The Windows Media Player window appears.

Note: The first time Windows Media Player starts, a Welcome to Windows Media Player wizard appears, helping you set up the Player. See the top of page 103 for more information on the wizard.

■ If you selected a video file, this area displays the video.

Note: If you selected a sound file, the sound plays. The area displays splashes of color and shapes that change as the sound plays.

■ This area displays the name of the video or sound file.

Tip

Why does a Welcome wizard appear when I try to play a video or sound file?

The first time Windows Media Player starts, a Welcome to Windows Media Player wizard appears, helping you set up the Player on your computer. In the wizard, click **Express Settings** (⦿ changes to ⦿) and then click **Finish** to finish setting up Windows Media Player.

Tip

Can I use the entire screen to view a video?

You can easily use your entire screen area to view a video. After performing step **1** below to start playing a video, click 🔲 at the bottom-right corner of the Windows Media Player window. The video will continue playing using your entire screen. To once again view the video in a window, press the Esc key on your keyboard.

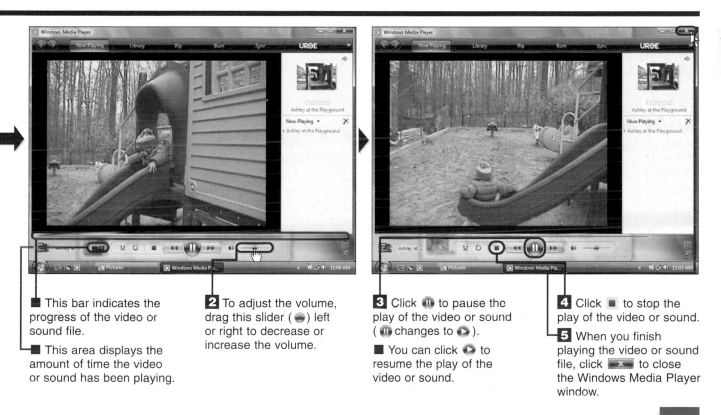

■ This bar indicates the progress of the video or sound file.

■ This area displays the amount of time the video or sound has been playing.

2 To adjust the volume, drag this slider (⬤) left or right to decrease or increase the volume.

3 Click ⏸ to pause the play of the video or sound (⏸ changes to ▶).

■ You can click ▶ to resume the play of the video or sound.

4 Click ■ to stop the play of the video or sound.

5 When you finish playing the video or sound file, click ✖ to close the Windows Media Player window.

PLAY A MUSIC CD

You can use your computer to play music CDs while you work.

The first time Windows Media Player starts, a Welcome to Windows Media Player wizard appears, helping you set up the Player. See the top of page 103 for information on using the wizard to set up the Player.

PLAY A MUSIC CD

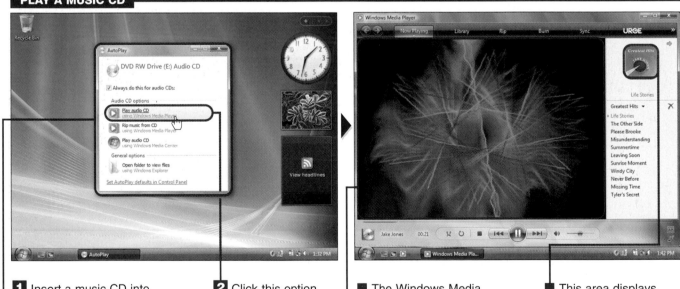

1 Insert a music CD into your computer's CD drive.

■ The first time you insert a music CD, the AutoPlay dialog box appears, allowing you to select what you want to do.

2 Click this option to play the music CD using Windows Media Player.

Note: You only need to perform step 2 once.

■ The Windows Media Player window appears and the CD begins to play.

■ This area displays splashes of color and shapes that change with the beat of the song that is currently playing.

■ This area displays the cover for the CD that is currently playing.

Tip

How does Windows Media Player know the CD cover and the name of each song on my music CD?

If you are connected to the Internet when you play a music CD, Windows Media Player attempts to obtain information about the CD from the Internet, including the CD cover and track names. If you are not connected to the Internet or information about the CD is unavailable, Windows Media Player displays a generic CD cover and the track number of each song instead. If Windows Media Player is able to obtain information about the CD, Windows will recognize the CD and display the appropriate information each time you insert the CD.

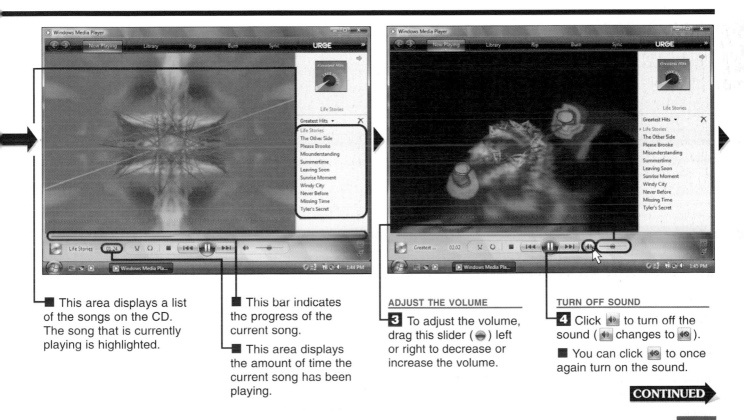

■ This area displays a list of the songs on the CD. The song that is currently playing is highlighted.

■ This bar indicates the progress of the current song.

■ This area displays the amount of time the current song has been playing.

ADJUST THE VOLUME

3 To adjust the volume, drag this slider (●) left or right to decrease or increase the volume.

TURN OFF SOUND

4 Click 🔊 to turn off the sound (🔊 changes to 🔇).

■ You can click 🔇 to once again turn on the sound.

CONTINUED ►

PLAY A MUSIC CD

When playing a music CD, you can pause or stop the play of the CD at any time. You can also play a specific song or play the songs in random order.

PLAY A MUSIC CD (CONTINUED)

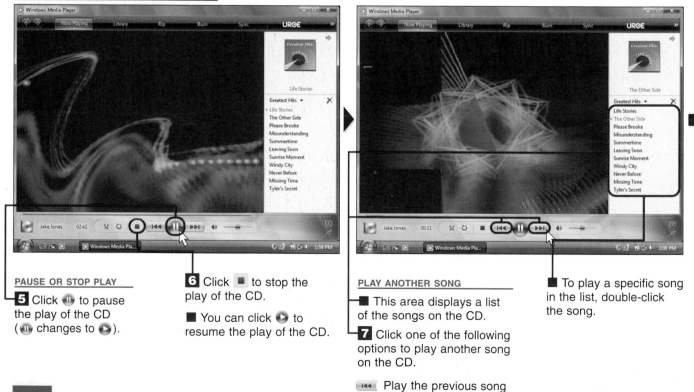

PAUSE OR STOP PLAY

5 Click ⏸ to pause the play of the CD (⏸ changes to ▶).

6 Click ■ to stop the play of the CD.

■ You can click ▶ to resume the play of the CD.

PLAY ANOTHER SONG

■ This area displays a list of the songs on the CD.

7 Click one of the following options to play another song on the CD.

⏮ Play the previous song

⏭ Play the next song

■ To play a specific song in the list, double-click the song.

Tip

Can I play a music CD while performing other tasks on my computer?

Yes. If you want to perform other tasks on your computer while playing a music CD, you can display the Windows Media Player window in the mini Player mode. The mini Player mode displays the most commonly used Windows Media Player playback controls in a toolbar on the taskbar. For information on the mini Player mode, see page 113.

Tip

Can I eject a CD using Windows Media Player?

When you are finished listening to a CD, you can easily eject the CD using Windows Media Player's controls. Right-click an empty area at the bottom of the Player window to display a menu of options and then click **Play**. In the menu that appears, click **Eject** to eject the CD from your CD drive.

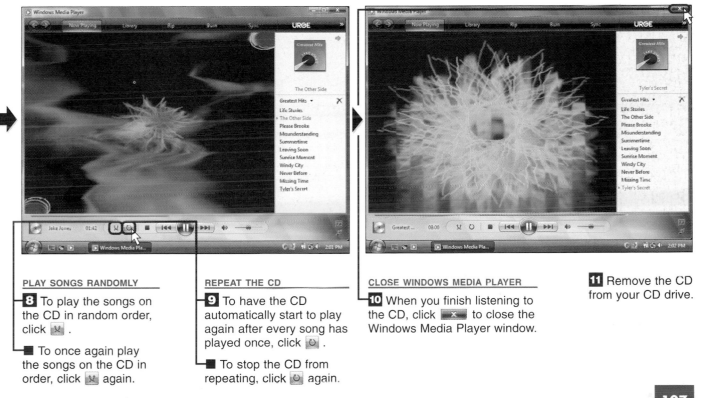

PLAY SONGS RANDOMLY

8 To play the songs on the CD in random order, click .

■ To once again play the songs on the CD in order, click again.

REPEAT THE CD

9 To have the CD automatically start to play again after every song has played once, click .

■ To stop the CD from repeating, click again.

CLOSE WINDOWS MEDIA PLAYER

10 When you finish listening to the CD, click to close the Windows Media Player window.

11 Remove the CD from your CD drive.

USING THE LIBRARY

You can use the Library to view, organize and play all the media files on your computer, such as music, pictures and videos.

The first time Windows Media Player starts, a Welcome to Windows Media Player wizard appears, helping you set up the Player. See the top of page 103 for information on using the wizard to set up the Player.

USING THE LIBRARY

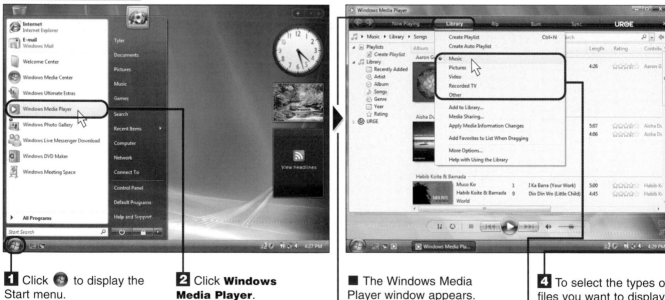

1 Click ⊕ to display the Start menu.

2 Click **Windows Media Player**.

*Note: If Windows Media Player does not appear on the Start menu, click **All Programs** on the Start menu and then click **Windows Media Player**.*

■ The Windows Media Player window appears.

3 Click **Library** to view and play the media files on your computer, including music, pictures and videos.

4 To select the types of files you want to display in the Library, click **Library** again. A menu appears.

5 Click the type of files you want to display.

Note: For information on the types of files you can display, see the top of page 109.

Tip

What types of files can I display and work with in the Library?

Music	All your music files, including files you have downloaded from the Internet or copied from a music CD.
Pictures	All your pictures files, including pictures you have obtained from the Internet or copied from a digital camera.
Video	All your video files, including videos you have downloaded from the Internet and movies you have created using Windows Movie Maker.
Recorded TV	Television shows you have recorded.
Other	Digital media files that do not belong in any other category.

Note: Windows may also automatically provide sample music, pictures and videos that you can display in the Library.

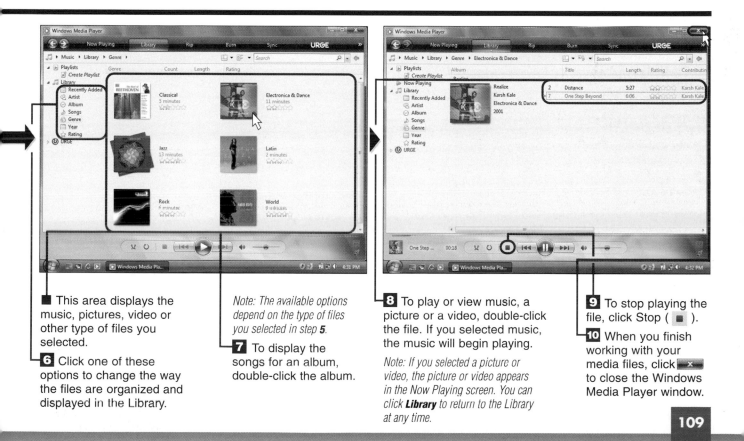

■ This area displays the music, pictures, video or other type of files you selected.

6 Click one of these options to change the way the files are organized and displayed in the Library.

Note: The available options depend on the type of files you selected in step 5.

7 To display the songs for an album, double-click the album.

8 To play or view music, a picture or a video, double-click the file. If you selected music, the music will begin playing.

*Note: If you selected a picture or video, the picture or video appears in the Now Playing screen. You can click **Library** to return to the Library at any time.*

9 To stop playing the file, click Stop (■).

10 When you finish working with your media files, click ✕ to close the Windows Media Player window.

CREATE A PLAYLIST

You can create personalized lists, called playlists, of your favorite sound, video and picture files.

When you play a playlist, Windows Media Player will play all the files in the playlist. For example, you can create a playlist that contains your favorite rock music or a playlist that contains the photos from your last family vacation.

The first time Windows Media Player starts, a Welcome to Windows Media Player wizard appears, helping you set up the Player. See the top of page 103 for information on using the wizard to set up the Player.

CREATE A PLAYLIST

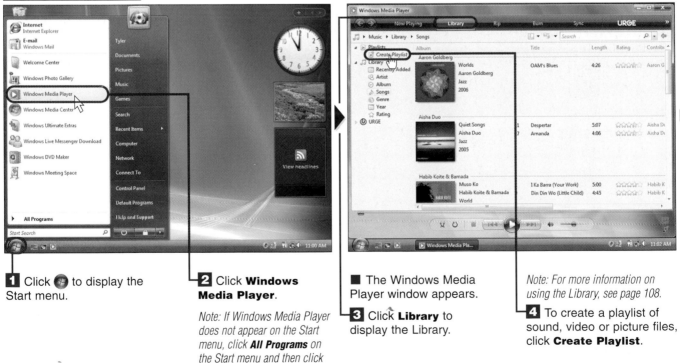

1 Click 🟦 to display the Start menu.

2 Click **Windows Media Player**.

*Note: If Windows Media Player does not appear on the Start menu, click **All Programs** on the Start menu and then click **Windows Media Player**.*

■ The Windows Media Player window appears.

3 Click **Library** to display the Library.

Note: For more information on using the Library, see page 108.

4 To create a playlist of sound, video or picture files, click **Create Playlist**.

Can I make changes to a playlist after I create it?

You can make changes to a playlist at any time. In the Windows Media Player window, display the Library and then click the name of the playlist you want to change. Click **Edit in List Pane** to make changes to the playlist.

To add a new item, drag the item to the playlist. To change the order of items, drag an item to a new location in the playlist. To remove an item from the playlist, right-click the item and click **Remove from List** in the menu that appears. When you have finished making changes, click **Save Playlist**.

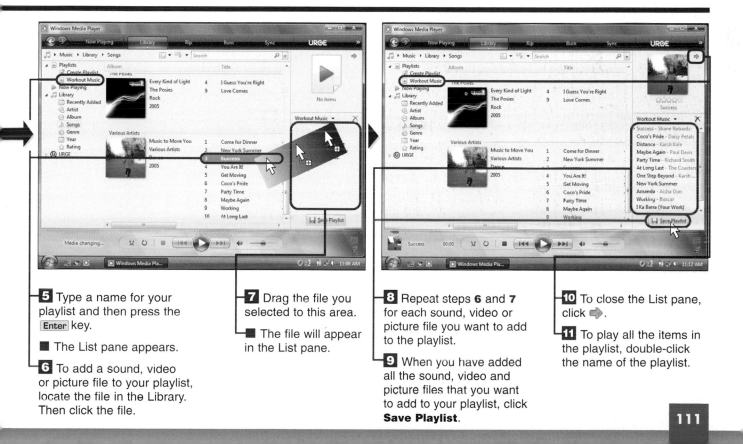

5 Type a name for your playlist and then press the Enter key.

■ The List pane appears.

6 To add a sound, video or picture file to your playlist, locate the file in the Library. Then click the file.

7 Drag the file you selected to this area.

■ The file will appear in the List pane.

8 Repeat steps **6** and **7** for each sound, video or picture file you want to add to the playlist.

9 When you have added all the sound, video and picture files that you want to add to your playlist, click **Save Playlist**.

10 To close the List pane, click ➡.

11 To play all the items in the playlist, double-click the name of the playlist.

SWITCH BETWEEN DISPLAY MODES

You can change the appearance of Windows Media Player by switching between three different display modes.

The first time Windows Media Player starts, a Welcome to Windows Media Player wizard appears, helping you set up the Player. See the top of page 103 for information on using the wizard to set up the Player.

Full

Compact

Mini Player

SWITCH BETWEEN DISPLAY MODES

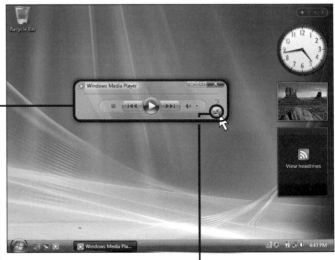

FULL MODE

■ Windows Media Player initially appears in the full mode. The full mode allows you to access all the features that Windows Media Player provides.

1 To display Windows Media Player in the compact mode, click ▣.

COMPACT MODE

■ The compact mode offers a distinct design and usually takes up less room on your screen, but offers fewer features than the full mode.

■ To once again display Windows Media Player in the full mode, click ▣.

What types of playback controls does the mini Player mode toolbar offer?

The Windows Media Player toolbar that appears on your taskbar in mini Player mode contains controls that allow you to play ( ), stop ( ) or pause ( ) the currently playing item, move forward ( ) or back ( ) through the items, turn the sound on or off ( ) and adjust the volume ( ). You can also use the button on the toolbar to display or hide a small window that shows the currently playing video or the splashes of color and shapes for the currently playing sound.

Can I stop Windows Media Player from appearing as a toolbar on the taskbar when I minimize the window?

Yes. If you want Windows Media Player to appear as a regular button on the taskbar when you minimize the window, perform steps **1** to **3** below to turn off the mini Player mode. Windows Media Player will no longer appear as a toolbar on the taskbar when you minimize the window.

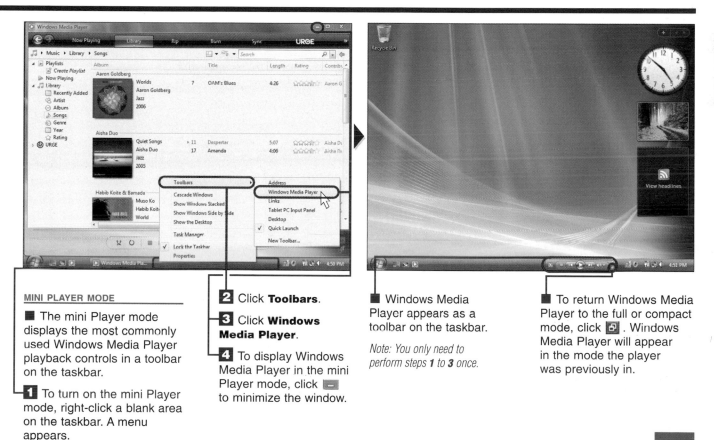

MINI PLAYER MODE

■ The mini Player mode displays the most commonly used Windows Media Player playback controls in a toolbar on the taskbar.

1 To turn on the mini Player mode, right-click a blank area on the taskbar. A menu appears.

2 Click **Toolbars**.

3 Click **Windows Media Player**.

4 To display Windows Media Player in the mini Player mode, click to minimize the window.

■ Windows Media Player appears as a toolbar on the taskbar.

Note: You only need to perform steps 1 to 3 once.

■ To return Windows Media Player to the full or compact mode, click . Windows Media Player will appear in the mode the player was previously in.

COPY SONGS FROM A MUSIC CD

You can copy songs from a music CD onto your computer.

Copying songs from a music CD, also known as "ripping" music, allows you to play the songs at any time without having to insert the CD into your computer. Copying songs from a music CD also allows you to later copy the songs to a recordable CD or a portable device, such as an MP3 player.

The first time Windows Media Player starts, a Welcome to Windows Media Player wizard appears, helping you set up the Player. See the top of page 103 for information on using the wizard to set up the Player.

COPY SONGS FROM A MUSIC CD

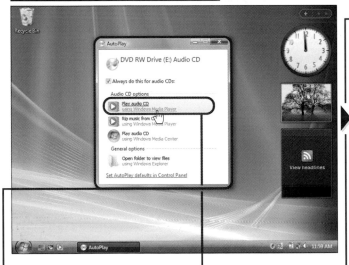

1 Insert a music CD into your computer's CD drive.

■ The first time you insert a music CD, the AutoPlay dialog box appears, allowing you to select what you want to do.

2 Click this option to play the music CD using Windows Media Player.

*Note: You only need to perform step **2** once.*

■ The Windows Media Player window appears and the CD begins to play.

3 Click **Rip** to copy songs from the music CD.

■ This area displays information about each song on the CD.

Note: For information on how Windows Media Player determines the name of each song on a CD, see the top of page 105.

Tip

How can I play a song I copied from a music CD?

Songs you copy from a music CD are listed in the Library in Windows Media Player. To play a song in the Library, see page 108. Songs you copy from a music CD are also stored in the Music folder on your computer. The Music folder contains a subfolder for each artist whose songs you have copied to your computer. To work with the Music folder, see page 38. To play a song in the Music folder, double-click the song.

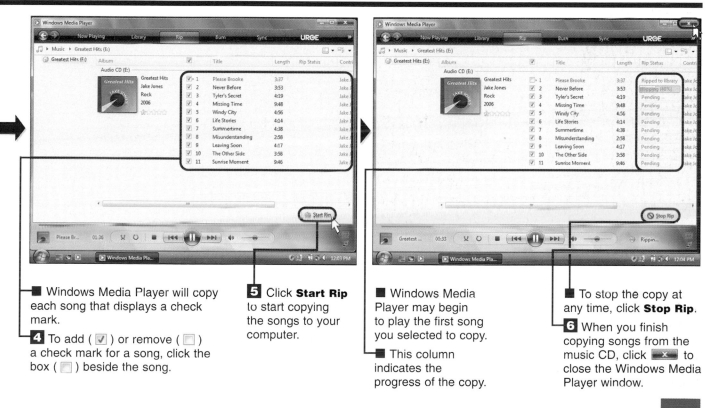

■ Windows Media Player will copy each song that displays a check mark.

4 To add (✓) or remove (☐) a check mark for a song, click the box (☐) beside the song.

5 Click **Start Rip** to start copying the songs to your computer.

■ Windows Media Player may begin to play the first song you selected to copy.

■ This column indicates the progress of the copy.

■ To stop the copy at any time, click **Stop Rip**.

6 When you finish copying songs from the music CD, click ▬✕▬ to close the Windows Media Player window.

COPY SONGS TO A CD

You can use Windows Media Player to copy songs on your computer to a CD. Copying songs to a CD is also known as "burning" a CD.

The first time Windows Media Player starts, a Welcome to Windows Media Player wizard appears, helping you set up the Player. See the top of page 103 for information on using the wizard to set up the Player.

COPY SONGS TO A CD

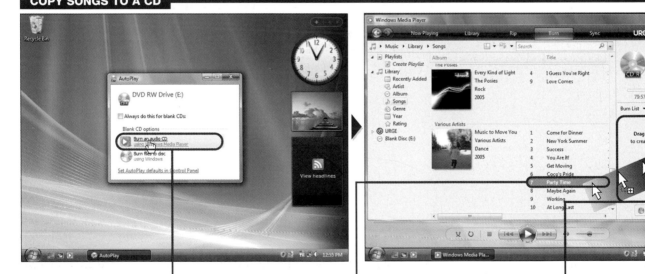

1 To copy songs to a CD, insert a blank, recordable CD into your recordable CD drive.

■ A dialog box appears, allowing you to select what you want to do.

2 Click **Burn an audio CD**.

■ The Windows Media Player window appears.

3 To specify a song you want to copy to the CD, locate the song in the Library. Then click the file.

Note: For information on using the Library, see page 108.

4 Drag the file you selected to this area.

■ The file will appear in the List pane.

Tip

Can I copy songs to more than one CD at a time?

If you want to copy more songs than will fit on a single CD, the List pane will divide the songs into several CDs for you. The List pane displays the words "Next Disc" between the songs for each CD you will copy to. When Windows Media Player has finished copying songs to the first CD, the completed CD is automatically ejected from the CD drive. Insert the next blank CD into the drive and click **Start Burn** again.

Tip

Can I copy songs to a CD at different times?

You can copy songs to a CD only once using Windows Media Player. Since you must copy all the songs to a CD at the same time, make sure you carefully select all the songs you want to copy.

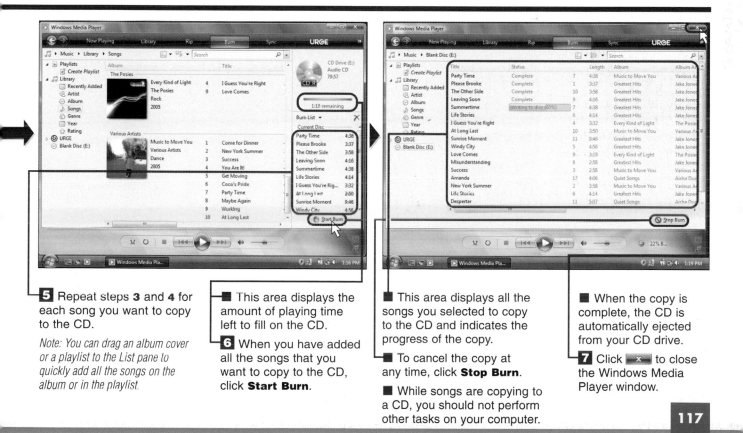

5 Repeat steps **3** and **4** for each song you want to copy to the CD.

Note: You can drag an album cover or a playlist to the List pane to quickly add all the songs on the album or in the playlist.

■ This area displays the amount of playing time left to fill on the CD.

6 When you have added all the songs that you want to copy to the CD, click **Start Burn**.

■ This area displays all the songs you selected to copy to the CD and indicates the progress of the copy.

■ To cancel the copy at any time, click **Stop Burn**.

■ While songs are copying to a CD, you should not perform other tasks on your computer.

■ When the copy is complete, the CD is automatically ejected from your CD drive.

7 Click ▓▓▓ to close the Windows Media Player window.

COPY SONGS TO A PORTABLE DEVICE

You can use Windows Media Player to copy songs on your computer to a portable device, such as an MP3 player.

You can copy songs that you have copied from a music CD or downloaded from the Internet to a portable device. Copying songs to a portable device is also known as "synchronizing" or "syncing" songs.

The first time Windows Media Player starts, a Welcome to Windows Media Player wizard appears, helping you set up the Player. See the top of page 103 for information on using the wizard to set up the Player.

COPY SONGS TO A PORTABLE DEVICE

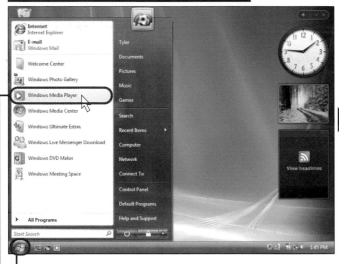

1 Click ⊕ to display the Start menu.

2 Click **Windows Media Player**.

*Note: If Windows Media Player does not appear on the Start menu, click **All Programs** on the Start menu and then click **Windows Media Player**.*

■ The Windows Media Player window appears.

3 Connect the portable device to your computer.

■ The List pane appears.

4 To specify a song you want to copy to the portable device, locate the song in the Library. Then click the file.

Note: For information on using the Library, see page 108.

5 Drag the file you selected to this area.

■ The file will appear in the List pane.

Tip

Why does a Device Setup wizard appear when I connect a portable device to my computer?

The first time you connect a portable device, such as an MP3 player, to your computer, the Device Setup wizard may appear. The wizard may allow you to specify how you want to copy, or synchronize, songs to the portable device and ask you to name the device. Follow the instructions in the wizard to continue.

Tip

Can I have Windows Media Player compile an assortment of songs to copy to my portable device?

You can use Windows Media Player's shuffle feature to create a list of songs from throughout your Library to copy to your portable device. After connecting the portable device to your computer, click the **Shuffle music** link in the List pane at the right side of the Player window to have Windows Media Player compile a list of songs to copy. Then click **Shuffle now** to copy the songs to your portable device.

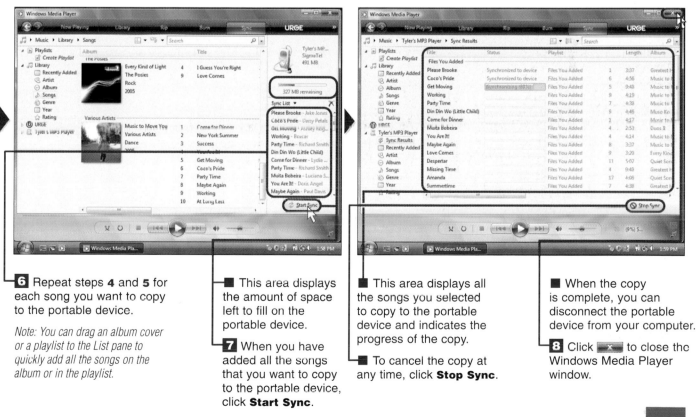

◾6 Repeat steps **4** and **5** for each song you want to copy to the portable device.

Note: You can drag an album cover or a playlist to the List pane to quickly add all the songs on the album or in the playlist.

◾ This area displays the amount of space left to fill on the portable device.

◾7 When you have added all the songs that you want to copy to the portable device, click **Start Sync**.

◾ This area displays all the songs you selected to copy to the portable device and indicates the progress of the copy.

◾ To cancel the copy at any time, click **Stop Sync**.

◾ When the copy is complete, you can disconnect the portable device from your computer.

◾8 Click ✕ to close the Windows Media Player window.

PLAY A DVD MOVIE

You can use Windows Media Player to play DVD movies on your computer.

If you have a notebook computer, using your computer to play DVD movies can be especially useful when traveling.

The first time Windows Media Player starts, a Welcome to Windows Media Player wizard appears, helping you set up the Player. See the top of page 103 for information on using the wizard to set up the Player.

PLAY A DVD MOVIE

1 Insert a DVD movie into your computer's DVD drive.

■ The first time you insert a DVD movie, the AutoPlay dialog box appears, allowing you to select what you want to do.

2 Click this option to play the DVD movie using Windows Media Player.

Note: You only need to perform step 2 once.

■ The DVD movie begins playing, filling your entire screen.

■ After a few moments, the DVD's main menu usually appears, displaying options you can select, such as playing the movie or a specific scene. To select an option, click the option.

3 To display controls you can use to adjust the playback of the movie, move the mouse ⃗ on your screen.

■ The playback controls will appear at the bottom of the screen.

Tip

Why can't I play a DVD movie?

Before you can play DVD movies, your computer must have a DVD drive and a DVD decoder installed. A DVD decoder is software that allows your computer to play DVD movies. Most new computers with a DVD drive come with a DVD decoder installed. If your computer has a DVD drive but does not have a DVD decoder installed, you can purchase a DVD decoder for Windows Vista from companies such as InterVideo (www.intervideo.com) and CyberLink (www.gocyberlink.com).

Tip

Do I have to use the entire screen to watch a DVD movie?

No. Playing a DVD movie within the Windows Media Player window allows you to perform other tasks on your computer while the movie plays. To view a movie in the Windows Media Player window at any time, press the Esc key. To once again view the movie using the full screen, click at the bottom-right corner of the window.

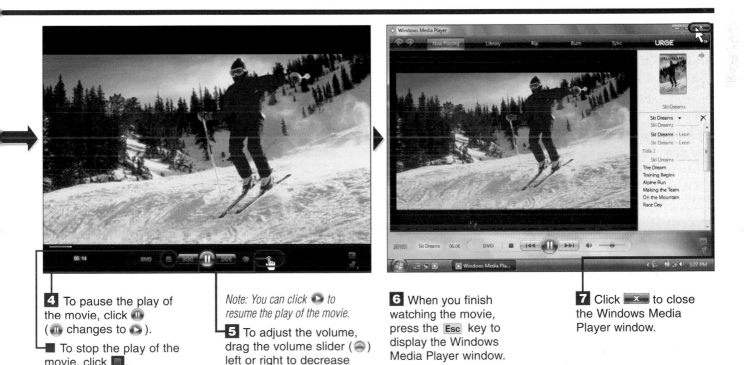

4 To pause the play of the movie, click (changes to).

To stop the play of the movie, click .

Note: You can click to resume the play of the movie.

5 To adjust the volume, drag the volume slider () left or right to decrease or increase the volume.

6 When you finish watching the movie, press the Esc key to display the Windows Media Player window.

7 Click to close the Windows Media Player window.

Create Movies

TRANSFER VIDEO TO YOUR COMPUTER

You can use Windows Movie Maker to transfer home movies from your camcorder to your computer.

After you transfer video to your computer, you can edit the video on your computer to create your own movies.

For the best results when working with Windows Movie Maker, your screen resolution should be set at 1024x768 or higher.
To change your screen resolution, see page 160.

TRANSFER VIDEO TO YOUR COMPUTER

START WINDOWS MOVIE MAKER

1 Click 🔵 to display the Start menu.

2 Click **All Programs** to view a list of the programs on your computer.

3 Click **Windows Movie Maker**.

■ The Windows Movie Maker window appears.

TRANSFER VIDEO

1 Connect your camcorder to your computer, turn the camcorder on and set it to the mode that plays back recorded video. Make sure the video tape is at the point where you want to begin transferring the video.

Tip

Which format should I choose when transferring video to my computer?

Audio Video Interleaved (single file)	This format is useful if you plan to record your final video back to the tape cartridge in your camcorder. This option produces high quality video, but very large file sizes.
Windows Media Video (single file)	This format is useful if you want to play the final video on your computer, copy the video to a CD or DVD or send the video in an e-mail message. The entire video will be saved as one file on your computer.
Windows Media Video (one file per scene)	This format is the same as Windows Media Video (single file), but the video will be broken into small, manageable segments, called clips, that you can work with in Windows Movie Maker. *Note: A clip is created each time Windows Movie Maker detects a different sequence in a video, such as when you turn on your camcorder.*

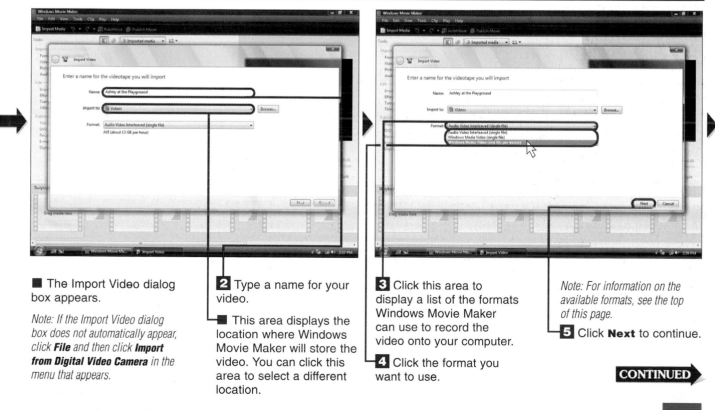

■ The Import Video dialog box appears.

*Note: If the Import Video dialog box does not automatically appear, click **File** and then click **Import from Digital Video Camera** in the menu that appears.*

2 Type a name for your video.

■ This area displays the location where Windows Movie Maker will store the video. You can click this area to select a different location.

3 Click this area to display a list of the formats Windows Movie Maker can use to record the video onto your computer.

4 Click the format you want to use.

Note: For information on the available formats, see the top of this page.

5 Click **Next** to continue.

CONTINUED

TRANSFER VIDEO TO YOUR COMPUTER

When you transfer video to your computer, you can choose to transfer all the video on the tape at once or only portions of the video that you select.

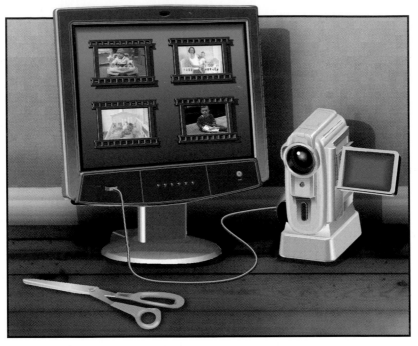

TRANSFER VIDEO TO YOUR COMPUTER (CONTINUED)

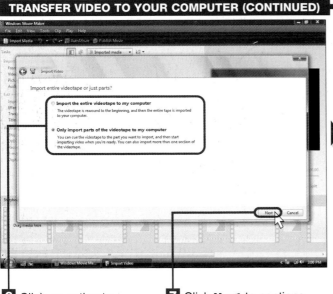

6 Click an option to specify whether you want to transfer all the video on the entire tape or only part of the video on the tape (⊙ changes to ⊙).

7 Click **Next** to continue.

Note: If you selected to transfer all the video on the entire tape in step 6, Windows Movie Maker will transfer the contents of the entire tape in your camcorder. When the transfer is complete, skip to step 10.

■ To move through the video on your camcorder, you can use these controls to play (▶), stop (■), rewind (◀◀) and fast forward (▶▶) the video. You can also use the controls on your camcorder.

■ This area will display the video.

8 When you are ready to start transferring the video to your computer, click **Start Video Import**.

■ This area will display the time that has passed since you started transferring the video and the current size of the video file.

Tip

When transferring video to my computer, can I perform other tasks on my computer?

Transferring video from a camcorder to a computer requires a lot of computer processing power. To ensure the best quality of the transferred video, you should avoid performing any tasks on your computer, such as browsing the Web or editing a document, while the video transfers.

Tip

Can I use video I have recorded on another digital device, such as a digital camera, to make a movie?

You can use video from a digital device to make a movie, but you cannot import video from a digital device directly into Windows Movie Maker. You must first copy the video to your computer. You can copy video from a digital camera to your computer the same way you copy photos. See page 90.

After copying the video to your computer, start Windows Movie Maker and click **Import Media**. In the Import Media Items dialog box, locate and click the video you want to use for your movie and then click **Import**.

9 When you want to stop transferring the video, click **Stop Video Import**.

■ If you want to transfer another part of the video on your camcorder, use the controls in the wizard or the controls on your camcorder to move to the point in the video where you want to start the next transfer. Then repeat steps **8** and **9**.

10 Click **Finish** to close the Import Video dialog box.

■ When Windows Movie Maker has finished transferring the video to your computer, this area displays the video.

■ If you selected to create clips during the transfer, the clips appear. To help you identify the video clips, Windows Movie Maker displays the first frame of each clip.

ADD A VIDEO CLIP TO YOUR PROJECT

You must add each video clip that you want to include in your movie to the storyboard.

The storyboard displays the order in which video clips will play in your movie.

You can play a video clip before adding it to your movie to determine if you want to include the video clip in your movie.

Video Clips

ADD A VIDEO CLIP TO YOUR PROJECT

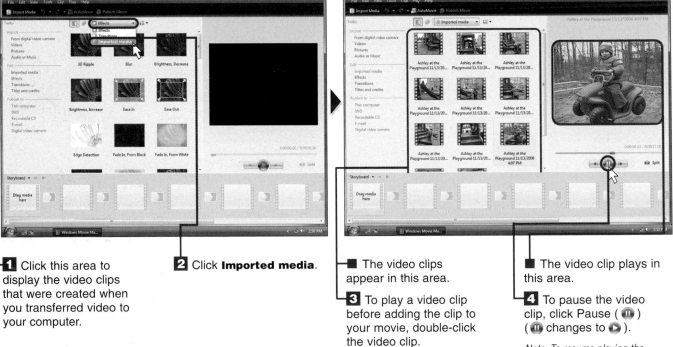

1 Click this area to display the video clips that were created when you transferred video to your computer.

2 Click **Imported media**.

■ The video clips appear in this area.

3 To play a video clip before adding the clip to your movie, double-click the video clip.

■ The video clip plays in this area.

4 To pause the video clip, click Pause (▮▮) (▮▮ changes to ▶).

Note: To resume playing the video clip, click ▶ .

Tip

Can I change the order of the video clips on the storyboard?

Yes. Changing the order of the video clips on the storyboard allows you to change the order in which the clips will play in your movie. To change the location of a video clip in your movie, position the mouse ⬉ over the video clip on the storyboard and then drag the video clip to a new location on the storyboard. A vertical bar will indicate where the video clip will appear. When you move a video clip, the surrounding video clips will move to make room for the video clip.

Tip

How can I break a long video clip into smaller clips?

You can break a long video clip into smaller clips before you add the clips to the storyboard. Double-click the clip you want to break into smaller sections. When you want to end the clip and begin a new clip, click 🎬 Split below the area where the clip is playing. The original clip will end and a new clip appears.

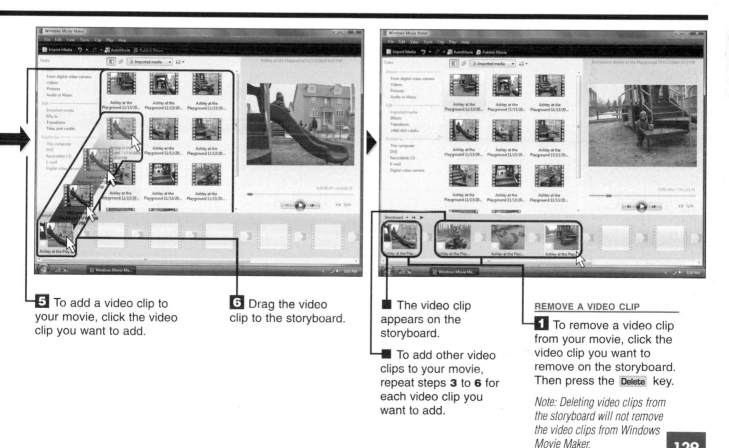

5 To add a video clip to your movie, click the video clip you want to add.

6 Drag the video clip to the storyboard.

■ The video clip appears on the storyboard.

■ To add other video clips to your movie, repeat steps **3** to **6** for each video clip you want to add.

REMOVE A VIDEO CLIP

1 To remove a video clip from your movie, click the video clip you want to remove on the storyboard. Then press the Delete key.

Note: Deleting video clips from the storyboard will not remove the video clips from Windows Movie Maker.

129

SAVE A PROJECT

You can save a project so you can later review and make changes to the project.

A project is a rough draft of your movie that contains all the video clips you added to the storyboard. You should regularly save changes you make to a project to avoid losing your work.

SAVE A PROJECT

1 Click **File**.

2 Click **Save Project**.

■ The Save Project As dialog box appears.

Note: If you previously saved your project, the Save Project As dialog box will not appear since you have already named the project.

3 Type a name for your project.

■ This area shows the location where Windows Movie Maker will store your project.

4 Click **Save** to save your project.

OPEN A PROJECT

You can open a
saved project to
display the video
clips in the project.
Opening a project
allows you to review
and make changes
to the project.

A project is a rough
draft of your movie
that contains all the
video clips you added
to the storyboard.

You can work with
only one project at
a time. If you are
currently working with
a project, make sure
you save the project
before opening another
project. To save a
project, see page 130.

OPEN A PROJECT

1 Click **File**.

2 Click **Open Project**.

■ The Open Project
dialog box appears.

■ This area shows the
location of the displayed
projects. Click ▾ in this
area to change the location.

3 Click the name of the
project you want to open.

4 Click **Open** to open
the project.

■ The project opens and
the video clips in the project
appear on the storyboard.
You can now review and
make changes to the project.

TRIM A VIDEO CLIP

You can trim a video clip to remove parts of the clip you do not want to play in your movie.

You can trim the beginning of a video clip, the end of a video clip, or both. Trimming a video clip in your movie will not affect the original video clip stored in Windows Movie Maker.

TRIM A VIDEO CLIP

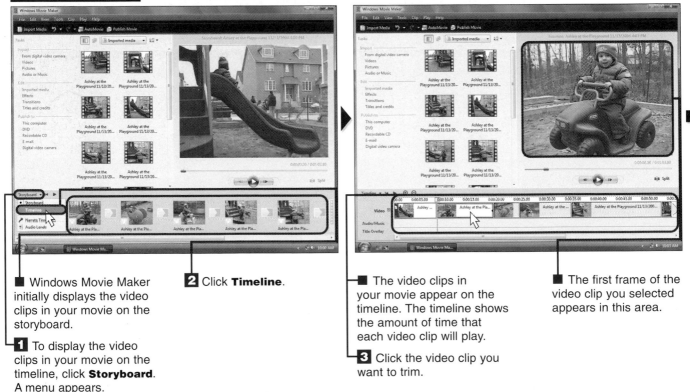

■ Windows Movie Maker initially displays the video clips in your movie on the storyboard.

1 To display the video clips in your movie on the timeline, click **Storyboard**. A menu appears.

2 Click **Timeline**.

■ The video clips in your movie appear on the timeline. The timeline shows the amount of time that each video clip will play.

3 Click the video clip you want to trim.

■ The first frame of the video clip you selected appears in this area.

Tip 💡

After I trim a video clip, can I undo the change I made?

Yes. If you trimmed too much or too little of a video clip or decide that you no longer want to trim a video clip in your movie, you can undo the change you made. To return a video clip to its original length, click the video clip on the timeline, perform step **6** below to display a menu and then click **Clear Trim Points**.

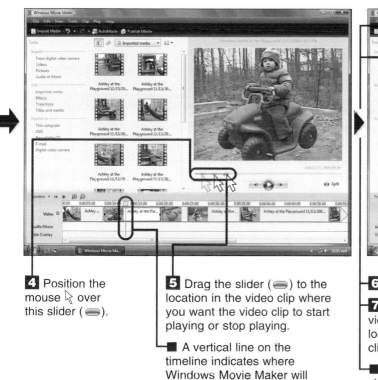

4 Position the mouse ⟡ over this slider (⬭).

5 Drag the slider (⬭) to the location in the video clip where you want the video clip to start playing or stop playing.

■ A vertical line on the timeline indicates where Windows Movie Maker will trim the video clip.

6 Click **Clip**.

7 To remove the part of the video clip before the current location of the slider (⬭), click **Trim Beginning**.

■ To remove the part of the video clip after the current location of the slider (⬭), click **Trim End**.

8 To once again display the storyboard, repeat steps **1** and **2**, selecting **Timeline** in step **1** and **Storyboard** in step **2**.

Note: To preview how the trimmed video clip will appear in your movie, see page 136 to preview a movie.

ADD A VIDEO TRANSITION

You can create a smooth video transition from one video clip to another in your movie. The first video clip will fade out as the following video clip fades in.

ADD A VIDEO TRANSITION

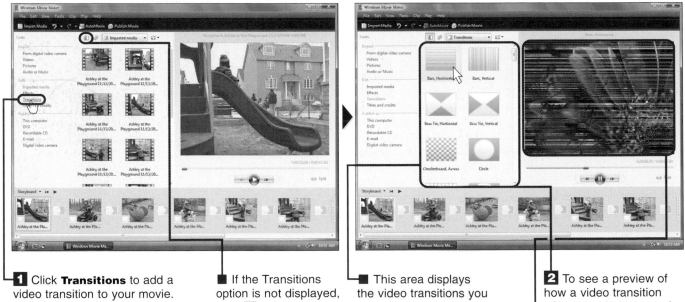

1 Click **Transitions** to add a video transition to your movie.

■ If the Transitions option is not displayed, click [▣] to display the Task pane.

■ This area displays the video transitions you can add to your movie. You can use the scroll bar to browse through the available transitions.

2 To see a preview of how a video transition will appear in your movie, double-click the transition.

■ This area displays a preview of the video transition.

Tip 💡 **How do I remove a video transition from my movie?**

To remove a video transition, click the picture representing the transition between the video clips on the storyboard. Then press the `Delete` key.

Tip 💡 **What should I consider when adding video transitions to a movie?**

Although Windows Movie Maker offers many different types of video transitions, using too many different transitions in a movie can distract the audience from your movie. If you are trying to create a professional-looking movie, use similar video transitions throughout your movie and add video transitions sparingly.

3 To add a video transition to your movie, position the mouse ⌖ over the transition you want to add.

4 Drag the video transition between the video clips on the storyboard where you want to add the transition.

■ A small picture representing the video transition appears between the video clips.

■ To add additional video transitions to your movie, repeat steps **2** to **4** for each transition you want to add.

5 To once again view your video clips instead of the list of available video transitions, click **Imported media**.

Note: To see how your movie plays with the video transitions you have added, see page 136.

PREVIEW AND SAVE A MOVIE

You can preview and save your movie.

Preview a Movie

You can preview a movie by playing all the video clips you have added to the storyboard. Before you save a completed movie, you should preview the movie to make sure you are happy with the movie. You can also preview a movie at any time while you create a movie.

Save a Movie

When your movie is complete, you can save the movie on your computer. Saving a movie allows you to share the movie with family and friends.

PREVIEW A MOVIE

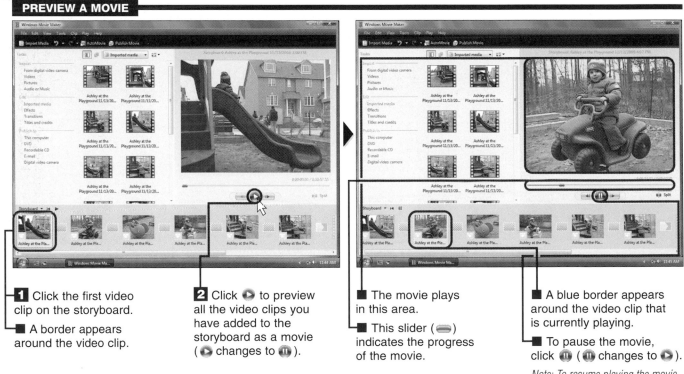

1 Click the first video clip on the storyboard.

■ A border appears around the video clip.

2 Click ▶ to preview all the video clips you have added to the storyboard as a movie (▶ changes to ⏸).

■ The movie plays in this area.

■ This slider (⬭) indicates the progress of the movie.

■ A blue border appears around the video clip that is currently playing.

■ To pause the movie, click ⏸ (⏸ changes to ▶).

Note: To resume playing the movie, click ▶.

Tip

Can I share a movie I have created with other people?

Yes. Windows Movie Maker lets you easily share your movie with other people in several ways, including copying the movie to a recordable CD that you can share and sending the movie in an e-mail message.

If you have a recordable CD drive, insert a blank, recordable CD into the drive. Then perform steps **1** to **6** starting below, except click **Recordable CD** in step **1**.

To send your movie in an e-mail message, click **E-mail** in step **1** below. Then click **Attach Movie** in the wizard that appears. For more information on sending e-mail messages, see page 228.

SAVE A MOVIE

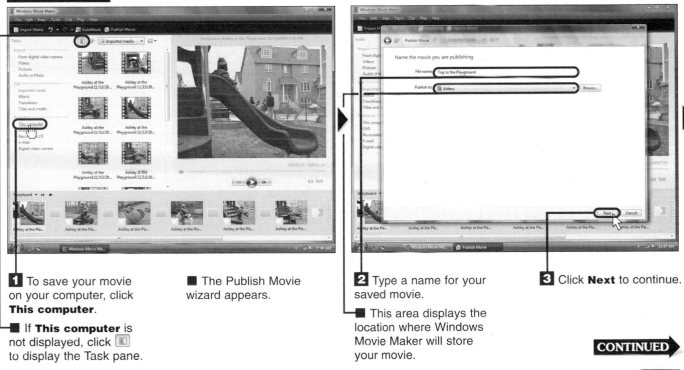

1 To save your movie on your computer, click **This computer**.

■ If **This computer** is not displayed, click 🔲 to display the Task pane.

■ The Publish Movie wizard appears.

2 Type a name for your saved movie.

■ This area displays the location where Windows Movie Maker will store your movie.

3 Click **Next** to continue.

CONTINUED

PREVIEW AND SAVE A MOVIE

After you save
a movie on
your computer,
the wizard will
automatically
play the movie
in Windows
Media Player.

SAVE A MOVIE (CONTINUED)

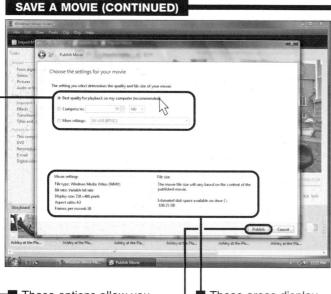

■ These options allow you
to determine the quality
and file size of your movie.

4 To save your movie
using the best video
quality, click the first option
(○ changes to ⊙).

■ These areas display
information about the
movie and the amount of
storage space available
on your hard drive.

5 Click **Publish** to
continue.

■ This area indicates
the progress of the
creation of the movie.

■ This area displays the
file name of the movie
and the location on your
computer where the
wizard is saving the movie.

How can I later play a movie I have saved?

Windows Movie Maker automatically stores your movies in the Videos folder, which is located in the User folder. You can double-click a movie in the Videos folder to play the movie. To view the contents of the User folder, see page 38.

Note: The name of the User folder is the same as the name you use to log on to your computer.

Can I make changes to a movie I have saved?

No. You cannot make changes to a movie you have saved. Windows Movie Maker only allows you to make changes to a project, which is a rough draft of a movie. To open a project so you can make changes to the project, see page 131.

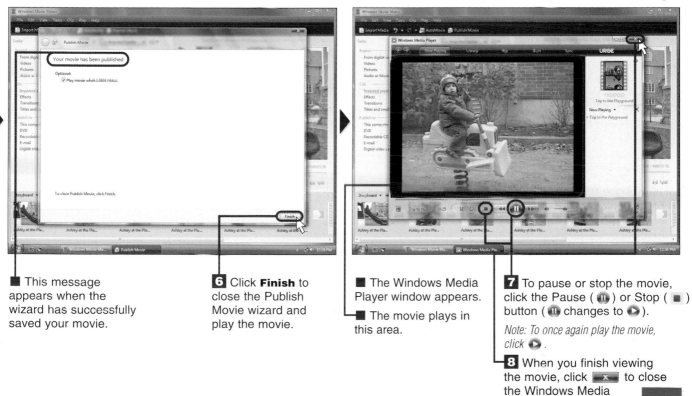

■ This message appears when the wizard has successfully saved your movie.

6 Click **Finish** to close the Publish Movie wizard and play the movie.

■ The Windows Media Player window appears.

■ The movie plays in this area.

7 To pause or stop the movie, click the Pause ( ) or Stop ( ) button (changes to).

Note: To once again play the movie, click .

8 When you finish viewing the movie, click to close the Windows Media Player window.

139

Using Windows Media Center

Windows Media Center allows you to enjoy your favorite entertainment in one place. You can view pictures, watch and record live television, listen to music, watch videos and more.

Windows Media Center is only available in the Home Premium and Ultimate editions of Windows Vista.

If your computer came with a Windows Media Center remote control, you can use the control to operate Windows Media Center. You can also purchase a Windows Media Center remote control at local computer stores.

START WINDOWS MEDIA CENTER

1 Click ⊕ to display the Start menu.

2 Click **Windows Media Center**.

Note: If Windows Media Center does not appear on the Start menu, click **All Programs** on the Start menu and then click **Windows Media Center**.

■ The Windows Media Center start screen appears.

Note: The first time you start Windows Media Center, the welcome dialog box appears. Click **OK** to set up Windows Media Center.

3 To browse through the main categories, position the mouse ▷ over this area and then click the arrow (⌃) that appears.

Note: You can also roll the wheel on your mouse to move through the categories.

4 To browse through the options in the selected category, click the arrow (⟨ or ⟩) at the left or right side of your screen.

WINDOWS MEDIA CENTER FEATURES

TV + Movies

recorded tv—play a recorded television show

live tv—watch live television

guide—find television shows

movies guide—find movies on television

play dvd—play a DVD

search—find television shows and movies

Pictures + Videos

picture library—find and view pictures

play all—display all of your pictures in a slide show

video library—find and play a video

Music

music library—find music you want to listen to

play all—play all of your music

radio—listen to radio stations

search—search for music

Online Media

program library—play games, access television shows, find music and radio stations, share pictures, get news and download movies over the Internet

Tasks

settings—adjust Windows Media Center settings

shutdown—close Windows Media Center, log off, shut down or restart Windows or put your computer to sleep

burn cd/dvd—copy pictures, music, videos and recorded television shows to CDs and DVDs

sync—keep your files synchronized between your computer and mobile devices, such as portable music players, personal digital assistants (PDAs) and mobile phones

add extender—set up a Windows Media Center Extender device, such as an Xbox 360, TV or DVD player, so you can enjoy music, pictures, video and recorded television shows stored on your computer anywhere in your home

media only—always keep Windows Media Center displayed in a full screen

WATCH A TELEVISION SHOW

You can watch live
television shows
on your computer
screen.

To be able to watch
live television on your
computer screen, your
computer needs a TV
tuner card.

While watching live
television, you can
change the channel
and adjust the volume.
You can also pause
live television if you
will be away from your
computer for a short
time and do not want
to miss parts of a show.

WATCH A TELEVISION SHOW

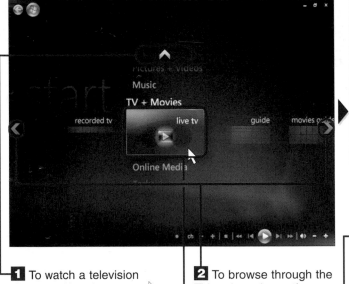

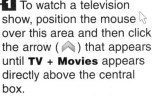

1 To watch a television
show, position the mouse
over this area and then click
the arrow (⌃) that appears
until **TV + Movies** appears
directly above the central
box.

2 To browse through the
TV and movies options,
click the arrow (❮ or ❯)
at the left or right side of
your screen until you see
the **live tv** option.

3 To begin watching live
television, click **live tv**.

■ A live television show
plays on your computer
screen.

4 To display the
controls for watching
live television at any
time, move the mouse
on your desk.

CHANGE THE CHANNEL

1 To change the channel,
click ▬ or ➕ to move
down or up one channel.

■ When you change the
channel, a box will temporarily
appear, displaying information
about the television show
playing on your screen.

Tip

Is there anything I need to do before I can watch live television?

You need to set up your TV signal before you can watch live television. To do so, perform steps **1** to **3** on page 144, selecting **set up tv** in steps **2** and **3**. Then follow the instructions in the wizard that appears.

Tip

How can I display information about a television show?

To display information about a television show you are watching, right-click the television show and then click **Mini Guide** on the menu that appears. Information about the television show will appear.

Tip

Can I watch a television show in a window?

Yes. To watch a television show in a window so you can perform other tasks on your computer, move the mouse on your desk to display the menu bar. Then click ▣ at the top-right corner of your screen to display the television show in a window. You can move and resize the window as you would move and resize any window. To once again display the television show using the entire screen, click ▣ .

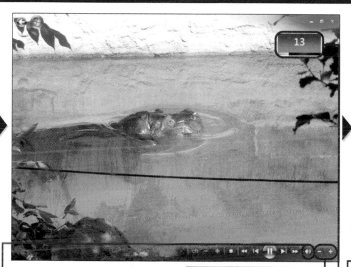

TURN OFF SOUND

1 Click ◀》 to turn off the sound (◀》 changes to ◀✕).

■ To once again turn on the sound, click ◀✕ .

ADJUST THE VOLUME

1 To decrease or increase the volume, click ▬ or ✚ .

■ A box will temporarily appear, displaying the volume setting.

PAUSE LIVE TV

1 While watching live television, click ⏸ to pause the television show (⏸ changes to ▶).

■ To resume playing the television show, click ▶ .

STOP PLAYING LIVE TV

1 While watching live television, click ■ to stop playing live television.

■ You are returned to the Windows Media Center start screen.

RECORD A TELEVISION SHOW

You can record a television show that you are watching. Recording a television show allows you to watch the show again at a later time.

When you record a live television show, Windows records the show from the moment you start recording. If you are halfway through a show, Windows will only record the second half of the show.

RECORDING...
16 World of Animals
9:00 PM – 9:30 PM

RECORD A TELEVISION SHOW

1 To record a live television show that you are watching, move the mouse on your desk to display the controls.

Note: To record a scheduled television show, see the top of page 149.

2 Click ● to record the television show.

PLAY A RECORDED TELEVISION SHOW

start

Pictures + Videos
Music
TV + Movies

recorded tv   live tv   guide   movies g...

Online Media

1 To play a recorded television show, position the mouse ⌖ over this area and then click the arrow (⌃) that appears until **TV + Movies** appears directly above the central box.

2 To browse through the TV and movies options, click the arrow (⟨ or ⟩) at the left or right edge of your screen until you see the **recorded tv** option.

3 To play a recorded television show, click **recorded tv**.

Tip

Can I fast forward through a recorded television show?

Yes. To move through a recorded television show that you are watching, move the mouse on your desk to display the controls. Then click a control to rewind ( ), skip backward ( ), skip forward ( ) or fast forward ( ) through the television show. Moving through a recorded television show is especially useful when you do not want to watch any commercials.

■ This area displays the television shows you have recorded as well as recorded television shows that come with Windows Media Center.

4 To browse through the recorded television shows, position the mouse at the left or right edge of your screen over a recorded television show.

5 Click the television show you want to watch.

■ Information about the recorded television show appears.

6 To watch the television show, click **Play**.

■ The television show plays on your computer screen.

Note: When the television show finishes playing, a menu will appear, allowing you to display information about the show by selecting Done, restart the show, delete the show or keep the show. Click the option you want to use.

DISPLAY THE TELEVISION GUIDE

You can display a
television guide,
which displays the
television shows
that are available
on each channel.

DISPLAY THE TELEVISION GUIDE

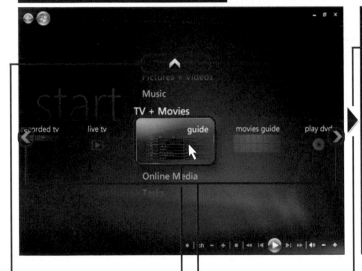

1 To display the television guide, position the mouse over this area and then click the arrow ( ) that appears until **TV + Movies** appears directly above the central box.

2 To browse through the TV and movies options, click the arrow (◀ or ▶) at the left or right side of your screen until you see the **guide** option.

3 To display the television guide, click **guide**.

■ The guide appears, displaying the television shows that are available on each channel.

■ This area displays the current date and the times of the displayed television shows.

■ This area displays the channel number, channel name and the title of each television show.

■ This area displays information about the highlighted show.

4 To move up, down, left or right through the channels, one at a time, press the ⬆, ⬇, ⬅ or ➡ key.

5 To move through the channels one screen at a time, press the Page Up or Page Down key.

6 To instantly move to a specific channel in the guide, type the channel number.

7 To use the mouse to move through the channels, move the mouse on your desk to display the arrows. Then click an arrow to move left (❮), right (❯), up (⌃) or down (⌄) through the channels.

Note: You can also roll the wheel on your mouse to move up and down through the channels.

8 To watch a television show that is currently playing, click the television show.

■ The television show will play on your computer screen.

149

CHAPTER 8

Customize Windows

CHANGE THE DESKTOP BACKGROUND

You can change the picture used to decorate your desktop.

Windows comes with many desktop backgrounds that you can choose from, including black and white pictures, paintings and solid colors.

You can also display your own pictures on the desktop by selecting a picture from the Pictures folder.

CHANGE THE DESKTOP BACKGROUND

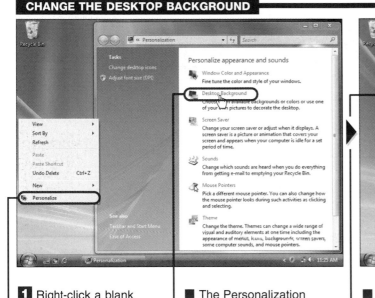

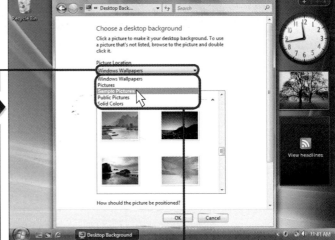

1 Right-click a blank area on your desktop. A menu appears.

2 Click **Personalize** to personalize your computer.

■ The Personalization window appears.

3 Click **Desktop Background** to personalize your desktop background.

■ The Desktop Background window appears.

4 Click this area to display a list of locations and types of pictures you can choose from.

5 Click the location or type of picture you want to choose from.

Note: You can select from wallpapers and sample pictures that come with Windows, pictures located in the Pictures folder, shared pictures located in the Public Pictures folder and solid colors.

Tip **I cannot find the picture I want to use as my desktop background. What can I do?**

If you cannot find the picture you want to use as your desktop background, click **Browse** in the Desktop Background window to locate the picture on your computer. When you find the picture you want to use in the dialog box that appears, double-click the picture.

Tip **How can I change the color that surrounds my picture?**

If you choose to position a picture in the middle of your screen, you can change the color that surrounds the picture. To change this color, click **Change background color** in the Desktop Background window. In the dialog box that appears, click the color you want to use and then click **OK**.

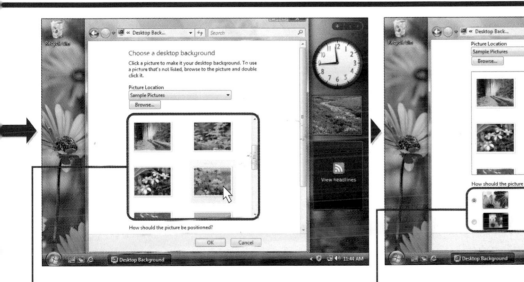

■ This area displays the pictures stored in the location you selected.

6 Click the picture you want to display on your desktop.

■ The picture you selected immediately appears on your desktop.

7 Click the way you want to position the picture on your desktop (⦾ changes to ⦿).

■ You can have the picture cover your entire screen, repeat until it fills the entire screen or appear in the middle of your screen.

*Note: If you selected a large picture, selecting an option in step **7** will have little effect on the way the picture will appear on your screen.*

8 Click **OK** to add the picture to your desktop.

CHANGE THE SCREEN SAVER

A screen saver is a picture or animation that appears on the screen when you do not use your computer for a period of time.

You can use a screen saver to hide your work while you are away from your desk.

By default, Windows will display a screen saver when you do not use your computer for ten minutes.

CHANGE THE SCREEN SAVER

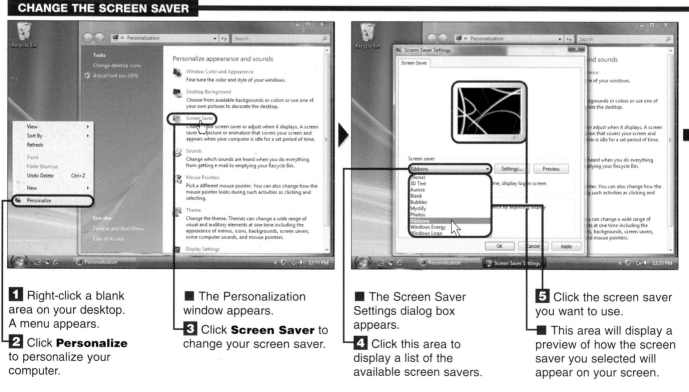

1 Right-click a blank area on your desktop. A menu appears.

2 Click **Personalize** to personalize your computer.

■ The Personalization window appears.

3 Click **Screen Saver** to change your screen saver.

■ The Screen Saver Settings dialog box appears.

4 Click this area to display a list of the available screen savers.

5 Click the screen saver you want to use.

■ This area will display a preview of how the screen saver you selected will appear on your screen.

Tip **What does the Photos screen saver do?**

You can select the Photos screen saver to have the pictures stored in your Pictures folder appear as your screen saver. Windows will rotate through all the pictures in the folder. To view the contents of your Pictures folder, see page 38.

Tip **Can I customize my screen saver?**

After you select the screen saver you want to use, you can click the **Settings** button to customize some screen savers. For example, if you select the 3D Text screen saver, you can customize the text that you want to appear on your screen, such as your company's name.

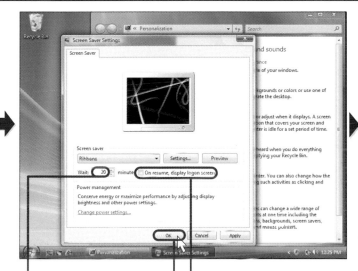

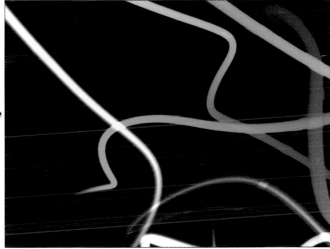

6 To specify the number of minutes your computer must be inactive before the screen saver will appear, double-click this area. Then type the number of minutes.

7 To make your computer more secure, this option requires you to log on to Windows each time you remove the screen saver. You can click this option to turn the option on (☑) or off (☐).

Note: For information on logging on to Windows, see page 191.

8 Click **OK**.

■ The screen saver appears when you do not use your computer for the number of minutes you specified.

■ You can move the mouse or press a key on the keyboard to remove the screen saver from your screen.

■ To stop a screen saver from appearing, perform steps **1** to **5**, selecting **(None)** in step **5**. Then perform step **8**.

CHANGE THE COLOR OF WINDOWS

You can add a personal touch to your computer by changing the colors used to display windows on your screen.

You may see different options, depending on your computer hardware, the settings in Windows Vista and the edition of Windows Vista you are using.

CHANGE THE COLOR OF WINDOWS

1 Right-click a blank area on your desktop. A menu appears.

2 Click **Personalize** to personalize your computer.

■ The Personalization window appears.

3 Click **Window Color and Appearance** to personalize the color and style of windows displayed on your screen.

■ The Window Color and Appearance window appears.

4 Click the color you want to use for your windows.

■ The windows displayed on your screen instantly display the new color.

156

Tip

Can I create my own color for windows?

Yes. If you do not see a color you like in the Window Color and Appearance window, click **Show color mixer** to create your own color. Drag the sliders ( ) that appear beside Hue (color), Saturation (intensity of color) and Brightness until the windows on your screen display the color you like.

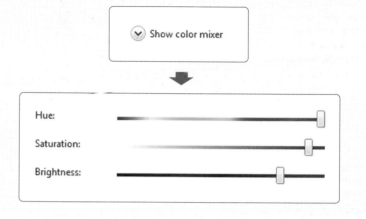

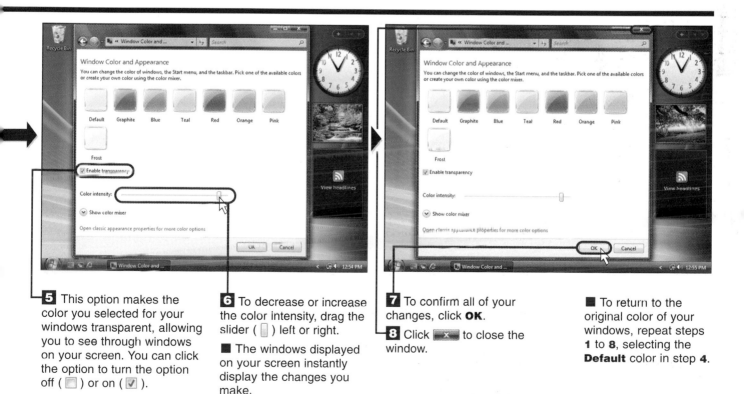

5 This option makes the color you selected for your windows transparent, allowing you to see through windows on your screen. You can click the option to turn the option off ( ) or on ( ).

6 To decrease or increase the color intensity, drag the slider ( ) left or right.

■ The windows displayed on your screen instantly display the changes you make.

7 To confirm all of your changes, click **OK**.

8 Click to close the window.

■ To return to the original color of your windows, repeat steps **1** to **8**, selecting the **Default** color in step **4**.

CHANGE THE DESKTOP THEME

You can use a desktop theme to personalize the overall appearance of Windows.

Each desktop theme contains several coordinated items, including a desktop background, screen saver, colors, sounds, mouse pointers, icons and fonts.

If you have multiple user accounts set up on your computer, each person can choose a different desktop theme. To create user accounts, see page 182.

CHANGE THE DESKTOP THEME

1 Right-click a blank area on your desktop. A menu appears.

2 Click **Personalize**.

■ The Personalization window appears.

3 Click **Theme** to change the desktop theme.

■ The Theme Settings dialog box appears.

4 Click this area to display a list of the available desktop themes.

5 Click the desktop theme you want to use.

What desktop themes come with Windows?

Windows provides a few desktop themes that you can choose from. *My Current Theme* is the theme you are currently using. *Windows Vista* is the theme that is initially displayed on a Windows Vista computer. *Windows Classic* is a theme that resembles the look and feel of previous versions of Windows. If you make changes to a theme, such as changing the desktop background, *Modified Theme* appears in the list of available themes.

Where can I get more desktop themes?

You can obtain additional desktop themes on the Internet, such as at the Microsoft Web site (www.microsoft.com), or buy desktop themes that are compatible with Windows Vista at local computer stores. You can find many different types of desktop themes, such as desktop themes to turn your computer into a virtual underwater aquarium, an outer space adventure or a peaceful, picturesque nature setting.

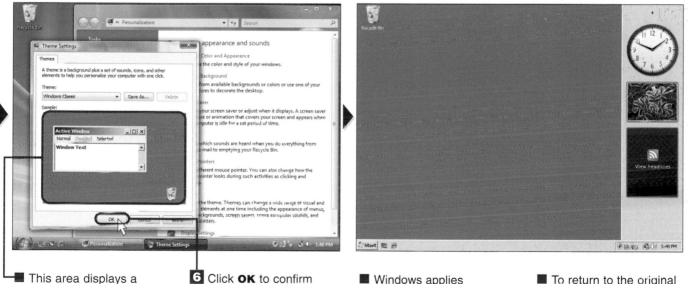

■ This area displays a preview of the desktop theme you selected.

6 Click **OK** to confirm your change.

■ Windows applies the desktop theme you selected.

■ To return to the original desktop theme, perform steps **1** to **6**, selecting **Windows Vista** in step **5**.

CHANGE THE SCREEN RESOLUTION

You can change the screen resolution to adjust the amount of information that can fit on your screen.

Your monitor and video card determine which screen resolutions are available on your computer.

When you change the screen resolution, it affects all users set up on the computer.

CHANGE THE SCREEN RESOLUTION

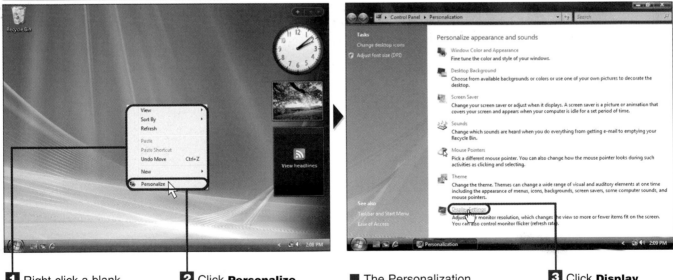

1 Right-click a blank area on your desktop. A menu appears.

2 Click **Personalize** to personalize your computer.

■ The Personalization window appears.

3 Click **Display Settings** to change your screen resolution.

Which screen resolution should I use?

The screen resolution is measured by
the number of horizontal and vertical
pixels displayed on a screen. A pixel
is the smallest point on a screen. The
screen resolution you should choose
depends on the size of your monitor
and the amount of information you want
to view on your screen at once.

Lower screen resolutions display larger
images so you can see the information
on your screen more clearly. Higher
screen resolutions display smaller
images so you can display more
information on your screen at once.

**Can I change the screen resolution for
an LCD monitor?**

You will not usually change the screen
resolution of a Liquid Crystal Display
(LCD) monitor, since this can reduce
the image quality. LCD monitors should
remain at their native resolution, which
is the resolution a monitor is designed
to best display images. An LCD monitor
is a thin, lightweight monitor compared
to the bulkier Cathode Ray Tube (CRT)
monitor.

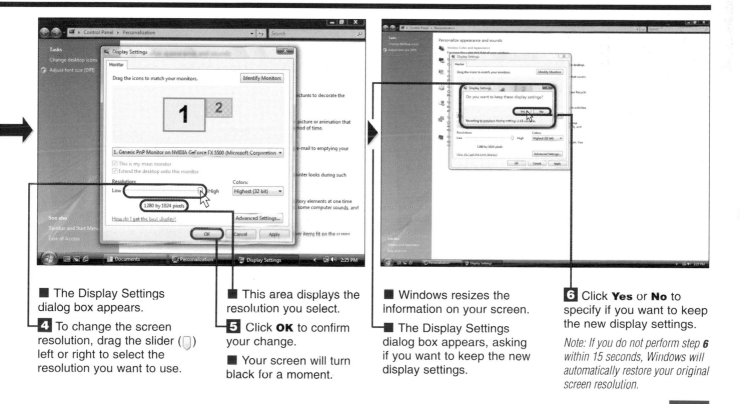

■ The Display Settings
dialog box appears.

■ 4 To change the screen
resolution, drag the slider (⬜)
left or right to select the
resolution you want to use.

■ This area displays the
resolution you select.

■ 5 Click **OK** to confirm
your change.

■ Your screen will turn
black for a moment.

■ Windows resizes the
Information on your screen.

■ The Display Settings
dialog box appears, asking
if you want to keep the new
display settings.

6 Click **Yes** or **No** to
specify if you want to keep
the new display settings.

*Note: If you do not perform step 6
within 15 seconds, Windows will
automatically restore your original
screen resolution.*

ADJUST THE VOLUME

You can adjust the volume of sound on your computer.

Windows allows you to quickly and easily adjust the volume of your speakers. You can also adjust the volume of individual devices and programs on your computer without affecting the volume of other devices and programs.

ADJUST THE SPEAKER VOLUME

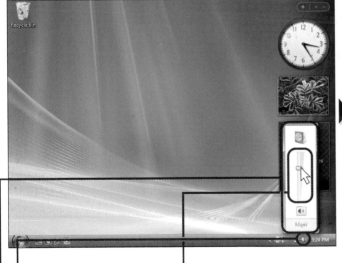

1 Click 🔊 to display the Volume control.

■ The Volume control appears.

2 To adjust the speaker volume, drag the slider (⬜) up or down to increase or decrease the volume.

3 To turn off the sound coming from your speakers, click 🔊 (🔊 changes to 🔇).

Note: When you turn off the sound, the speaker icon 🔊 on the taskbar changes to 🔇 .

■ To once again turn on the sound, click 🔇 (🔇 changes to 🔊).

4 When you finish adjusting the speaker volume, click a blank area on your desktop to hide the Volume control.

Tip **What devices and programs can appear in the Volume Mixer dialog box?**

The devices and programs that appear in the Volume Mixer dialog box depend on the devices that are connected to your computer and the programs you have open that produce sound. Here are some devices and programs you may see in the dialog box.

Speakers—Adjusts the volume of your speakers.

Windows Sounds—Adjusts the volume of sounds that play when certain events, such as the arrival of new e-mail messages, occur on your computer.

Windows Movie Maker—Adjusts the sounds playing in Windows Movie Maker.

Windows Media Player—Adjusts the sounds playing in Windows Media Player.

Tip **Is there a quick way to adjust the speaker volume?**

Many speakers have a volume control that you can use to adjust the volume. Your speakers may also have a power button that you can use to turn the sound on or off.

ADJUST THE VOLUME OF INDIVIDUAL DEVICES

1 Click 🔊 to display the Volume control.

■ The Volume control appears.

2 Click **Mixer** to adjust the volume of individual devices and programs on your computer.

■ The Volume Mixer dialog box appears.

■ This area displays each device and program that you can adjust the volume for.

3 To adjust the volume for a device or program, drag the slider (⬜) up or down to increase or decrease the volume.

4 To turn off the sound for a device or program, click 🔊 (🔊 changes to 🔇).

5 When you finish adjusting the volume for individual devices and programs, click ✖ to close the Volume Mixer dialog box.

CHANGE THE COMPUTER SOUNDS

You can change the sounds that your computer plays when certain events occur on your computer. For example, you can hear a short tune when you start Windows.

You can change the sounds that your computer plays for many events at once by selecting a sound theme. A sound theme consists of a set of related sounds.

CHANGE THE COMPUTER SOUNDS

DISPLAY THE SOUND SETTINGS

1 Click  to display the Start menu.

2 Click **Control Panel** to change your computer's settings.

■ The Control Panel window appears.

3 Click **Hardware and Sound**.

■ The Hardware and Sound window appears.

4 Click **Change system sounds** to change your computer's sounds.

■ The Sound dialog box appears.

Tip

What events can Windows play sounds for?

Windows can play sounds for over 45 events on your computer. Here are some examples.

Exit Windows—A sound will play each time you exit Windows.

New Mail Notification—A sound will play each time you receive a new e-mail message.

Print Complete—A sound will play when the printing of a file is complete.

Device Connect—A sound will play each time you connect a device to your computer.

Windows Logon—A sound will play each time you log on to Windows.

Tip

When I try to change the sound theme, why does the Save previous scheme dialog box appear?

Windows wants to know if you want to save your previous sound theme. Click **Yes** or **No** to specify if you want to save the previous sound theme. If you select **Yes**, type a name for the sound theme in the dialog box that appears and then click **OK**. The sound theme will appear in the list of available sound themes.

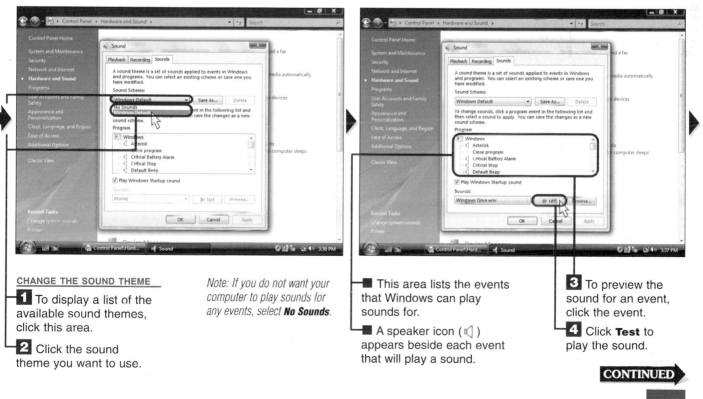

CHANGE THE SOUND THEME

1 To display a list of the available sound themes, click this area.

2 Click the sound theme you want to use.

*Note: If you do not want your computer to play sounds for any events, select **No Sounds**.*

■ This area lists the events that Windows can play sounds for.

■ A speaker icon (◁) appears beside each event that will play a sound.

3 To preview the sound for an event, click the event.

4 Click **Test** to play the sound.

CONTINUED

CHANGE THE COMPUTER SOUNDS

When changing the sounds that your computer plays, you can select sounds that you want to play when certain events occur.

For example, you may want to play dialogue or music from your favorite cartoon when you close a program or hear a sigh of relief when you exit Windows.

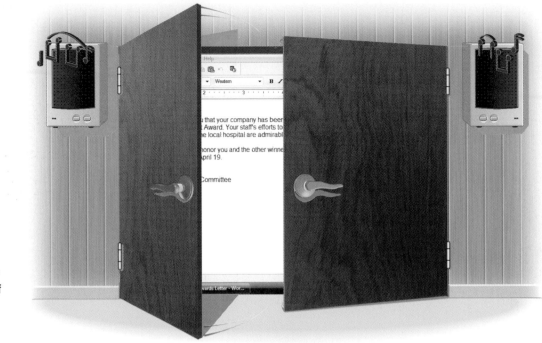

CHANGE THE COMPUTER SOUNDS (CONTINUED)

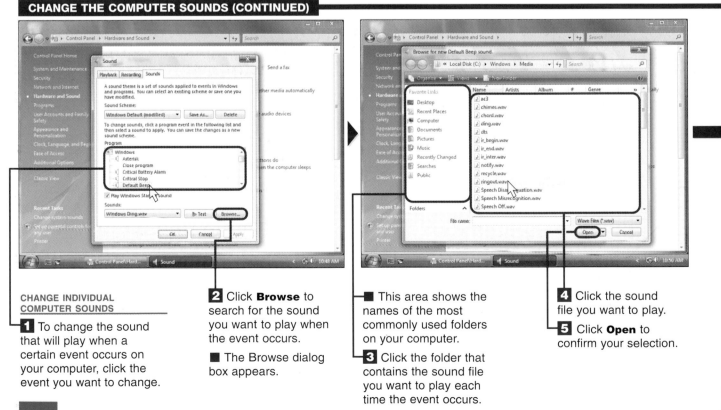

CHANGE INDIVIDUAL COMPUTER SOUNDS

1 To change the sound that will play when a certain event occurs on your computer, click the event you want to change.

2 Click **Browse** to search for the sound you want to play when the event occurs.

■ The Browse dialog box appears.

■ This area shows the names of the most commonly used folders on your computer.

3 Click the folder that contains the sound file you want to play each time the event occurs.

4 Click the sound file you want to play.

5 Click **Open** to confirm your selection.

Tip

Where can I get sounds that I can have Windows play?

You can use the sounds included with Windows or obtain sounds on the Internet. The sounds you use must be in the Wave format. Wave files have the .wav extension, such as chimes.wav.

Tip

How can I stop a sound from playing when a certain event occurs on my computer?

In the Sound dialog box, click the event you no longer want to play a sound. Click ▼ below Sounds: and then select **(None)** from the top of the list.

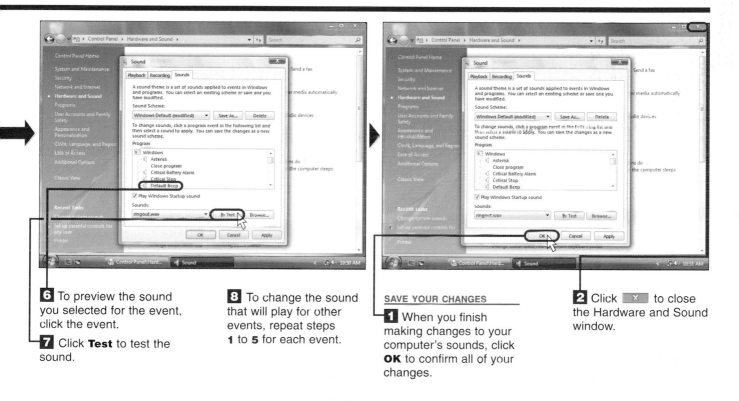

6 To preview the sound you selected for the event, click the event.

7 Click **Test** to test the sound.

8 To change the sound that will play for other events, repeat steps **1** to **5** for each event.

SAVE YOUR CHANGES

1 When you finish making changes to your computer's sounds, click **OK** to confirm all of your changes.

2 Click ❌ to close the Hardware and Sound window.

167

VIEW AND CHANGE THE DATE AND TIME

You can view and change your computer's date and time settings. Windows uses the date and time to record when you create and update your files.

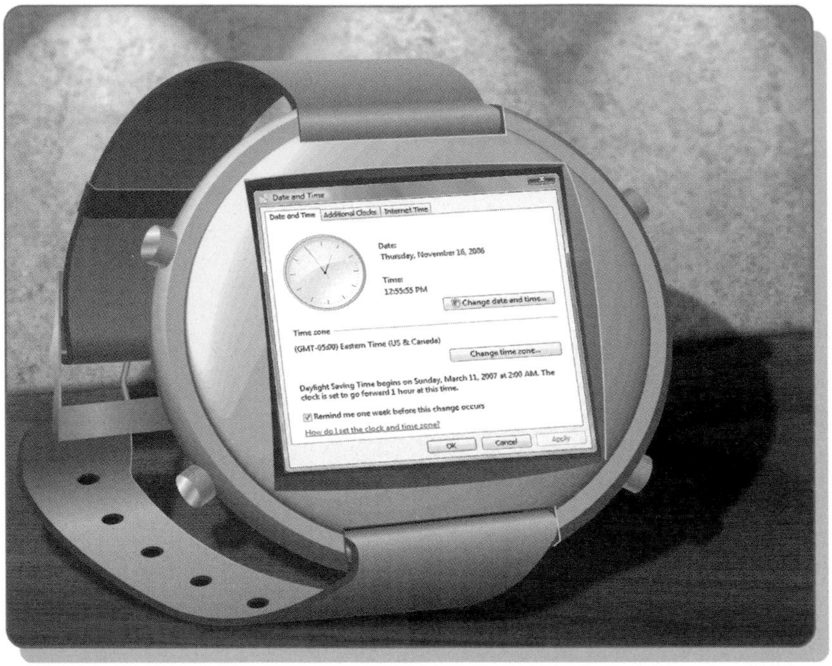

Your computer has a built-in clock that keeps track of the date and time even when you turn off your computer.

To help ensure that your computer's clock is accurate, Windows automatically synchronizes your computer's clock with a time server on the Internet about once a week. Your computer must be connected to the Internet for the synchronization to occur.

VIEW THE DATE AND TIME

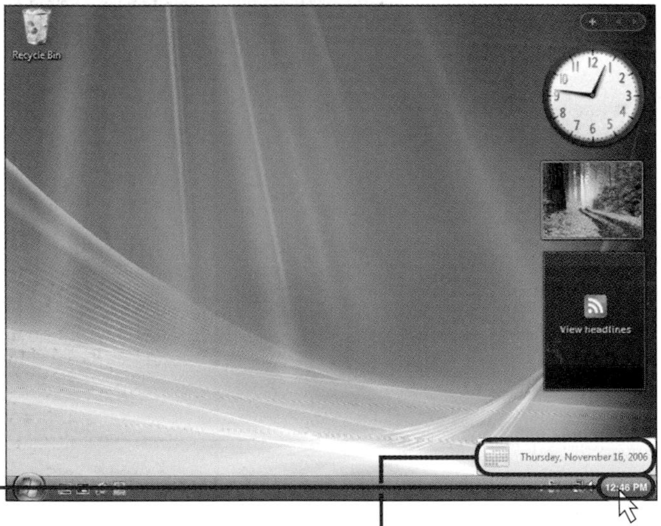

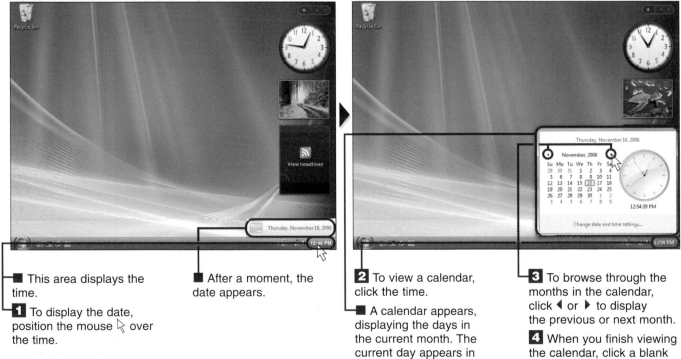

- This area displays the time.

1 To display the date, position the mouse over the time.

- After a moment, the date appears.

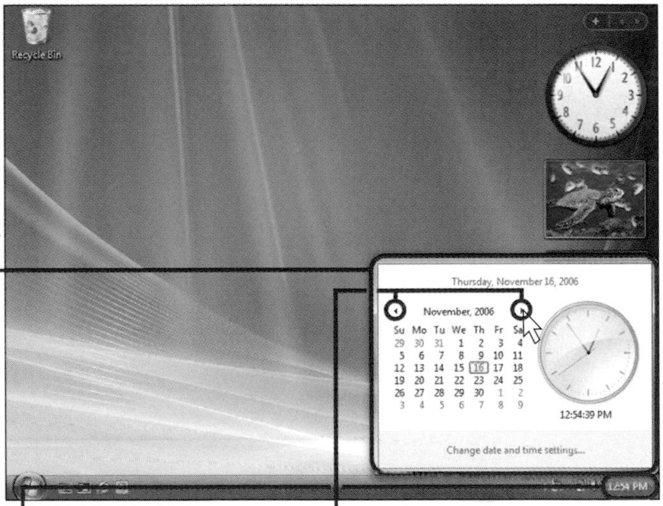

2 To view a calendar, click the time.

- A calendar appears, displaying the days in the current month. The current day appears in blue and displays a blue border.

3 To browse through the months in the calendar, click ◀ or ▶ to display the previous or next month.

4 When you finish viewing the calendar, click a blank area on your screen to close the calendar.

Tip

How do I change the date and time?

To change the date and time, click **Change date and time** in the Date and Time dialog box. To continue, you will need to click **Continue** or type an administrator password and click **OK**. In the dialog box that appears, click the correct day and then double-click the part of the time you want to change and type the correct information. Click **OK** to save your changes.

Tip

How do I change the time zone?

To change the time zone, click **Change time zone** in the Date and Time dialog box. In the dialog box that appears, select a time zone from the list of available time zones and then click **OK** to save your change. You may want to change the time zone when traveling or after you move to a new city.

VIEW THE DATE AND TIME SETTINGS

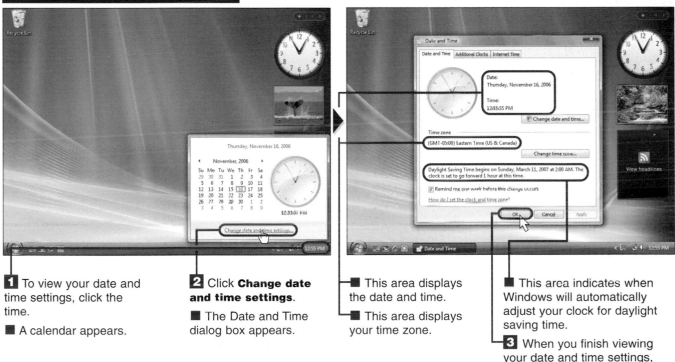

1 To view your date and time settings, click the time.

■ A calendar appears.

2 Click **Change date and time settings**.

■ The Date and Time dialog box appears.

■ This area displays the date and time.

■ This area displays your time zone.

■ This area indicates when Windows will automatically adjust your clock for daylight saving time.

3 When you finish viewing your date and time settings, click **OK** to close the dialog box.

START A PROGRAM AUTOMATICALLY

If you use the same program every day, you can have the program start automatically each time you start Windows.

To have a program start automatically, you need to place a shortcut for the program in the Startup folder. A shortcut is a link to the program.

START A PROGRAM AUTOMATICALLY

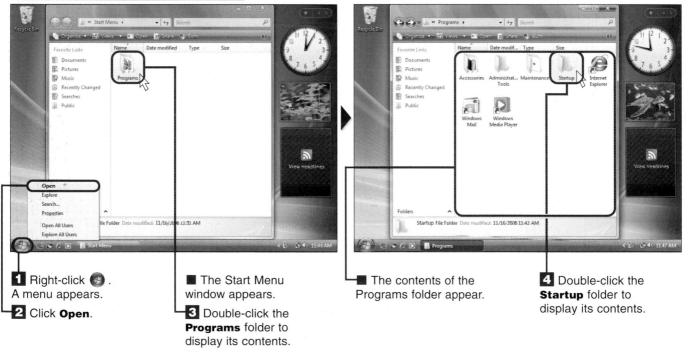

1 Right-click 🔵. A menu appears.

2 Click **Open**.

■ The Start Menu window appears.

3 Double-click the **Programs** folder to display its contents.

■ The contents of the Programs folder appear.

4 Double-click the **Startup** folder to display its contents.

How do I stop a program from starting automatically?

To stop a program from starting automatically, you must remove the shortcut for the program from the Startup folder. Deleting a shortcut for a program will not remove the program from your computer.

To remove a shortcut for a program from the Startup folder, perform steps **1** to **4** below to display the contents of the Startup folder. Click the shortcut for the program you no longer want to start automatically and then press the Delete key. In the confirmation dialog box that appears, click **Yes** to delete the shortcut for the program.

Can I have a file open automatically?

Yes. You can set up a file you frequently use to open automatically each time you start Windows. To do so, create a shortcut for the file (see page 66) and then perform steps **1** to **4** below to display the contents of the Startup folder. Then drag the shortcut you created to a blank area in the Startup window.

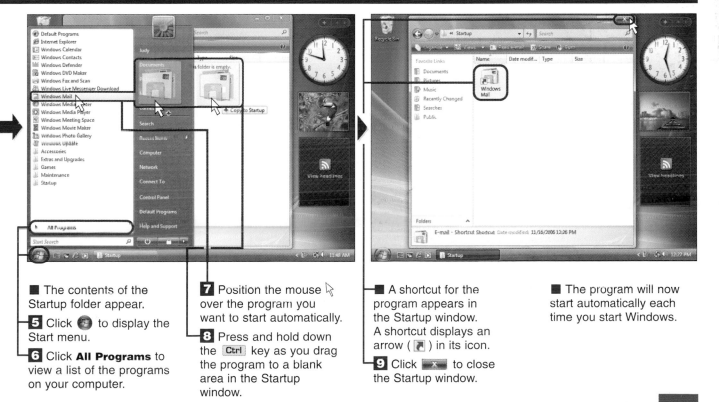

■ The contents of the Startup folder appear.

5 Click 🪟 to display the Start menu.

6 Click **All Programs** to view a list of the programs on your computer.

7 Position the mouse ▷ over the program you want to start automatically.

8 Press and hold down the Ctrl key as you drag the program to a blank area in the Startup window.

■ A shortcut for the program appears in the Startup window. A shortcut displays an arrow (🠝) in its icon.

9 Click ✕ to close the Startup window.

■ The program will now start automatically each time you start Windows.

WORKING WITH GADGETS

Windows Sidebar contains gadgets, which are mini-programs that provide continuously updated information and quick access to frequently used tools.

Windows comes with a variety of gadgets. Windows initially displays the Clock gadget, which displays the current time, the Slide Show gadget, which plays a slide show of your pictures, and the Feed Headlines gadget, which tracks the latest news, sports and entertainment headlines.

You can choose which gadgets you want to appear on your Windows Sidebar.

ADD A GADGET

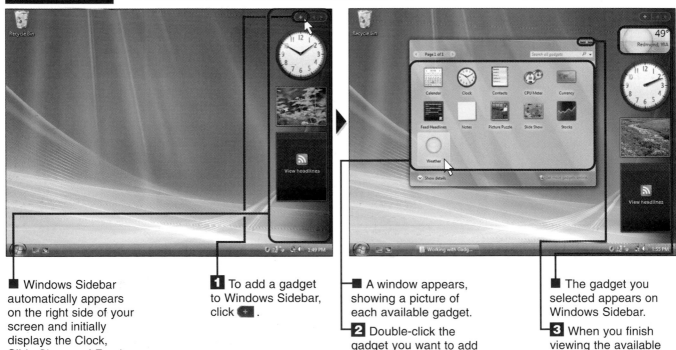

■ Windows Sidebar automatically appears on the right side of your screen and initially displays the Clock, Slide Show and Feed Headlines gadgets.

1 To add a gadget to Windows Sidebar, click ⊕.

■ A window appears, showing a picture of each available gadget.

2 Double-click the gadget you want to add to Windows Sidebar.

■ The gadget you selected appears on Windows Sidebar.

3 When you finish viewing the available gadgets, click ✕ to close the window.

Tip

Where can I get more gadgets?

You can find more gadgets on the Internet. When adding a gadget, click **Get more gadgets online** in the window that shows a picture of each available gadget. A Microsoft Web page appears, showing a list of the available gadgets that you can download and use on your computer. You need to install a gadget before the gadget will appear in your list of available gadgets.

Tip

How can I get information about a gadget?

When adding a gadget, click **Show details** in the window that shows a picture of each available gadget. A description of the selected gadget appears at the bottom of the window. You can click another gadget to display its description.

REMOVE A GADGET

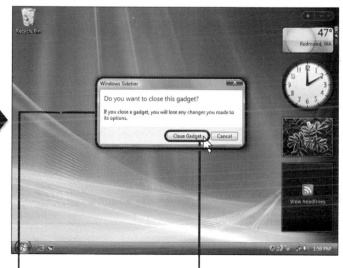

1 Position the mouse ▷ over the gadget you want to remove from your screen.

■ A toolbar appears beside the gadget.

2 Click ✕ to remove the gadget.

■ A dialog box may appear, confirming that you want to close the gadget. When you close a gadget, you will lose any changes you made to the gadget's options.

Note: To change a gadget's options, see page 174.

3 Click **Close Gadget** to remove the gadget from your screen.

■ The gadget disappears from your screen.

CONTINUED

WORKING WITH GADGETS

You can customize each gadget displayed on the Windows Sidebar to suit your preferences.

For example, you can choose which city's weather forecast is shown by the Weather gadget and change the time zone used for the Clock gadget.

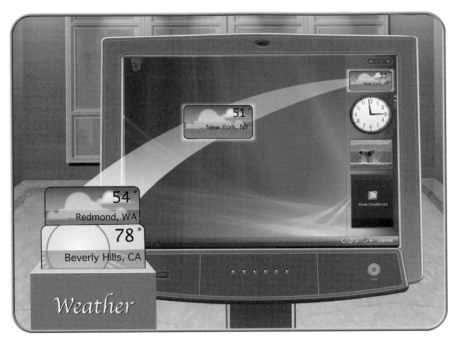

CUSTOMIZE A GADGET

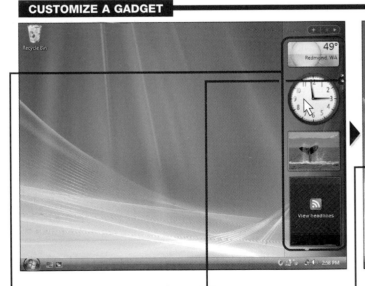

1 Position the mouse ⌖ over the gadget you want to customize.

■ A toolbar appears beside the gadget.

2 Click ⊘ to customize the gadget.

Note: If ⊘ is not displayed, you cannot customize the gadget.

■ A dialog box appears, allowing you to customize the gadget. The available options depend on the gadget you selected. In this example, we customize the Clock gadget.

3 To change the look of the clock, click ◀ or ▶ until the clock you like appears.

4 To change the time zone used by the clock, you can click this area and then select a different time zone.

5 To show the second hand on the clock, click this option (☐ changes to ☑).

6 Click **OK** to save your changes.

Tip

Can I change the order of gadgets?

Yes. You can change the order of the gadgets on the Windows Sidebar. For example, you may want the Clock gadget to appear as the last gadget on the Windows Sidebar. To move a gadget, position the mouse ⬍ over the gadget and then drag the gadget to a new location on the Windows Sidebar.

Tip

Can a gadget appear anywhere on my desktop?

Yes. You can detach a gadget from the Windows Sidebar and place the gadget anywhere on your desktop. Position the mouse ⬍ over the gadget and then drag the gadget to the location on your desktop where you want it to appear. If you close the Windows Sidebar, the gadget will remain on your desktop. To once again display the gadget on the Windows Sidebar, position the mouse ⬍ over the gadget and then drag the gadget to a blank area on the Windows Sidebar.

CLOSE WINDOWS SIDEBAR

1 To close Windows Sidebar, right-click a blank area on the Windows Sidebar. A menu appears.

2 Click **Close Sidebar**.

■ Windows Sidebar disappears from your screen.

REDISPLAY WINDOWS SIDEBAR

1 To once again display the Windows Sidebar on your screen, click the Windows Sidebar icon (▨).

*Note: You can also right-click the Windows Sidebar icon (▨) and then select **Open** from the menu that appears.*

175

ADD A BLUETOOTH DEVICE

You can add a Bluetooth device to your computer so you can use the device with your computer.

Bluetooth wireless technology allows computers and devices, such as a mouse, keyboard, cell phone or printer, to communicate without cables. Bluetooth devices use radio signals to transmit information and operate over a distance of up to 30 feet.

PREPARE A BLUETOOTH DEVICE

■ Before you can add a Bluetooth device to your computer, you must make sure the device is ready to be added.

1 Insert batteries into the Bluetooth device.

2 Turn the Bluetooth device on.

3 If you are adding a Bluetooth mouse or keyboard, make sure a mouse or keyboard with a cable is connected to your computer. You will need to use the mouse or keyboard to add the Bluetooth mouse or keyboard to your computer.

4 Make sure the Bluetooth device is discoverable, which means that your computer can see the device.

■ If you are adding a Bluetooth mouse or keyboard, the device may have a button at the bottom of the device that you can press to make the device discoverable.

Note: To determine how to make your Bluetooth device discoverable, refer to the documentation that came with your device.

**What are some of the benefits of using
Bluetooth devices with my computer?**

You can use a Bluetooth wireless
mouse, keyboard, printer or headset
to prevent cables from cluttering your
desk. Bluetooth technology also allows
you to transfer information wirelessly
between a computer and a Personal
Digital Assistant (PDA).

Can my computer use Bluetooth devices?

Computers do not usually come with
the capability to use Bluetooth devices.
To add Bluetooth capability to a computer,
you can plug an external Bluetooth adapter
into the computer. Bluetooth adapters often
connect to a computer through a USB port.
After you have added Bluetooth capability
to your computer, any Bluetooth device
can communicate with the computer.

ADD A BLUETOOTH DEVICE

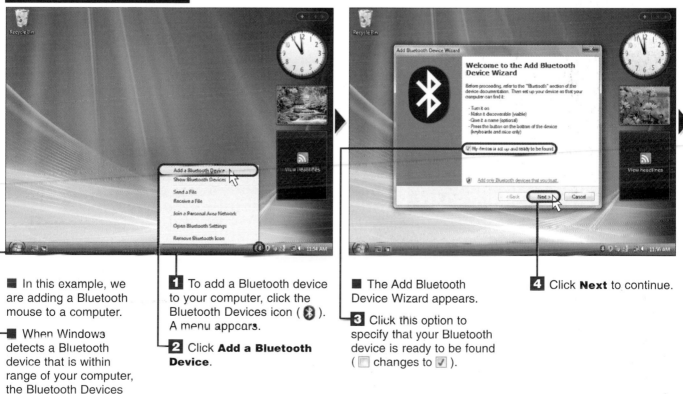

■ In this example, we
are adding a Bluetooth
mouse to a computer.

■ When Windows
detects a Bluetooth
device that is within
range of your computer,
the Bluetooth Devices
icon (🛦) appears on
the taskbar.

1 To add a Bluetooth device
to your computer, click the
Bluetooth Devices icon (🛦).
A menu appears.

2 Click **Add a Bluetooth
Device**.

■ The Add Bluetooth
Device Wizard appears.

3 Click this option to
specify that your Bluetooth
device is ready to be found
(☐ changes to ☑).

4 Click **Next** to continue.

CONTINUED

ADD A BLUETOOTH DEVICE

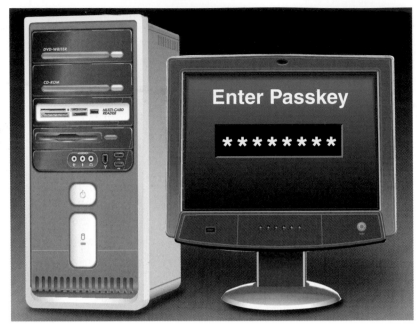

When adding a
Bluetooth device to
your computer, you
may need to enter a
passkey for the device.

A passkey enables
Windows to identify your
Bluetooth device and
helps to secure the data
passing between your
computer and the device.
Some Bluetooth devices
do not use a passkey.

You should refer to
the documentation
that came with your
Bluetooth device to
determine if your
device requires a
specific passkey.

ADD A BLUETOOTH DEVICE (CONTINUED)

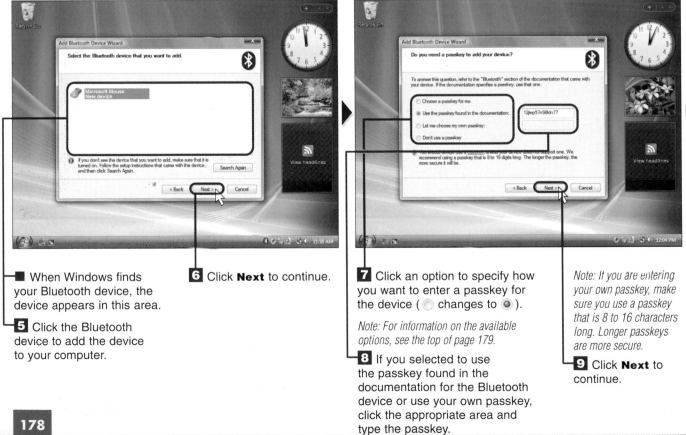

■ When Windows finds
your Bluetooth device, the
device appears in this area.

5 Click the Bluetooth
device to add the device
to your computer.

6 Click **Next** to continue.

7 Click an option to specify how
you want to enter a passkey for
the device (○ changes to ●).

*Note: For information on the available
options, see the top of page 179.*

8 If you selected to use
the passkey found in the
documentation for the Bluetooth
device or use your own passkey,
click the appropriate area and
type the passkey.

*Note: If you are entering
your own passkey, make
sure you use a passkey
that is 8 to 16 characters
long. Longer passkeys
are more secure.*

9 Click **Next** to
continue.

When adding a Bluetooth device, how can I enter a passkey for the device?

Choose a passkey for me

Select this option if the documentation for the Bluetooth device does not specify a passkey, but the device can accept a passkey. Typically, Bluetooth devices such as keyboards, cell phones and Personal Digital Assistants (PDAs) can accept a passkey.

Let me choose my own passkey

Select this option if you want to create your own passkey.

Use the passkey found in the documentation

Select this option if the documentation for the Bluetooth device specifies a passkey. Typically, devices such as Bluetooth headsets and mice specify a passkey in the documentation.

Don't use a passkey

Select this option if the documentation for the Bluetooth device does not specify a passkey and the device cannot accept a passkey.

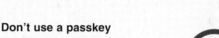

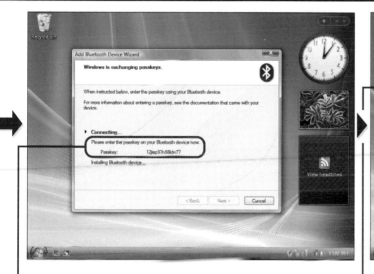

■ Windows starts adding the Bluetooth device to your computer.

■ If your Bluetooth device requires a passkey, the wizard indicates when you must enter the passkey on your device and displays the passkey you need to enter.

Note: You can refer to the documentation that came with your Bluetooth device to determine how to enter a passkey on the device.

■ This message appears when you have successfully added the Bluetooth device to your computer. Your computer and the device can now communicate whenever the device is within range of your computer.

10 Click **Finish** to close the wizard.

Note: Depending on the Bluetooth device you added, you may need to perform other steps to allow the device to communicate with your computer. You can refer to the documentation that came with your device to determine what steps, if any, you need to perform.

Share Your Computer

CREATE A USER ACCOUNT

If you share your computer with other people, you can create a personalized user account for each person.

Even if you do not share your computer with other people, Windows recommends that you create a standard user account and use that account instead of the administrator account that was automatically set up when Windows was installed.

CREATE A USER ACCOUNT

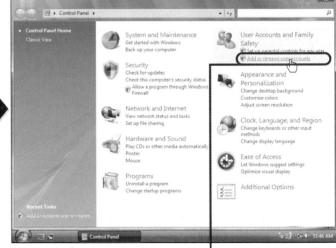

1 Click 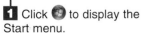 to display the Start menu.

2 Click **Control Panel** to change your computer's settings.

■ The Control Panel window appears.

3 Click **Add or remove user accounts** to add or remove user accounts on your computer.

Tip

Will Windows keep my personal files separate from the files of other users?

Yes. Windows will keep your personal files separate from the personal files created by other users. For example, your Documents, Pictures and Music folders display only the files you have created. Internet Explorer also keeps your lists of recently visited Web pages and favorite Web pages separate from the lists of other users.

Tip

How can I personalize Windows for my user account?

You can personalize the appearance of Windows for your user account by changing the screen saver, desktop background and many other computer settings. You can see chapter 8 for information on some of the ways that you can personalize Windows.

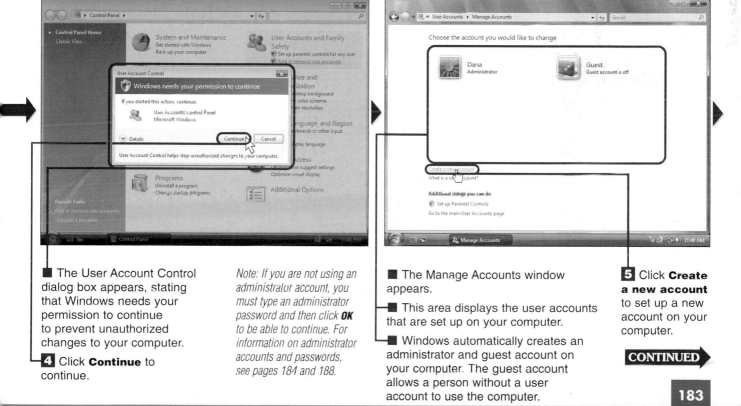

■ The User Account Control dialog box appears, stating that Windows needs your permission to continue to prevent unauthorized changes to your computer.

4 Click **Continue** to continue.

Note: If you are not using an administrator account, you must type an administrator password and then click OK to be able to continue. For information on administrator accounts and passwords, see pages 184 and 188.

■ The Manage Accounts window appears.

■ This area displays the user accounts that are set up on your computer.

■ Windows automatically creates an administrator and guest account on your computer. The guest account allows a person without a user account to use the computer.

5 Click **Create a new account** to set up a new account on your computer.

CONTINUED

CREATE A USER ACCOUNT

When you create a user account, you must select the type of account you want to create.

Standard user

You can perform almost any task on the computer. However, you cannot perform tasks that might affect every user or the security of the computer without first entering an administrator password. Windows recommends that you make each new account you create a standard user account.

Administrator

You can perform any task on the computer. Windows does not recommend this type of account for daily use.

CREATE A USER ACCOUNT (CONTINUED)

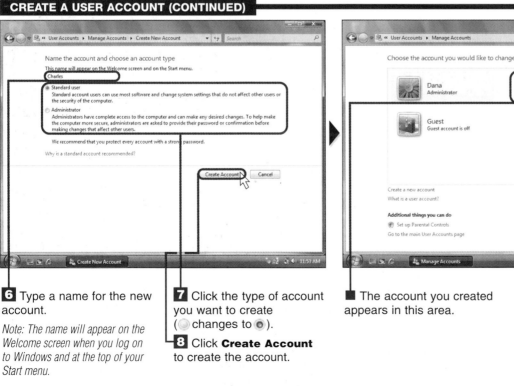

6 Type a name for the new account.

Note: The name will appear on the Welcome screen when you log on to Windows and at the top of your Start menu.

7 Click the type of account you want to create (○ changes to ◉).

8 Click **Create Account** to create the account.

■ The account you created appears in this area.

9 Click ❎ to close the Manage Accounts window.

If a person no longer
uses your computer,
you can delete the
person's user account
from your computer.

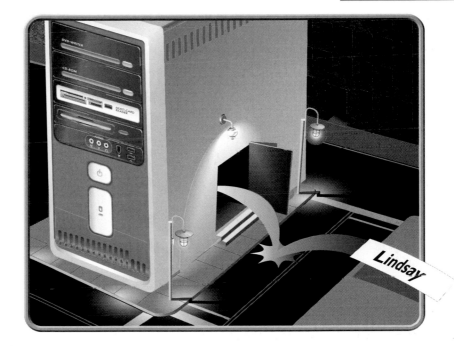

DELETE A USER ACCOUNT

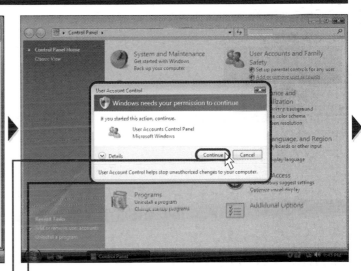

1 Click 🟦 to display
the Start menu.

2 Click **Control Panel**
to change your
computer's settings.

■ The Control Panel
window appears.

3 Click **Add or remove
user accounts** to add or
remove user accounts on
your computer.

■ The User Account
Control dialog box appears,
stating that Windows needs
your permission to continue
to prevent unauthorized
changes to your computer.

4 Click **Continue** to
continue.

*Note: If you are not using an
administrator account, you must
type an administrator password and
then click **OK** to be able to continue.
For information on administrator
accounts and passwords, see pages
184 and 188.*

CONTINUED

DELETE A USER ACCOUNT

When you delete a user account, you can choose to delete or keep the user's personal files.

If you choose to delete a user's personal files, Windows will permanently delete the files from your computer.

DELETE A USER ACCOUNT (CONTINUED)

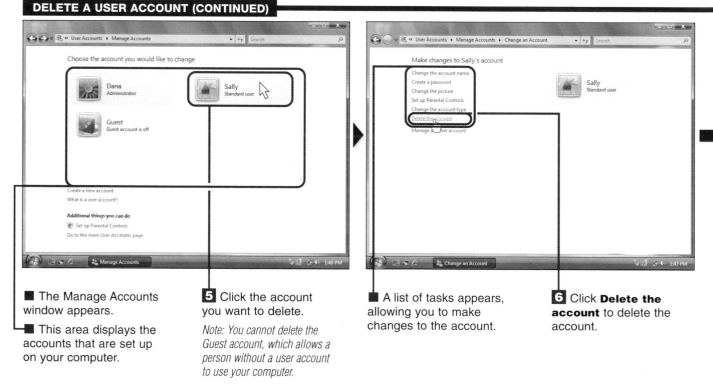

■ The Manage Accounts window appears.

■ This area displays the accounts that are set up on your computer.

5 Click the account you want to delete.

Note: You cannot delete the Guest account, which allows a person without a user account to use your computer.

■ A list of tasks appears, allowing you to make changes to the account.

6 Click **Delete the account** to delete the account.

Tip

If I choose to keep the personal files for a deleted user account, which files will Windows save?

Windows will save the user's personal files that are displayed on the desktop and stored in the Documents, Music, Pictures and Videos folders. Windows will also save the user's list of favorite Web pages. The files will be saved on your desktop in a new folder that has the same name as the deleted account. Windows will not save the user's e-mail messages and computer settings.

Tip

Can I delete an administrator account?

Yes. You can delete administrator accounts. However, Windows will not allow you to delete the last administrator account on your computer. This ensures that one administrator account always exists on the computer.

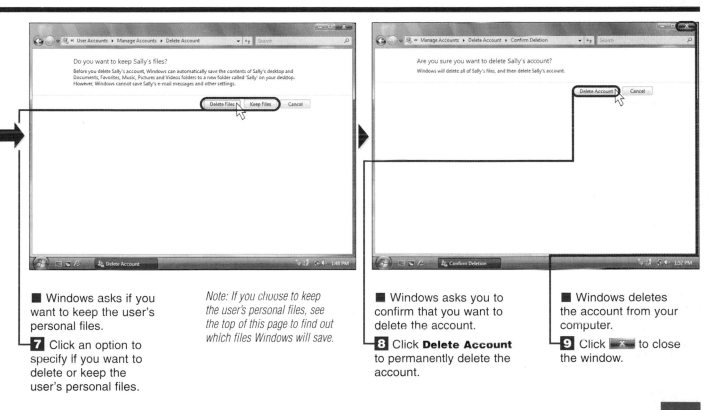

■ Windows asks if you want to keep the user's personal files.

7 Click an option to specify if you want to delete or keep the user's personal files.

Note: If you choose to keep the user's personal files, see the top of this page to find out which files Windows will save.

■ Windows asks you to confirm that you want to delete the account.

8 Click **Delete Account** to permanently delete the account.

■ Windows deletes the account from your computer.

9 Click ▣ to close the window.

CREATE A PASSWORD

You can add a password to your user account to prevent other people from accessing the account. You will need to enter the password each time you want to use Windows.

If your password contains capital letters, you will need to type the letters in the same way each time you enter your password.

When you create a password, you can enter a password hint that can help you remember the password. The hint will be available to everyone who uses the computer. To display a password hint, see page 191.

CREATE A PASSWORD

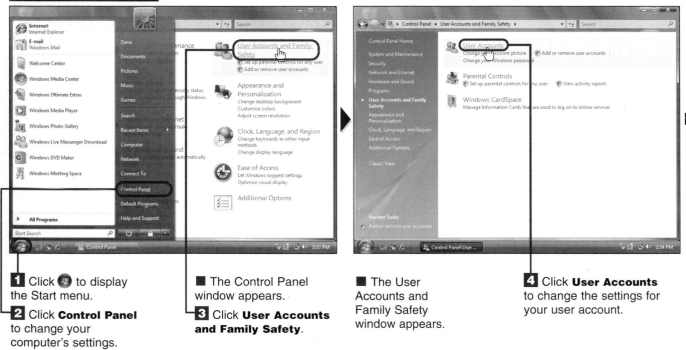

1 Click 🟦 to display the Start menu.

2 Click **Control Panel** to change your computer's settings.

■ The Control Panel window appears.

3 Click **User Accounts and Family Safety**.

■ The User Accounts and Family Safety window appears.

4 Click **User Accounts** to change the settings for your user account.

Tip

How do I create a good password?

A good password:

✓ Contains at least eight characters.

✓ Contains uppercase letters (A,B,C), lowercase letters (a,b,c), numbers (0,1,2,3), symbols found on the keyboard (!,@,#,$,%) and spaces.

✓ Does not contain your real name, company name or user name.

✓ Does not contain a complete word.

✓ Is easy to remember, such as:

Msb=8/Apr 94 ➜ "My son's birthday is April 8, 1994"
iL2e CwDp! ➜ "I like to eat chips with dip!"

Tip

How do I change my password?

To change your password, perform steps **1** to **4** below and then click **Change your password**. Type the current password and the new password you want to use. Then type the new password again to confirm the password. If you want to provide a password hint, type the hint and then click **Change password** to change the password.

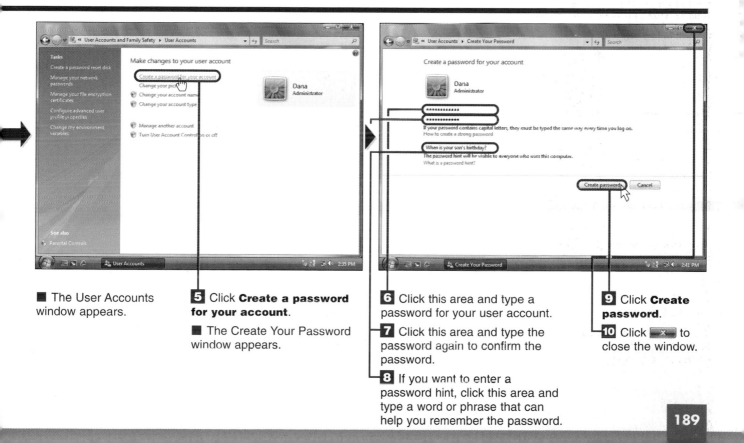

■ The User Accounts window appears.

5 Click **Create a password for your account**.

■ The Create Your Password window appears.

6 Click this area and type a password for your user account.

7 Click this area and type the password again to confirm the password.

8 If you want to enter a password hint, click this area and type a word or phrase that can help you remember the password.

9 Click **Create password**.

10 Click ✕ to close the window.

LOG OFF WINDOWS

When you finish using your computer, you can log off Windows to allow another person to log on to Windows to use the computer.

When you log off Windows, your computer remains on but your user account is closed.

LOG OFF WINDOWS

■ Before logging off Windows, you should close your open files and programs.

1 Click 🪟 to display the Start menu.

2 Click ▸ to display a list of options.

3 Click **Log Off** to log off Windows.

■ The Welcome screen appears, allowing another person to log on to Windows to use the computer. To log on to Windows, see page 191.

■ If another person turns off the computer, the person does not need to worry about losing your information since your user account is closed.

LOG ON TO WINDOWS

**If you have set up
user accounts on your
computer, you will
need to log on to
Windows to use the
computer.**

If you have only one user
account set up on your
computer and have assigned
a password to that account,
you will also need to log
on to Windows to use the
computer. To assign
a password to a user
account, see page 188.

LOG ON TO WINDOWS

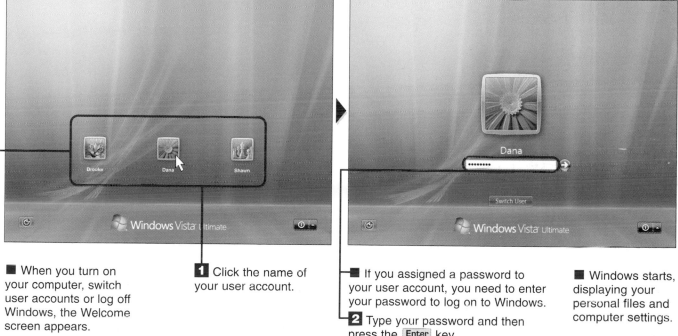

■ When you turn on
your computer, switch
user accounts or log off
Windows, the Welcome
screen appears.

■ This area displays
the user accounts set
up on your computer.

1 Click the name of
your user account.

■ If you assigned a password to
your user account, you need to enter
your password to log on to Windows.

2 Type your password and then
press the Enter key.

*Note: A message appears if you enter the
wrong password. Click **OK** to try entering
the password again. This time, Windows
will display the password hint you entered
when you created the password.*

■ Windows starts,
displaying your
personal files and
computer settings.

SWITCH USERS

If another person wants to use your computer, you can allow the person to switch to their user account. Windows will keep your files and programs open while the other person logs on to Windows to use the computer.

When you switch between users, you can quickly return to your files and programs after the other person finishes using the computer.

SWITCH USERS

■ Before switching users, you should save any files you have open.

Note: If another person turns off the computer, any unsaved changes you have made to your files will be lost.

1 Click ![start] to display the Start menu.

2 Click ![arrow] to display a list of options.

3 Click **Switch User**.

■ The Welcome screen appears, allowing another person to log on to Windows to use the computer. To log on to Windows, see page 191.

■ Windows keeps your user account "logged on," which means that your files and programs remain open on the computer.

SHARE FILES

You can share files with other users set up on your computer by adding the files to the Public folder. Every user set up on your computer can access the files stored in the Public folder.

The Public folder contains folders for sharing documents, downloaded files, music, pictures, videos and recorded TV programs.

SHARE FILES

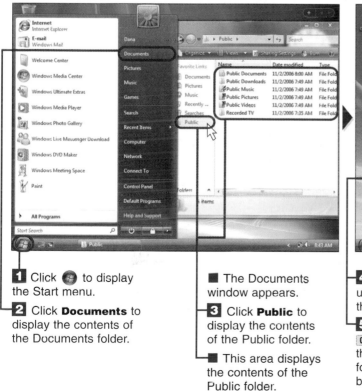

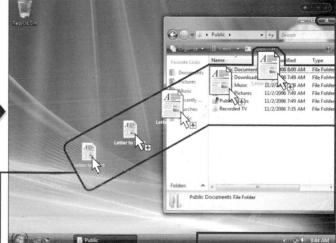

1 Click 🔵 to display the Start menu.

2 Click **Documents** to display the contents of the Documents folder.

■ The Documents window appears.

3 Click **Public** to display the contents of the Public folder.

■ This area displays the contents of the Public folder.

4 To share a file with every user on your computer, position the mouse ▹ over the file.

5 Press and hold down the **Ctrl** key as you drag a copy of the file to the appropriate Public folder. Release the left mouse button and then the **Ctrl** key.

Note: To display the contents of a Public folder, double-click the folder.

6 When you finish sharing files, click ✖ to close the window.

SET UP PARENTAL CONTROLS

You can set up parental controls to help control how your children use your computer.

For example, you can set up time limits to control when your children can use the computer. You can also limit the Web sites that your children can view on the Web.

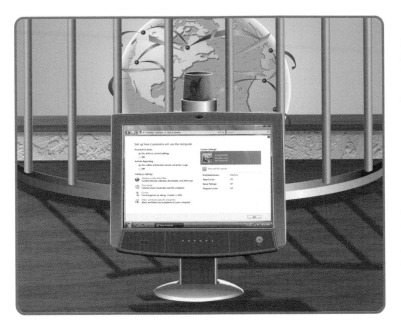

Parental controls are only available in the Home Basic, Home Premium and Ultimate editions of Windows Vista.

Before setting up parental controls, make sure your administrator accounts are password protected to prevent your children from bypassing or turning off parental controls. To create a password, see page 188.

SET UP PARENTAL CONTROLS

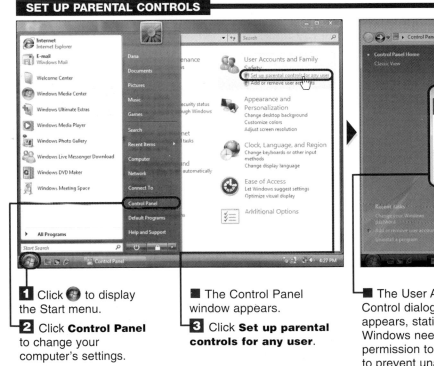

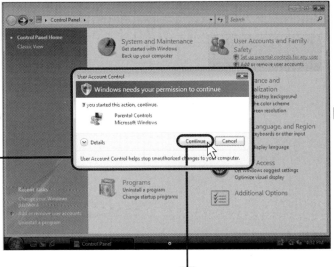

1 Click ⊕ to display the Start menu.

2 Click **Control Panel** to change your computer's settings.

■ The Control Panel window appears.

3 Click **Set up parental controls for any user**.

■ The User Account Control dialog box appears, stating that Windows needs your permission to continue to prevent unauthorized changes to your computer.

4 Click **Continue** to continue.

*Note: If you are not using an administrator account, you must type an administrator password and then click **OK** to be able to continue. For information on administrator accounts and passwords, see pages 184 and 188.*

Tip

How do I view the information about my child's computer activities?

To view a report that shows your child's computer activities, perform steps 1 to 4 below and then click the child's user account in the window that appears. Click **View activity reports** to display a report of your child's computer activities. When you finish viewing the report, click ▬✕▬ to close the window.

Tip

How do I turn off parental controls?

To turn off parental controls for your child, perform steps 1 to 4 below and then click the child's user account in the window that appears. Below Parental Controls, click **Off** and then click **OK** to save your changes. The child will now have full access to the computer and the Internet.

■ The Parental Controls window appears.

■ This area lists each user account set up on your computer.

Note: To set up a user account for each person who uses the computer, see page 182.

5 To set up parental controls for your child, click the child's user account.

■ The User Controls window appears.

6 To turn on parental controls for the child, click this option (◯ changes to ◉).

7 Click an option to specify if you want to collect information about the child's computer activities (◯ changes to ◉).

Note: Windows can collect information such as the top 10 Web sites visited, the total time spent on the computer and the games the child plays.

CONTINUED

SET UP PARENTAL CONTROLS

You can limit the Web sites that your children can view on the Web. You can also set up time limits to control when your children can use the computer.

When limiting the Web sites your children can view, you can choose a medium or high restriction level. The medium restriction level blocks children from viewing Web sites with inappropriate content. The high restriction level allows children to visit only children's Web sites.

SET UP PARENTAL CONTROLS (CONTINUED)

LIMIT WEB SITES

1 To limit the Web sites that your child can view on the Web, click **Windows Vista Web Filter**.

■ The Web Restrictions window appears.

2 Click an option to block some Web sites or allow your child to visit all Web sites (○ changes to ◉).

3 If you selected to block some Web sites, click a high or medium restriction level (○ changes to ◉).

4 To block your child from downloading files from the Internet, click this option (☐ changes to ☑).

5 Click **OK** to save your changes.

Tip

Can I specify which Web sites my child can and cannot visit?

Yes. In the Web Restrictions window, click **Block some websites or content** (○ changes to ●) and then click **Edit the Allow and block list**. In the window that appears, type a Web site address and then click **Allow** or **Block** to add the address to the allowed or blocked list. To allow your child to visit only the Web sites in your allow list, click **Only Allow websites which are on the allow list**. Click **OK** to save your changes.

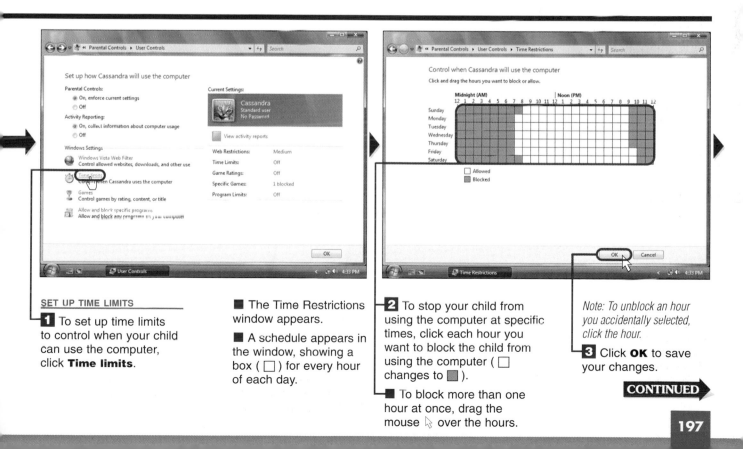

SET UP TIME LIMITS

1 To set up time limits to control when your child can use the computer, click **Time limits**.

■ The Time Restrictions window appears.

■ A schedule appears in the window, showing a box (□) for every hour of each day.

2 To stop your child from using the computer at specific times, click each hour you want to block the child from using the computer (□ changes to ■).

■ To block more than one hour at once, drag the mouse ⌖ over the hours.

Note: To unblock an hour you accidentally selected, click the hour.

3 Click **OK** to save your changes.

CONTINUED

SET UP PARENTAL CONTROLS

You can control which games your children can play on your computer.

For example, you can block your children from playing a game that is not age appropriate.

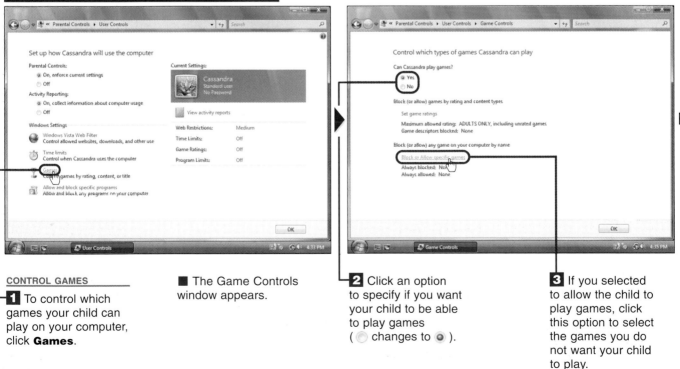

CONTROL GAMES

1 To control which games your child can play on your computer, click **Games**.

■ The Game Controls window appears.

2 Click an option to specify if you want your child to be able to play games (○ changes to ●).

3 If you selected to allow the child to play games, click this option to select the games you do not want your child to play.

Tip

How are games rated?

Most games sold in stores are rated to help you determine which games are appropriate for your children. You can look on the front of a game's box for the game's rating.

Rating	Suitable Ages
Early childhood (Ec)	3 and older
Everyone (E)	6 and older
Everyone 10+ (E10+)	10 and older
Teen (T)	13 and older
Mature (M)	17 and older
Adults Only (Ao)	18 and older

Tip

Can I use game ratings to control which games my child can play?

Yes. In the Game Controls window, click **Yes** to allow your child to play games and then click **Set game ratings**. In the window that appears, click a game rating that is appropriate for your child. At the top of the window, click an option to allow or block games with no rating. Click **OK** to save your changes. Your child can now play only the games with the rating you selected.

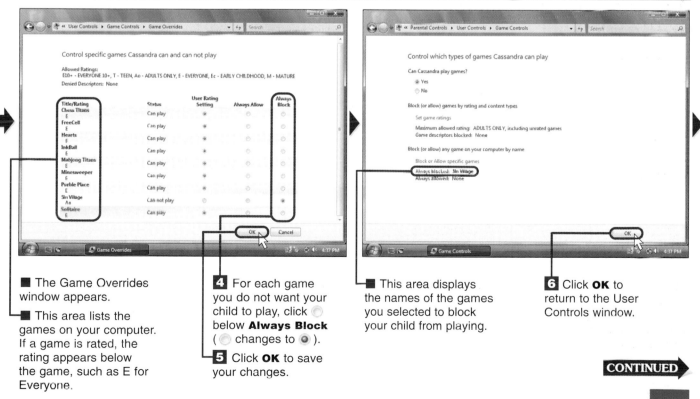

■ The Game Overrides window appears.

■ This area lists the games on your computer. If a game is rated, the rating appears below the game, such as E for Everyone.

4 For each game you do not want your child to play, click below **Always Block**.

5 Click **OK** to save your changes.

■ This area displays the names of the games you selected to block your child from playing.

6 Click **OK** to return to the User Controls window.

CONTINUED

SET UP PARENTAL CONTROLS

You can specify which programs your children can use on your computer.

For example, you can prevent your children from opening a program that you use to keep track of your finances.

SET UP PARENTAL CONTROLS (CONTINUED)

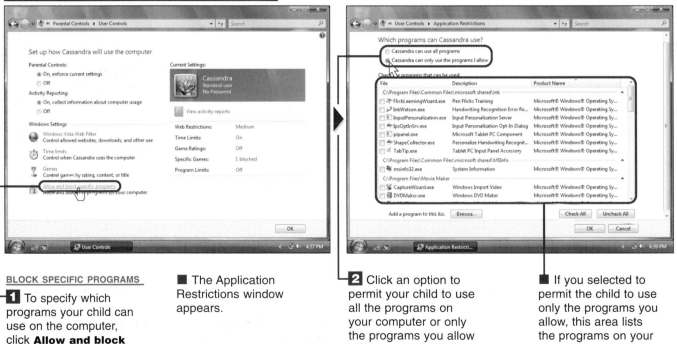

BLOCK SPECIFIC PROGRAMS

1 To specify which programs your child can use on the computer, click **Allow and block specific programs**.

■ The Application Restrictions window appears.

2 Click an option to permit your child to use all the programs on your computer or only the programs you allow (○ changes to ◉).

■ If you selected to permit the child to use only the programs you allow, this area lists the programs on your computer.

Tip

How can I further help protect my children when they use the computer?

Although the Parental Controls feature included with Windows can help manage how your children use the computer, it should not replace parental supervision. Constant adult supervision is the best way to help protect your children. Here are some tips:

✓ Keep the family computer in a high-traffic area in your house, such as the kitchen or family room, so you can monitor all activity.

✓ Maintain an ongoing conversation with your children about their computer activities.

✓ Tell your children not to provide their photo or personal information, such as their name, address, phone number or school name, to anyone they meet on the Internet.

✓ Tell your children not to meet with anyone they have met on the Internet.

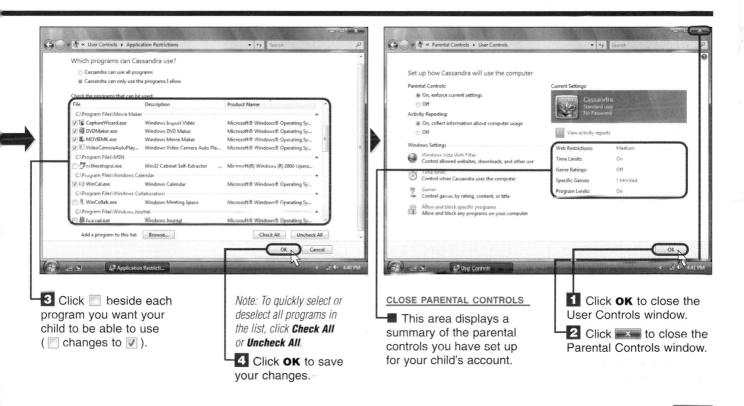

3 Click ☐ beside each program you want your child to be able to use (☐ changes to ☑).

*Note: To quickly select or deselect all programs in the list, click **Check All** or **Uncheck All**.*

4 Click **OK** to save your changes.

CLOSE PARENTAL CONTROLS

■ This area displays a summary of the parental controls you have set up for your child's account.

1 Click **OK** to close the User Controls window.

2 Click ✕ to close the Parental Controls window.

Browse the Web

START INTERNET EXPLORER

You can start Internet Explorer to browse through the information on the Web.

You need a connection to the Internet to browse information on the Web. Most people pay a company called an Internet Service Provider (ISP) to connect to the Internet.

START INTERNET EXPLORER

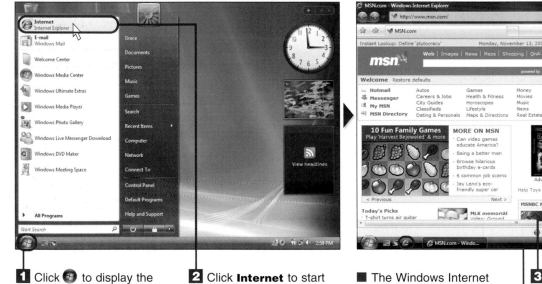

1 Click  to display the Start menu.

2 Click **Internet** to start Internet Explorer.

■ The Windows Internet Explorer window appears, displaying your home page.

Note: Your home page is the Web page that appears each time you start Internet Explorer. To change your home page, see page 214.

3 When you finish browsing the Web, click to close the window.

■ After you start Internet Explorer the first time, an icon appears in this area. You can click at any time to start Internet Explorer.

You can display any Web page on the Internet that you have heard or read about.

A Web page is a document that can include text, pictures, sounds and videos. Every Web page has a unique address. You need to know the address of the Web page you want to view.

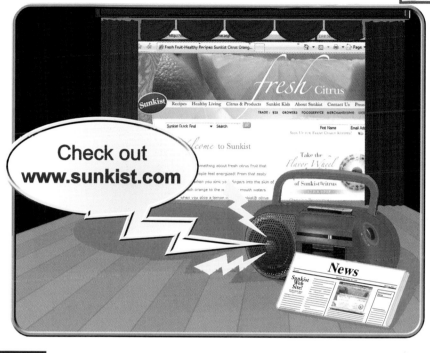

Internet Explorer blocks most pop-up windows and prevents Web pages from downloading potentially harmful files and running software on your computer without your knowledge. Pop-up windows are small windows that are often used to display advertisements and usually appear as soon as you visit a Web site.

DISPLAY A WEB PAGE

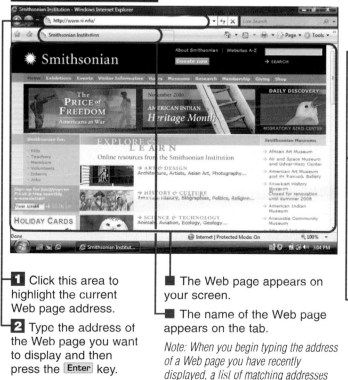

1 Click this area to highlight the current Web page address.

2 Type the address of the Web page you want to display and then press the Enter key.

■ The Web page appears on your screen.

■ The name of the Web page appears on the tab.

Note: When you begin typing the address of a Web page you have recently displayed, a list of matching addresses appears. You can click the address of the Web page you want to redisplay.

VIEW BLOCKED CONTENT

■ The Information Bar and Information Bar dialog box appear when Internet Explorer blocks a pop-up window or content that could harm your computer.

1 Click **Close** to close the dialog box.

2 If you want to view the blocked content, click the Information Bar. A menu appears.

3 Click the option that allows you to unblock the content.

205

WORK WITH WEB PAGES

There are many ways you can work with Web pages in Internet Explorer. For example, when you are viewing a Web page, you can select a link to display related information.

A link connects text or an image on one Web page to another Web page. When you select the text or image, the linked Web page appears.

When working with Web pages, you can also move back and forward through pages you have viewed and stop the transfer of a Web page to your computer.

SELECT A LINK

1 Position the mouse over a word or image of interest. The mouse changes to a hand when over a link.

■ This area displays the address of the Web page that the link will take you to.

2 Click the word or image to display the linked Web page.

■ The linked Web page appears.

■ This area displays the address of the Web page.

■ The name of the Web page appears on the tab.

Note: For information on working with tabs, see page 208.

Tip

Can I update the Web page displayed on my screen to view more recent information?

Yes. Transferring a fresh copy of a Web page to your computer, called refreshing a Web page, is useful for updating pages that contain regularly changing information, such as news or images from a live camera. To refresh the Web page currently displayed on your screen, click 🔄.

Tip

How can I enlarge the text displayed on a Web page?

If you have trouble reading small text on a Web page, you can use your mouse's wheel to change the size of the text. To enlarge the text, press and hold down the `Ctrl` key as you roll the wheel away from you.

Note: To reduce the size of text on a Web page, press and hold down the `Ctrl` key as you roll the mouse's wheel toward you.

MOVE THROUGH WEB PAGES

STOP TRANSFER OF A WEB PAGE

MOVE BACK

1 Click ⬅ to return to the last Web page you viewed.

Note: The ⬅ button is only available if you have viewed more than one Web page since you last started Internet Explorer.

MOVE FORWARD

1 Click ➡ to move forward through the Web pages you have viewed.

Note: The ➡ button is only available after you use the ⬅ button to return to a Web page.

■ If a Web page is taking a long time to appear on your screen or contains information that does not interest you, you can stop the transfer of the page.

■ This icon is animated as a Web page transfers to your computer.

1 Click ✕ to stop the transfer of the Web page.

WORK WITH TABS

You can use tabs to view and work with more than one Web page at a time within the Internet Explorer window.

When browsing the Web, you can choose which Web pages you want to open on new tabs.

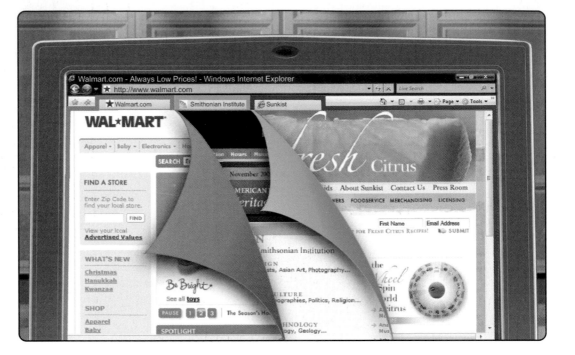

WORK WITH TABS

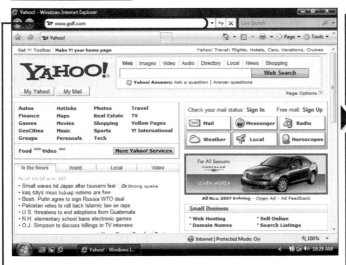

DISPLAY A WEB PAGE IN A NEW TAB

1 To display a Web page in a new tab, click this area and type the address of the Web page you want to display. Then press and hold down the `Alt` key as you press the `Enter` key.

■ To display a linked Web page in a new tab, press and hold down the `Ctrl` key as you click the link for the Web page.

■ A new tab for the Web page appears and the Web page is displayed.

MOVE BETWEEN TABS

1 Click the tab for the Web page you want to view.

■ The Web page will appear on your screen.

Tip

What happens if I have several tabs open when I exit Internet Explorer?

If you have several tabs open when you click ▨ to close the Internet Explorer window, a dialog box appears, asking if you want to close all the open tabs.

■ To close all the tabs and exit Internet Explorer, click **Close Tabs**.

■ To have Internet Explorer automatically redisplay all the current tabs the next time you start Internet Explorer, click **Show Options** in the dialog box and then click **Open these the next time I use Internet Explorer** (□ changes to ☑). Then click **Close Tabs**.

Tip

Are there other ways I can use tabs when working with Web pages?

Yes. You can also use tabs to set several Web pages as your home pages and to help you work with your favorite Web pages. For more information on working with tabs with your home pages, see page 214. For more information on using tabs with your list of favorite Web pages, see the top of page 219.

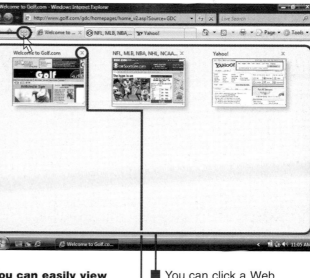

USING QUICK TABS

CLOSE A TAB

1 Click the tab you want to close.

2 Click ▨ on the tab to close the tab and remove it from your screen.

You can easily view and work with all the tabs you have open.

1 Click ▦ to display all the Web pages you currently have open.

■ This area displays each Web page you have open.

■ You can click a Web page to display the Web page on your screen.

■ You can click ✕ above a Web page you want to close.

2 To return to the last Web page you viewed, click ▦ again.

PRINT A WEB PAGE

You can produce a paper copy of the Web page displayed on your screen. Before printing a Web page, you can preview how the Web page will look when printed.

By default, the width of a Web page will be reduced to fit across a single piece of paper.

PREVIEW A WEB PAGE BEFORE PRINTING

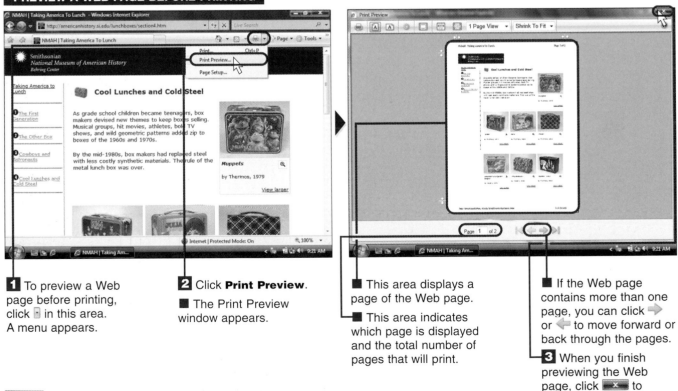

1 To preview a Web page before printing, click ⬇ in this area. A menu appears.

2 Click **Print Preview**.

■ The Print Preview window appears.

■ This area displays a page of the Web page.

■ This area indicates which page is displayed and the total number of pages that will print.

■ If the Web page contains more than one page, you can click ➡ or ⬅ to move forward or back through the pages.

3 When you finish previewing the Web page, click ✕ to close the window.

Tip

Why does the text on a Web page appear so small when it prints?

By default, the contents of a Web page are reduced to fit across a single piece of paper. This prevents the text or images at the right side of a Web page from being cut off but may make the text more difficult to read. To increase the size of the content on a Web page you will print, display the Web page in the Print Preview window and then click ⸱ beside **Shrink To Fit**. You can then choose a percentage you want the text and images to print at until the page appears the way you want.

Tip

Can I print only specific pages of a Web page?

After previewing how a Web page will print, you may want to print only specific pages. In the Print Preview window, click 🖨. The Print dialog box appears, displaying options you can select for printing the Web page. Double-click the number beside **Pages** and type the pages you want to print, such as 3 or 2-4. Then click **Print** to print the pages.

PRINT A WEB PAGE

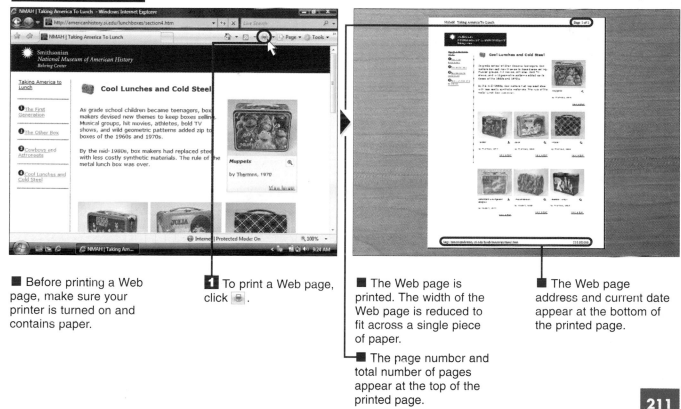

■ Before printing a Web page, make sure your printer is turned on and contains paper.

1 To print a Web page, click 🖨.

■ The Web page is printed. The width of the Web page is reduced to fit across a single piece of paper.

■ The page number and total number of pages appear at the top of the printed page.

■ The Web page address and current date appear at the bottom of the printed page.

SEARCH THE WEB

You can search for Web pages that discuss topics of interest to you.

Web sites that allow you to search for information on the Web are known as search providers. Google is the most popular search provider on the Web.

SEARCH THE WEB

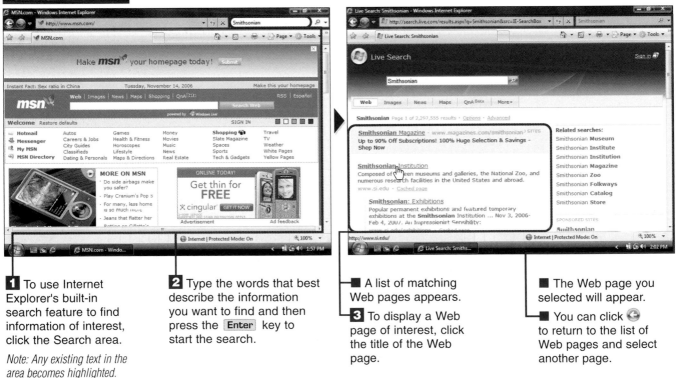

1 To use Internet Explorer's built-in search feature to find information of interest, click the Search area.

Note: Any existing text in the area becomes highlighted.

2 Type the words that best describe the information you want to find and then press the **Enter** key to start the search.

■ A list of matching Web pages appears.

3 To display a Web page of interest, click the title of the Web page.

■ The Web page you selected will appear.

■ You can click to return to the list of Web pages and select another page.

Tip

After searching, can I display a Web page of interest on a separate tab?

Yes. After performing steps 1 and 2 on page 212, right-click the title of the Web page of interest in the list of matching Web pages. In the menu that appears, click **Open in New Tab**. A new tab will appear at the top of the Internet Explorer window, displaying the name of the Web page you selected. You can click the tab to view the contents of the Web page. For more information on using tabs, see page 208.

Tip

Can I switch to a different search provider if the search does not provide the results I want?

You can change the search provider you use to perform a search at any time. Click ▾ in the Search area to display your list of search providers. Click the search provider you want to use and then perform steps 1 to 3 on page 212 to search the Web.

Note: To add a search provider to your list of providers in Internet Explorer, perform steps 1 to 4 below, except do not click the option in step 4.

CHANGE THE DEFAULT SEARCH PROVIDER

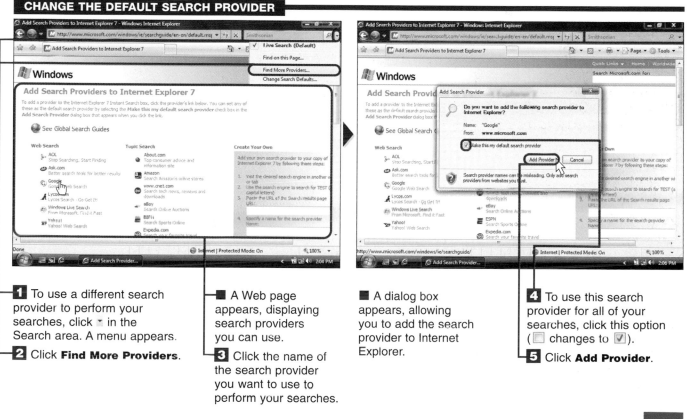

1 To use a different search provider to perform your searches, click ▾ in the Search area. A menu appears.

2 Click **Find More Providers**.

■ A Web page appears, displaying search providers you can use.

3 Click the name of the search provider you want to use to perform your searches.

■ A dialog box appears, allowing you to add the search provider to Internet Explorer.

4 To use this search provider for all of your searches, click this option (☐ changes to ☑).

5 Click **Add Provider**.

DISPLAY AND CHANGE YOUR HOME PAGE

You can display and change the Web page that appears each time you start Internet Explorer. This Web page is called your home page.

Internet Explorer also allows you to set up multiple home pages on tabs and display all of the tabs each time you start Internet Explorer. For more information on tabs, see page 208.

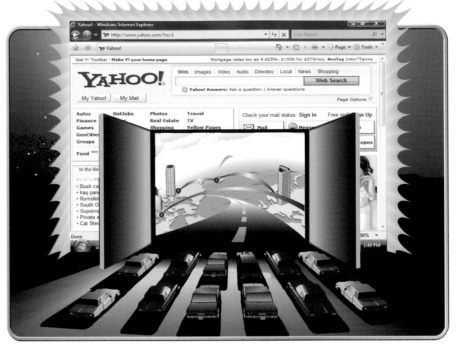

DISPLAY YOUR HOME PAGE

1 Click 🏠 to display your home page.

■ Your home page appears.

Note: Your home page may be different than the home page shown above.

CHANGE YOUR HOME PAGE

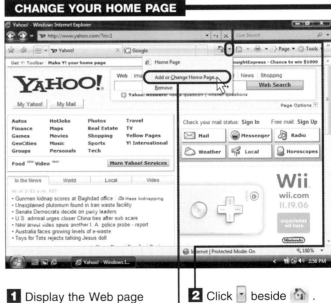

1 Display the Web page you want to set as your home page.

Note: To display a specific Web page, see page 205.

2 Click ▾ beside 🏠 .

3 Click **Add or Change Home Page**.

Tip

Which Web page should I set as my home page?

You can set any page on the Web as your home page. The Web page you choose should be a page you want to frequently visit. You may want to choose a Web page that provides a good starting point for exploring the Web, such as www.yahoo.com, or a page that provides information relevant to your personal interests or work.

Tip

How can I remove a home page I no longer want to display each time I start Internet Explorer?

Click ▾ beside ⌂ . In the menu that appears, click **Remove**. A list of your home pages appears. Click the home page you no longer want to display each time you start Internet Explorer and then click **Yes** in the confirmation dialog box that appears.

Note: If you remove all of your home pages, a blank page will appear when you start the Web browser.

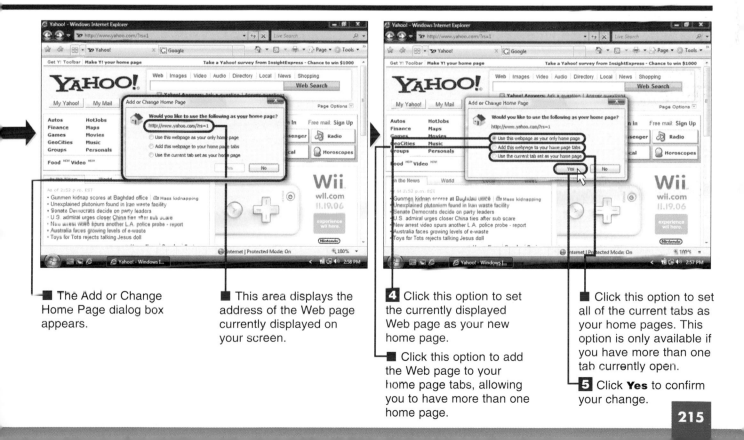

■ The Add or Change Home Page dialog box appears.

■ This area displays the address of the Web page currently displayed on your screen.

4 Click this option to set the currently displayed Web page as your new home page.

■ Click this option to add the Web page to your home page tabs, allowing you to have more than one home page.

■ Click this option to set all of the current tabs as your home pages. This option is only available if you have more than one tab currently open.

5 Click **Yes** to confirm your change.

DISPLAY HISTORY OF VIEWED WEB PAGES

Internet Explorer uses the History list to keep track of the Web pages you have recently viewed. You can display the History list at any time to redisplay a Web page.

The History list keeps track of the Web pages you have viewed over the last 20 days.

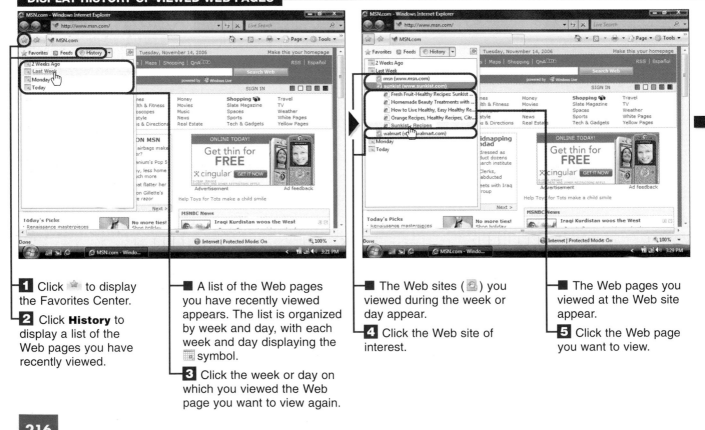

DISPLAY HISTORY OF VIEWED WEB PAGES

1 Click 🔖 to display the Favorites Center.

2 Click **History** to display a list of the Web pages you have recently viewed.

■ A list of the Web pages you have recently viewed appears. The list is organized by week and day, with each week and day displaying the 📅 symbol.

3 Click the week or day on which you viewed the Web page you want to view again.

■ The Web sites (📄) you viewed during the week or day appear.

4 Click the Web site of interest.

■ The Web pages you viewed at the Web site appear.

5 Click the Web page you want to view.

Tip

Can I change the way my list of recently viewed Web pages is organized?

Yes. You can sort the displayed Web pages in your History list. Click ⊡ beside History. A menu appears. Click the way you want to sort the list of Web pages you have recently visited. You can sort the displayed Web pages by date, Web site name, most frequently visited pages or most recently visited pages.

Tip

How can I stop my History list from disappearing when I click a Web page I want to view?

To more easily work with the Web pages in your History list, you can have the Favorites Center remain on your screen at all times. Click 📌 to keep the Favorites Center displayed on your screen until you are finished working with your History list. You can then click ✕ to remove the Favorites Center from your screen.

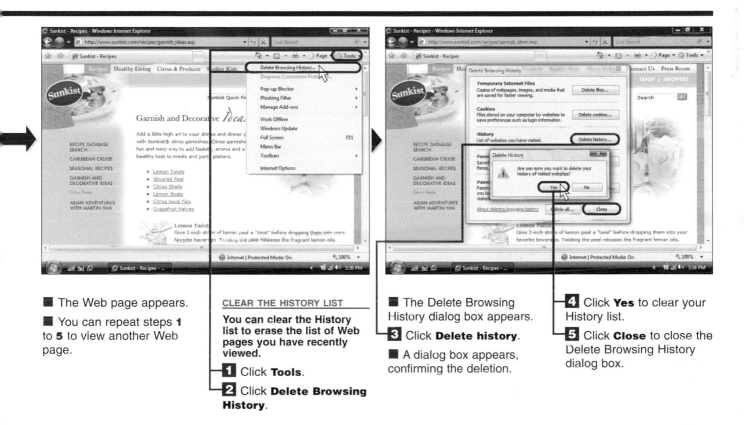

■ The Web page appears.

■ You can repeat steps **1** to **5** to view another Web page.

CLEAR THE HISTORY LIST

You can clear the History list to erase the list of Web pages you have recently viewed.

1 Click **Tools**.

2 Click **Delete Browsing History**.

■ The Delete Browsing History dialog box appears.

3 Click **Delete history**.

■ A dialog box appears, confirming the deletion.

4 Click **Yes** to clear your History list.

5 Click **Close** to close the Delete Browsing History dialog box.

ADD A WEB PAGE TO FAVORITES

You can use the Favorites feature to create a list of Web pages that you frequently visit. The Favorites feature allows you to quickly display a favorite Web page at any time.

Selecting Web pages from your list of favorites saves you from having to remember and constantly retype the same Web page addresses over and over again.

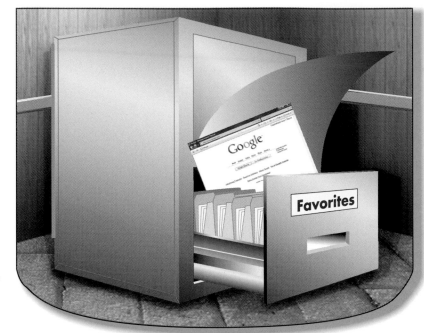

Internet Explorer automatically adds several folders of Web pages to your list of favorites, including the Links folder, the Microsoft Websites folder, the MSN Websites folder and the Windows Live folder.

ADD A WEB PAGE TO FAVORITES

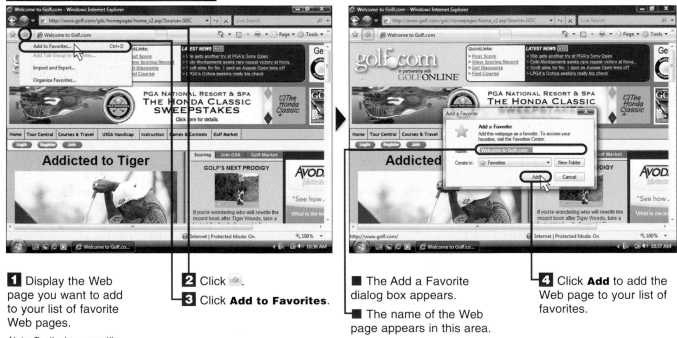

1 Display the Web page you want to add to your list of favorite Web pages.

Note: To display a specific Web page, see page 205.

2 Click ☆.

3 Click **Add to Favorites**.

■ The Add a Favorite dialog box appears.

■ The name of the Web page appears in this area.

4 Click **Add** to add the Web page to your list of favorites.

Tip

Can I create a group of several favorite Web pages?

If you have several Web pages open on tabs, you can save all the tabs as a group of favorites. For information on working with tabs, see page 208.

To save all the current tabs as a group of favorites, click ☆ and then click **Add Tab Group to Favorites** in the menu that appears. In the dialog box that appears, type a name for the group of tabs and then click **Add**.

To display all the tabs in a favorite group at once, perform steps **1** and **2** below. Position your mouse over the name of the group you want to display and then click ➜ that appears beside the name. A tab appears for each of the Web pages in the group you selected.

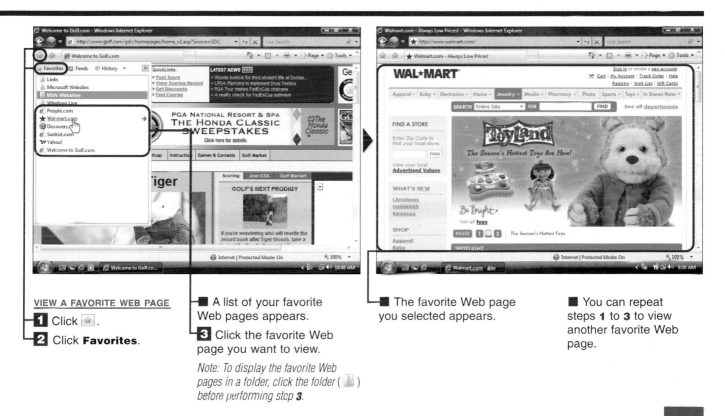

VIEW A FAVORITE WEB PAGE

1 Click ☆.

2 Click **Favorites**.

■ A list of your favorite Web pages appears.

3 Click the favorite Web page you want to view.

Note: To display the favorite Web pages in a folder, click the folder ( ) before performing step **3**.

■ The favorite Web page you selected appears.

■ You can repeat steps **1** to **3** to view another favorite Web page.

USING RSS FEEDS

You can use RSS feeds to quickly access up-to-date information on the Internet.

You can subscribe to an RSS feed offered by a Web site of interest to have new information from the Web site automatically delivered to your computer.

RSS stands for Really Simple Syndication and refers to the ability of Web sites to deliver up-to-date information to your computer any time you are connected to the Internet.

SUBSCRIBE TO AN RSS FEED

■ When you visit a Web page that has an RSS feed available, this icon (⬚) appears in color.

1 Click ⬚ to display information about the available RSS feed.

■ A Web page appears, displaying a list of articles that are currently available for the RSS feed.

2 Click **Subscribe to this feed** to add the RSS feed to your list of feeds.

Tip Why should I subscribe to RSS feeds instead of simply visiting Web sites of interest?

Subscribing to RSS feeds from Web sites of interest saves you time. You no longer have to visit each Web site and browse through all the information to determine what is new or changed since the last time you visited the Web site. After you subscribe to an RSS feed, all the new information for the Web site is delivered to your computer on a regular basis. You can then view all of the updates for the Web sites in one location in Internet Explorer.

Tip What are some popular Web sites that provide RSS feeds?

CBS SportsLine	www.sportsline.com
CNN Entertainment	www.cnn.com/showbiz
National Public Radio	www.npr.org
New York Times	www.nytimes.com
Rolling Stone	www.rollingstone.com
USA Today	www.usatoday.com

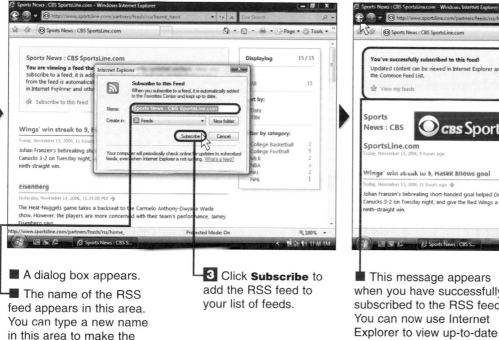

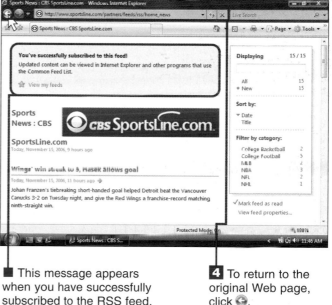

■ A dialog box appears.

■ The name of the RSS feed appears in this area. You can type a new name in this area to make the feed easier to identify.

3 Click **Subscribe** to add the RSS feed to your list of feeds.

■ This message appears when you have successfully subscribed to the RSS feed. You can now use Internet Explorer to view up-to-date content from the RSS feed.

4 To return to the original Web page, click ◉.

CONTINUED ▶

USING RSS FEEDS

After you subscribe to an RSS feed, your computer checks for updates to the feed at regular intervals, even when Internet Explorer is not open.

Having your computer automatically check for updates to Web pages helps ensure you always have access to the most up-to-date information.

Windows provides a gadget, which is a mini-program, that you can use to display RSS feeds you have subscribed to in Internet Explorer.

VIEW YOUR SUBSCRIBED RSS FEEDS

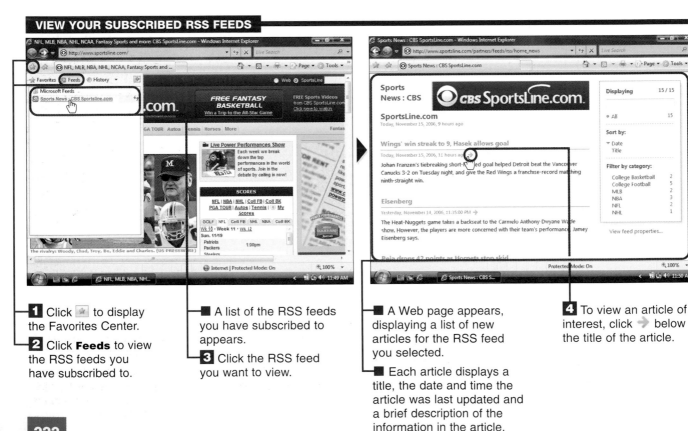

1 Click ![icon] to display the Favorites Center.

2 Click **Feeds** to view the RSS feeds you have subscribed to.

■ A list of the RSS feeds you have subscribed to appears.

3 Click the RSS feed you want to view.

■ A Web page appears, displaying a list of new articles for the RSS feed you selected.

■ Each article displays a title, the date and time the article was last updated and a brief description of the information in the article.

4 To view an article of interest, click ➡ below the title of the article.

Tip

Can I customize the Feed Headlines gadget to show only the articles for a specific RSS feed?

Yes. To customize the Feed Headlines gadget, position the mouse over the gadget and then click 🔍 In the dialog box that appears, click ⏷ below **Display this feed**. In the list that appears, select the name of the RSS feed you want to display articles for. Then click **OK**.

Tip

What is a netcast?

Netcasts, or podcasts, are similar to RSS feeds, but they are sound or video files that are automatically delivered to your computer. You can usually listen to or view a netcast on your computer or portable MP3 or media player. Web sites that offer netcasts usually provide an icon (RSS) you can click to subscribe to the netcast.

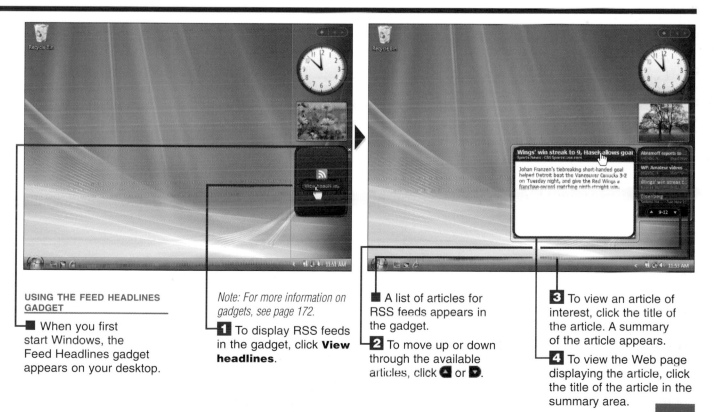

USING THE FEED HEADLINES GADGET

■ When you first start Windows, the Feed Headlines gadget appears on your desktop.

Note: For more information on gadgets, see page 172.

1 To display RSS feeds in the gadget, click **View headlines**.

■ A list of articles for RSS feeds appears in the gadget.

2 To move up or down through the available articles, click ◀ or ▶.

3 To view an article of interest, click the title of the article. A summary of the article appears.

4 To view the Web page displaying the article, click the title of the article in the summary area.

Exchange E-Mail

READ MESSAGES

You can start Windows Mail to open and read the contents of your e-mail messages.

The first time you start Windows Mail, a wizard will appear if you have not yet set up your e-mail account. Follow the instructions in the wizard to set up your e-mail account.

READ MESSAGES

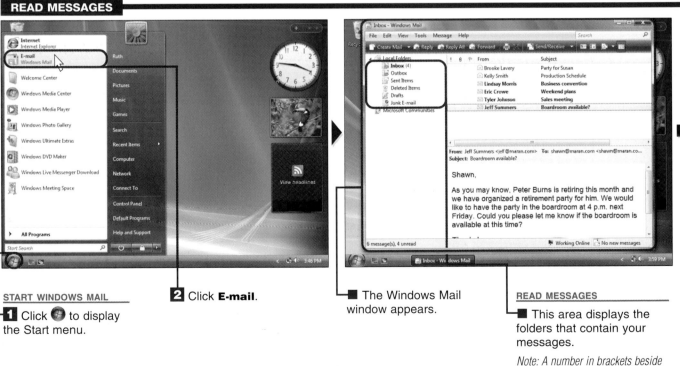

START WINDOWS MAIL

1 Click 🔵 to display the Start menu.

2 Click **E-mail**.

■ The Windows Mail window appears.

READ MESSAGES

■ This area displays the folders that contain your messages.

Note: A number in brackets beside a folder indicates how many unread messages the folder contains. The number disappears when you have read all the messages in the folder.

Tip

What folders does Windows Mail use to store my messages?

	Inbox
	Stores messages sent to you.
	Outbox
	Temporarily stores messages that have not yet been sent.
	Sent Items
	Stores copies of messages you have sent.
	Deleted Items
	Stores messages you have deleted.
	Drafts
	Stores messages you have not yet completed.
	Junk E-mail
	Stores junk messages sent to you.

Tip

Why does Windows Mail block pictures and other content in my e-mail messages?

Windows Mail blocks pictures and other content from displaying in your messages to help you avoid viewing potentially offensive material. Blocking content also helps reduce the amount of junk mail you receive. If pictures are displayed in junk mail, a message may be sent back to the sender, notifying the sender that your e-mail address works, which often results in you receiving more junk mail.

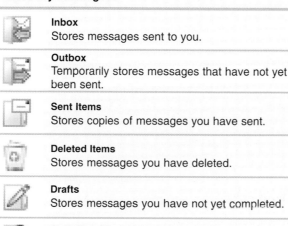

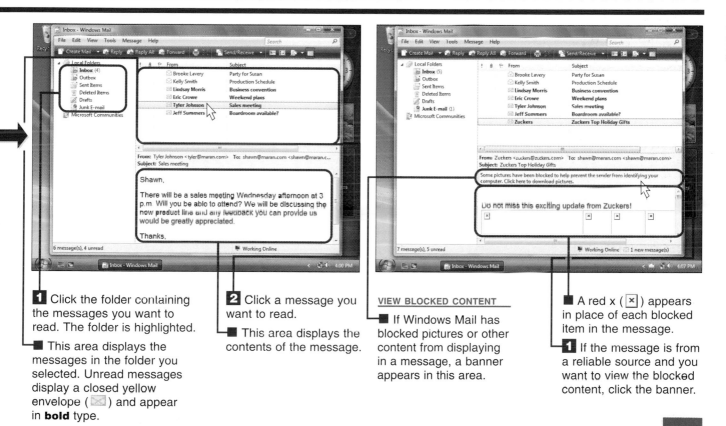

1 Click the folder containing the messages you want to read. The folder is highlighted.

■ This area displays the messages in the folder you selected. Unread messages display a closed yellow envelope (✉) and appear in **bold** type.

2 Click a message you want to read.

■ This area displays the contents of the message.

VIEW BLOCKED CONTENT

■ If Windows Mail has blocked pictures or other content from displaying in a message, a banner appears in this area.

■ A red x (✕) appears in place of each blocked item in the message.

1 If the message is from a reliable source and you want to view the blocked content, click the banner.

SEND A MESSAGE

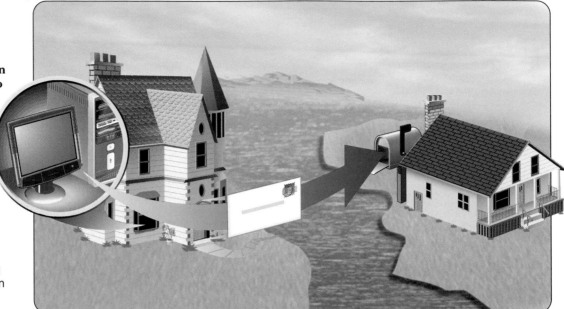

You can quickly and easily send an e-mail message to a friend, family member or colleague.

To practice sending a message, you can send a message to yourself.

SEND A MESSAGE

1 Click **Create Mail** to send a new message.

■ The New Message window appears.

2 Type the e-mail address of the person you want to receive the message.

3 To send a copy of the message to a person who is not directly involved but would be interested in the message, click this area and then type the person's e-mail address.

Note: To send the message to more than one person in step 2 or 3, separate each e-mail address with a semicolon (;).

Tip

Can I send decorative e-mail messages?

Yes. Windows Mail includes several stationery designs that you can use to enhance your e-mail messages. To send a message that displays a stationery design, click ■ beside **Create Mail** in the Windows Mail window. In the list of stationery designs that appears, click the stationery that you want to use, such as Stars, Roses or Garden. You can then perform steps **2** to **6** below to complete and send the e-mail message.

Tip

Is there another way to send a copy of a message?

Yes. In the New Message window, choose the **View** menu and then click **All Headers**. The Bcc: area appears in the window. You can type an e-mail address in this area to send someone a copy of the message without anyone else knowing that the person received the message. To no longer show the Bcc: area, choose the **View** menu and then click **All Headers** again.

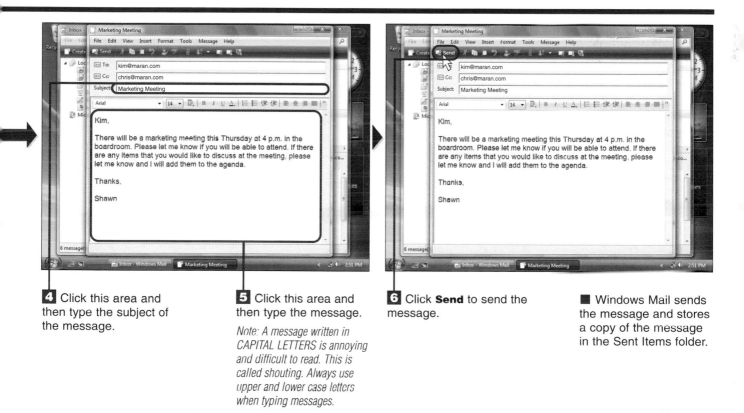

4 Click this area and then type the subject of the message.

5 Click this area and then type the message.

Note: A message written in CAPITAL LETTERS is annoying and difficult to read. This is called shouting. Always use upper and lower case letters when typing messages.

6 Click **Send** to send the message.

■ Windows Mail sends the message and stores a copy of the message in the Sent Items folder.

REPLY TO A MESSAGE

You can reply to a message to answer a question, express an opinion or supply additional information.

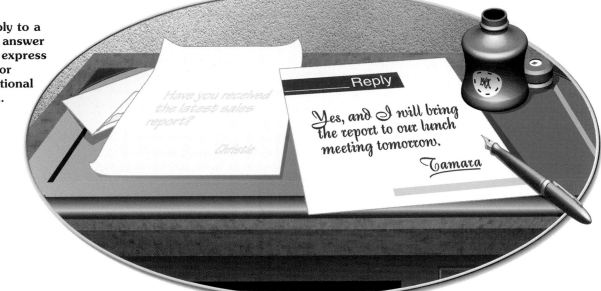

REPLY TO A MESSAGE

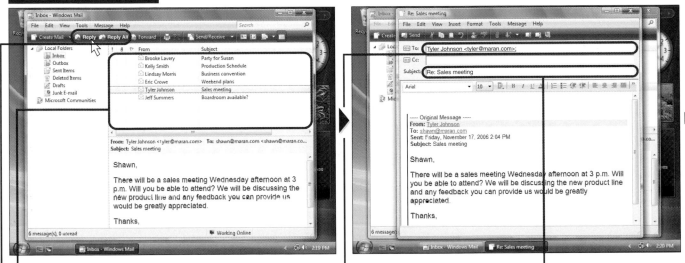

1 Click the message you want to reply to.

2 Click the reply option you want to use.

Reply
Sends a reply to only the author.

Reply All
Sends a reply to the author and everyone who received the original message.

■ A window appears for you to compose your reply.

■ Windows Mail fills in the e-mail address(es) for you.

■ Windows Mail also fills in the subject, starting the subject with **Re:**.

Tip

Can I format the text in my messages?

Yes. To format the text in a message, you first need to select the text you want to format by dragging the mouse I over the text. Then perform one of the following common formatting tasks.

- To change the font of text, click ▼ in the Font box and then select the font you want to use from the list of fonts that appears.

- To change the size of text, click the Font Size box and then select the font size you want to use from the list of sizes that appears.

- To bold, italicize or underline text, click the Bold (B), Italic (I) or Underline (U) button.

- To color text, click ▲ and then select the color you want to use from the list of colors that appears.

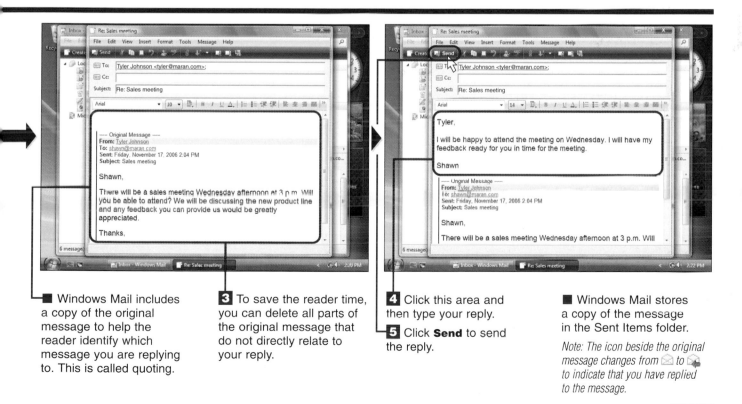

■ Windows Mail includes a copy of the original message to help the reader identify which message you are replying to. This is called quoting.

3 To save the reader time, you can delete all parts of the original message that do not directly relate to your reply.

4 Click this area and then type your reply.

5 Click **Send** to send the reply.

■ Windows Mail stores a copy of the message in the Sent Items folder.

Note: The icon beside the original message changes from ✉ to ✉ to indicate that you have replied to the message.

FORWARD A MESSAGE

After reading a message, you can add comments and then forward the message to a friend, family member or colleague.

Forwarding a message is useful when you know another person would be interested in a message.

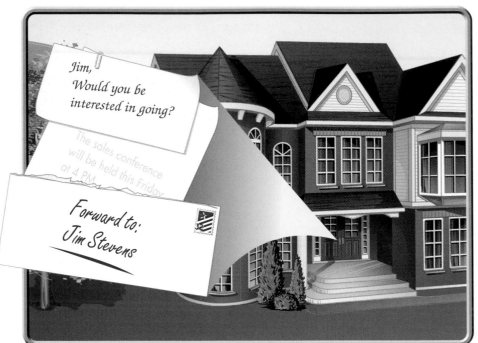

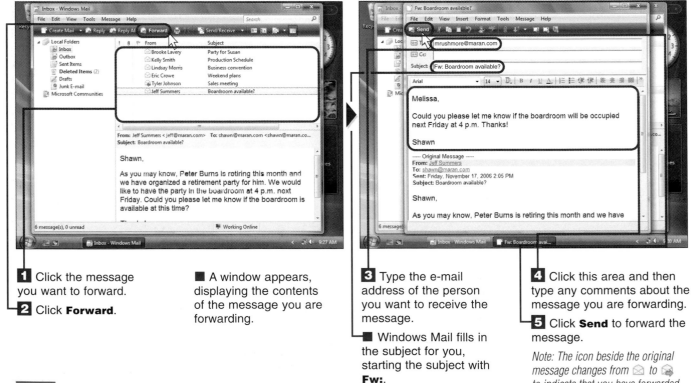

1 Click the message you want to forward.

2 Click **Forward**.

■ A window appears, displaying the contents of the message you are forwarding.

3 Type the e-mail address of the person you want to receive the message.

■ Windows Mail fills in the subject for you, starting the subject with **Fw:**.

4 Click this area and then type any comments about the message you are forwarding.

5 Click **Send** to forward the message.

Note: The icon beside the original message changes from ⊠ to ⧉ to indicate that you have forwarded the message.

CHECK FOR NEW MESSAGES

If you are waiting for an important message, you can have Windows Mail immediately check for new messages.

You can also change how often Windows Mail checks for new messages. Windows Mail initially checks for new messages every 30 minutes when you are connected to the Internet.

CHECK FOR NEW MESSAGES

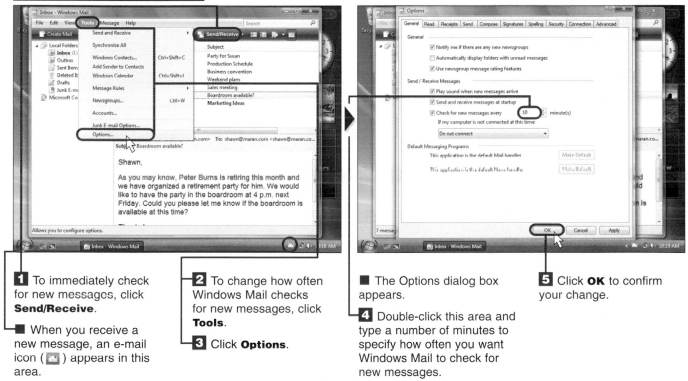

1 To immediately check for new messages, click **Send/Receive**.

■ When you receive a new message, an e-mail icon (📧) appears in this area.

2 To change how often Windows Mail checks for new messages, click **Tools**.

3 Click **Options**.

■ The Options dialog box appears.

4 Double-click this area and type a number of minutes to specify how often you want Windows Mail to check for new messages.

5 Click **OK** to confirm your change.

ATTACH A FILE TO A MESSAGE

You can attach a file to a message you are sending. Attaching a file to a message is especially useful when you want to include a photo or document with a message.

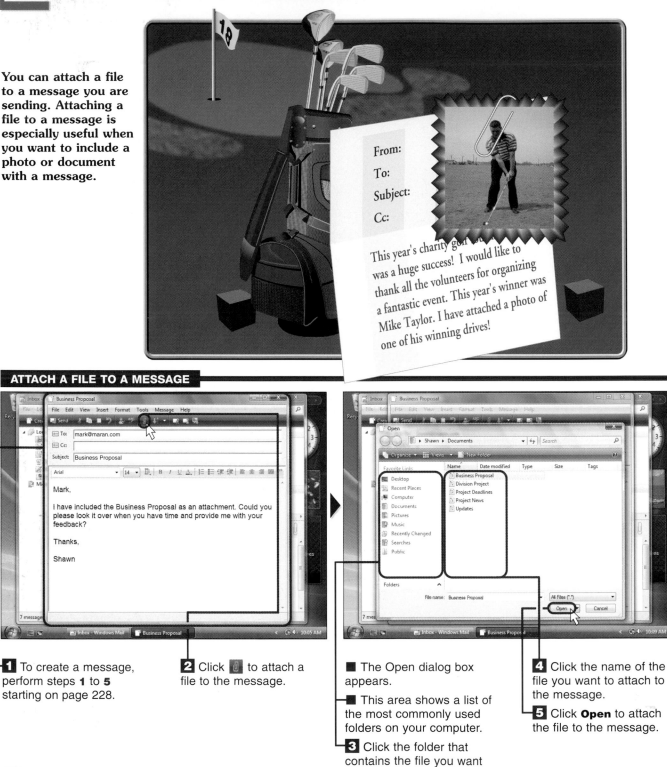

ATTACH A FILE TO A MESSAGE

1 To create a message, perform steps **1** to **5** starting on page 228.

2 Click 📎 to attach a file to the message.

■ The Open dialog box appears.

■ This area shows a list of the most commonly used folders on your computer.

3 Click the folder that contains the file you want to attach to the message.

4 Click the name of the file you want to attach to the message.

5 Click **Open** to attach the file to the message.

Tip

What types of files can I attach to a message?

You can attach any type of file to a message, including documents, photos, presentations, spreadsheets and videos. The computer receiving the message must have the necessary hardware and software installed to display or play the file you attach.

Tip

Can I attach a large file to a message?

The company that provides your e-mail account will usually limit the size of the messages that you can send and receive over the Internet. Most companies do not allow you to send or receive messages larger than 10 MB, which includes all attached files.

■ This area displays the name and size of the file you selected.

■ To attach additional files to the message, perform steps **2** to **5** for each file you want to attach.

6 Click **Send** to send the message.

■ Windows Mail will send the message and the attached file(s) to the e-mail address(es) you specified.

OPEN AN ATTACHED FILE

You can easily open a file attached to a message you receive.

Before opening an attached file, make sure the file is from a person you trust. Some files can contain a virus, which can damage the information on your computer. You can use an antivirus program to check files for viruses. To obtain an antivirus program, see page 277.

OPEN AN ATTACHED FILE

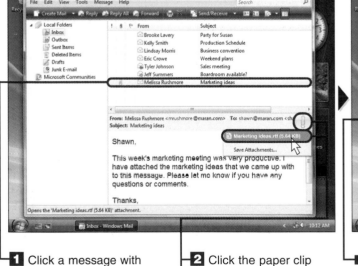

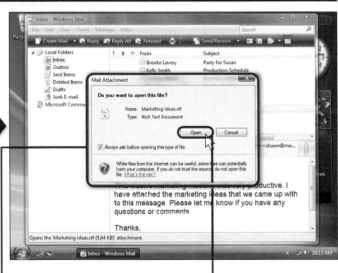

1 Click a message with an attached file. A message with an attached file displays a paper clip icon (🔗).

Note: If the attached file is a picture, the picture will usually appear in the contents of the message.

2 Click the paper clip icon (🔗) in this area to display a list of the files attached to the message.

3 Click the name of the file you want to open.

■ A dialog box may appear, asking if you want to open the file.

4 Click **Open** to open the file.

*Note: If you no longer want to open the file, click **Cancel**.*

DELETE A MESSAGE

You can delete a
message you no
longer need. Deleting
messages prevents
your folders from
becoming cluttered
with messages.

DELETE A MESSAGE

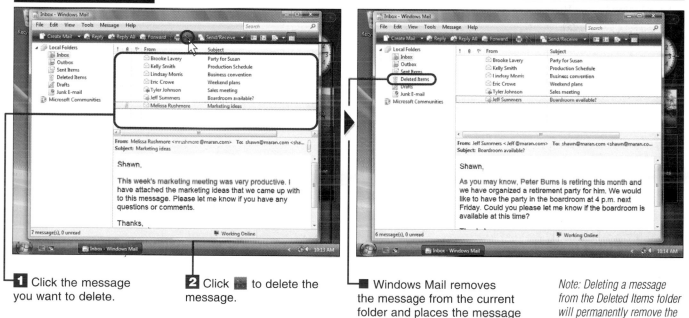

1 Click the message
you want to delete.

2 Click ▓ to delete the
message.

■ Windows Mail removes
the message from the current
folder and places the message
in the Deleted Items folder.

*Note: Deleting a message
from the Deleted Items folder
will permanently remove the
message from your computer.*

You can use the Contacts feature to store e-mail addresses and other information about friends, family members and clients, including phone numbers, addresses, birthdays and anniversaries.

When you send an e-mail message, you can use the Contacts feature to quickly fill in the e-mail address of a person you have added to your list of contacts.

ADD A CONTACT

1 Click ▣ to display the Contacts window.

■ The Contacts window appears.

■ This area displays each person in your list of contacts.

2 To add a new contact, click **New Contact**.

■ The Properties dialog box appears.

3 Type the first name of the person you want to add to your list of contacts.

4 Click this area and then type the last name of the person.

5 Click this area and then type the e-mail address of the person.

Tip

How do I change the information for a contact?

To change the information for a contact, display the Contacts window and then double-click the contact you want to change. Click the tab that contains the information you want to change and then make the necessary changes. When you finish making your changes, click **OK**.

Tip

Can I add a picture to a contact?

Yes. To add a picture to a contact, display the Contacts window and then double-click the contact you want to add a picture to. Click the current picture and then select **Change picture** from the menu that appears. Locate the picture you want to use and then click the picture. Click **Set** to add the picture and then click **OK** to close the dialog box.

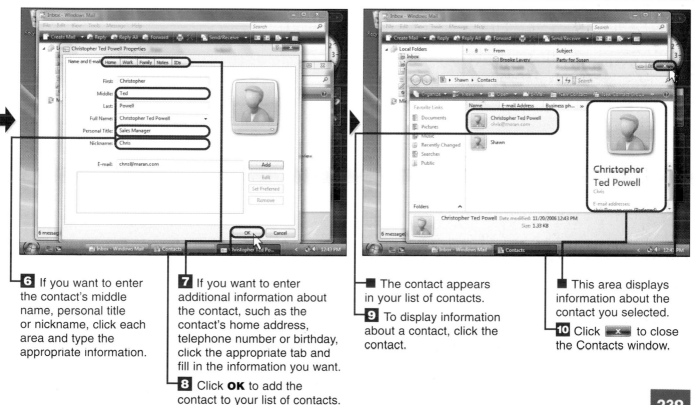

6 If you want to enter the contact's middle name, personal title or nickname, click each area and type the appropriate information.

7 If you want to enter additional information about the contact, such as the contact's home address, telephone number or birthday, click the appropriate tab and fill in the information you want.

8 Click **OK** to add the contact to your list of contacts.

■ The contact appears in your list of contacts.

9 To display information about a contact, click the contact.

■ This area displays information about the contact you selected.

10 Click [x] to close the Contacts window.

SEND A MESSAGE TO A CONTACT

When sending a message, you can select the name of the person you want to receive the message from your list of contacts.

jthomas@abc.com

E-MAIL ADDRESS			
Name		**Name**	**Address**
Jack Thomas	jthomas@abc.com	Silvia Parker	sparker@abc.com
Sue Jones	sjones@abc.com	Joy Smart	jsmart@abc.com
Bill Carey	bcarey@abc.com		
Henry Kim	hkim@abc.com		

Selecting names from your list of contacts saves you from having to remember the e-mail addresses of people you often send messages to.

SEND A MESSAGE TO A CONTACT

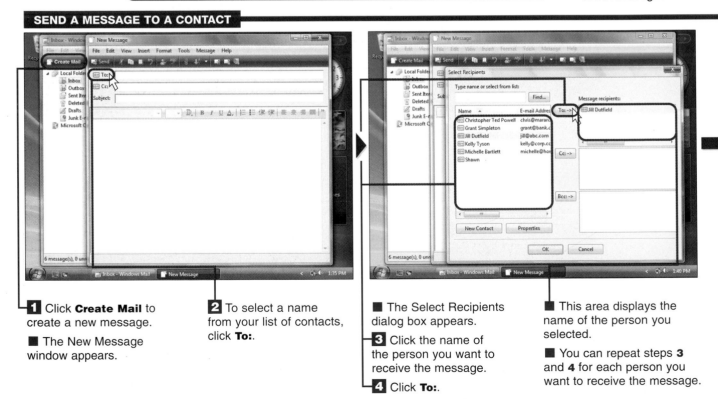

1 Click **Create Mail** to create a new message.

■ The New Message window appears.

2 To select a name from your list of contacts, click **To:**.

■ The Select Recipients dialog box appears.

3 Click the name of the person you want to receive the message.

4 Click **To:**.

■ This area displays the name of the person you selected.

■ You can repeat steps **3** and **4** for each person you want to receive the message.

Tip

How can I address a message I want to send?

To
Sends the message to the person you specify.

Carbon Copy (Cc)
Sends an exact copy of the message to a person who is not directly involved, but would be interested in the message.

Blind Carbon Copy (Bcc)
Sends an exact copy of the message to a person without anyone else knowing that the person received the message.

Tip

How do I delete a contact from my list of contacts?

If your list of contacts is getting cluttered, you can delete a contact you no longer correspond with. In the Windows Mail window, click 🔳 to display the Contacts window. Click the contact you want to delete and then press the Delete key. In the confirmation dialog box that appears, click **Yes** to delete the contact. Then click ✕ to close the Contacts window.

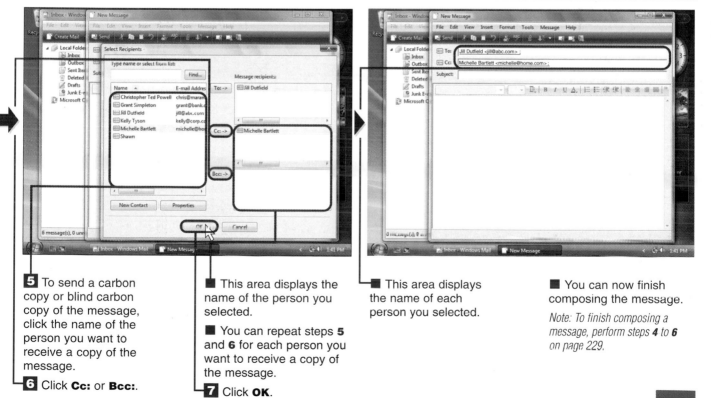

5 To send a carbon copy or blind carbon copy of the message, click the name of the person you want to receive a copy of the message.

6 Click **Cc:** or **Bcc:**.

■ This area displays the name of the person you selected.

■ You can repeat steps **5** and **6** for each person you want to receive a copy of the message.

7 Click **OK**.

■ This area displays the name of each person you selected.

■ You can now finish composing the message.

*Note: To finish composing a message, perform steps **4** to **6** on page 229.*

FIND A MESSAGE

If you cannot find a message, you can have Windows search for the message.

1 Click the folder you want to search.

2 Click this area and type the word, or part of the word, that appears in the subject or in the contents of the message you want to find.

■ As you type, Windows immediately displays the matching messages.

3 To display the contents of a matching message, click the message.

■ This area displays the contents of the message.

■ To once again display all of the messages in the folder, click ☒.

Windows examines messages you receive to determine if the messages are junk mail. Messages that appear to be junk mail are automatically moved to a special Junk E-mail folder.

Windows Mail is set up to move the most obvious junk mail to the Junk E-mail folder. You should regularly check the messages in the Junk E-mail folder to make sure Windows did not incorrectly identify a message you received as junk mail.

WORK WITH JUNK E-MAIL

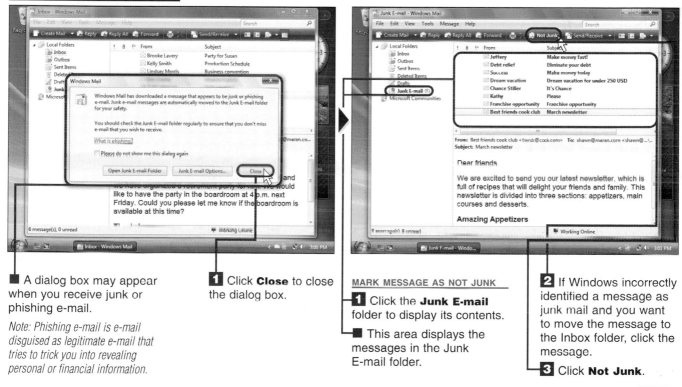

■ A dialog box may appear when you receive junk or phishing e-mail.

Note: Phishing e-mail is e-mail disguised as legitimate e-mail that tries to trick you into revealing personal or financial information.

1 Click **Close** to close the dialog box.

MARK MESSAGE AS NOT JUNK

1 Click the **Junk E-mail** folder to display its contents.

■ This area displays the messages in the Junk E-mail folder.

2 If Windows incorrectly identified a message as junk mail and you want to move the message to the Inbox folder, click the message.

3 Click **Not Junk**.

ADD A SIGNATURE TO MESSAGES

You can have Windows Mail automatically add personal information to the end of every message you send. This information is called a signature.

A signature saves you from having to type the same information every time you send a message.

ADD A SIGNATURE TO MESSAGES

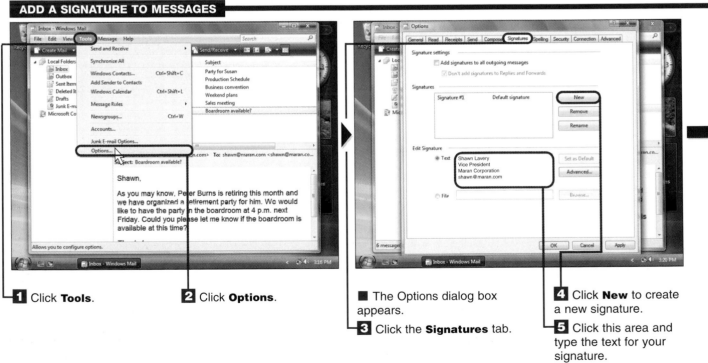

1 Click **Tools**.

2 Click **Options**.

■ The Options dialog box appears.

3 Click the **Signatures** tab.

4 Click **New** to create a new signature.

5 Click this area and type the text for your signature.

What can I include in a signature?

A signature can include information such as your name, e-mail address, mailing address, phone number, occupation, favorite quotation and Web page address. As a courtesy to people who will receive your messages, you should limit your signature to four or five lines.

Can I add a signature to just certain messages?

Yes. If you want to choose which messages you add a signature to, do not perform step **6** below when creating your signature. When you want to add a signature to a message you are sending, click the location in the message where you want to place the signature. Then choose the **Insert** menu and click **Signature**.

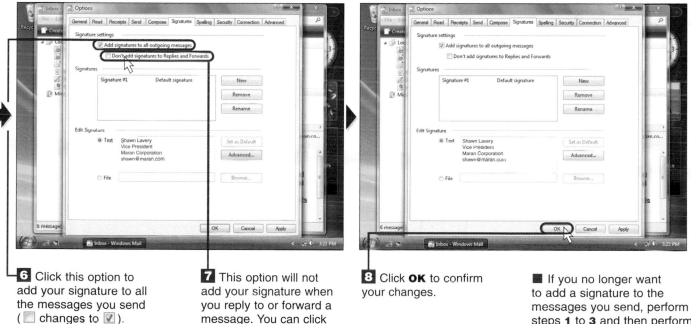

6 Click this option to add your signature to all the messages you send (☐ changes to ☑).

7 This option will not add your signature when you reply to or forward a message. You can click the option to turn the option on (☑) or off (☐).

8 Click **OK** to confirm your changes.

■ If you no longer want to add a signature to the messages you send, perform steps **1** to **3** and then perform step **6** (☑ changes to ☐). Then press the Enter key.

CHAPTER 12

Work on a Network

LINTRODUCTION TO NETWORKS

If you have more than one computer at home or at a small office, you can set up a network so the computers can exchange information as well as share equipment and an Internet connection.

WIRED NETWORKS

A wired network uses wires, or cables, to connect equipment and computers together.

Advantages of Wired Networks

✓ Fast, reliable transfer of data between computers on the network.

✓ Secure. To connect to a wired network, a computer must physically connect to the network's router using a cable.

✓ Ideal when computers and equipment on a network are close to each other.

EQUIPMENT NEEDED

Ethernet Network Card

Each computer requires an Ethernet network card or connection. An Ethernet network card or connection attaches each computer to a network and allows the computers on a network to communicate.

Router

A router is a device that provides a central location where all the cables on the network meet. A router also allows all the computers on the network to share one Internet connection.

Internet Connection Device

An Internet connection device, such as a cable modem or Digital Subscriber Line (DSL), allows you to connect to the Internet.

Cables

Ethernet cables physically connect each computer and device to the network.

SET UP A WIRED NETWORK

To set up a wired network, you simply set up and turn on the equipment you want to use on the network. Windows will automatically recognize the computers and devices on the network for you.

WIRELESS NETWORKS

A wireless network uses radio signals instead of cables to connect computers and devices together.

Advantages of Wireless Networks

✓ No cables to connect.

✓ Useful when computers are located where cables are not practical or economical.

✓ Ideal for allowing notebook computers to access a network from many locations in a home or office.

EQUIPMENT NEEDED

Wireless Network Card

Each computer requires an internal wireless network card or an external wireless network adapter. A wireless network card or adapter allows computers on a wireless network to communicate.

Wireless Router

A wireless router is a device that transmits and receives data between computers on a network. A wireless router also allows all the computers on the network to share one Internet connection.

Internet Connection Device

An Internet connection device, such as a cable modem or Digital Subscriber Line (DSL), allows you to connect to the Internet. The Internet connection device usually connects to the wireless router using a cable.

SET UP A WIRELESS NETWORK

To set up a wireless network, you simply set up and turn on the computers and devices you want to use on the network. Windows will automatically recognize the network devices for you.

To protect the information on your wireless network, you should adjust the security settings on the network, as shown on page 262.

BROWSE THROUGH A NETWORK

You can browse through the files and folders available on your network.

Depending on the way the owner of a computer set up file sharing, you may be able to only view the shared files or you may be able to make changes to the files.

To access a folder on the network, the computer that stores the folder must be turned on and the owner of the computer must have set up file sharing.

BROWSE THROUGH A NETWORK

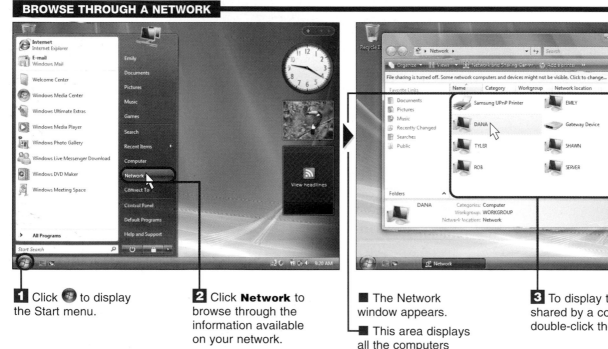

1 Click 🟦 to display the Start menu.

2 Click **Network** to browse through the information available on your network.

■ The Network window appears.

■ This area displays all the computers and devices that are available on your network.

3 To display the items shared by a computer, double-click the computer.

Work on a Network 12

Tip

Why can't I see any other computers or devices on the network?

The network discovery option may not be turned on for your computer, preventing you from seeing other computers and devices on the network. To turn on the network discovery option, click 🔵 to display the Start menu and then click **Control Panel**. Click **Network and Internet** and then click **Network and Sharing Center**. Click ⊗ beside **Network discovery**, click **Turn on network discovery** (◯ changes to ◉) and then click **Apply**.

Tip

Why does a dialog box appear when I try to display the items shared by a computer?

A dialog box may appear if the owner of the computer has not set up file sharing. Click **Cancel** to close the dialog box. For information about setting up file sharing, see page 252.

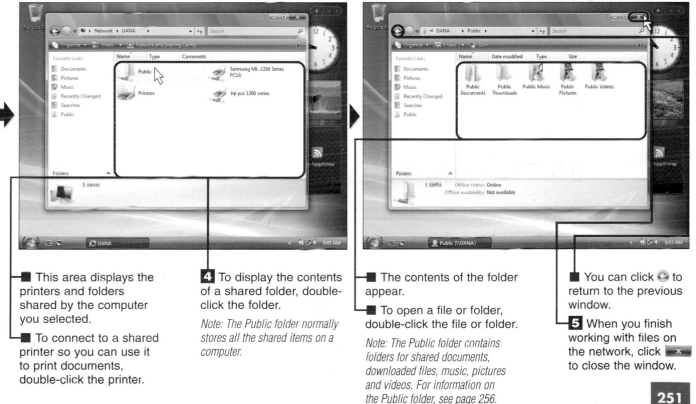

■ This area displays the printers and folders shared by the computer you selected.

■ To connect to a shared printer so you can use it to print documents, double-click the printer.

4 To display the contents of a shared folder, double-click the folder.

Note: The Public folder normally stores all the shared items on a computer.

■ The contents of the folder appear.

■ To open a file or folder, double-click the file or folder.

Note: The Public folder contains folders for shared documents, downloaded files, music, pictures and videos. For information on the Public folder, see page 256.

■ You can click 🔙 to return to the previous window.

5 When you finish working with files on the network, click ❌ to close the window.

TURN ON FILE AND PRINTER SHARING

If you want to share your files and printer with other people on your network, you must turn on file and printer sharing on your computer.

Sharing files is useful when other people on your network need to access your files. Sharing a printer allows you to reduce costs since several people on a network can use the same printer.

TURN ON FILE AND PRINTER SHARING

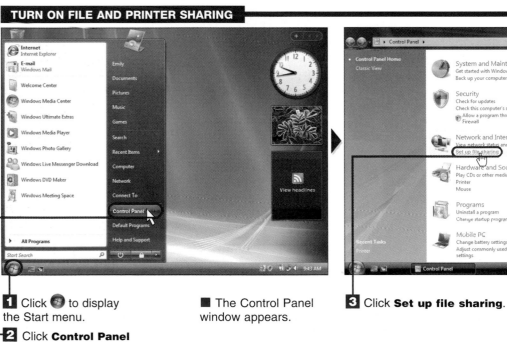

1 Click ⊕ to display the Start menu.

2 Click **Control Panel** to change your computer's settings.

■ The Control Panel window appears.

3 Click **Set up file sharing**.

■ The Network and Sharing Center window appears.

Tip

How can people access my files and printer after I turn on sharing?

To give other people on the network access to your files, you must first copy the files you want to share into the Public folder on your computer. For information on using the Public folder, see page 256.

Other people on the network can print files to the printer connected to your computer as if the printer was directly connected to their computers. Once a person on the network has connected to a shared printer, the shared printer will appear in the list of available printers when the person prints a file. To connect to a shared printer, see page 251.

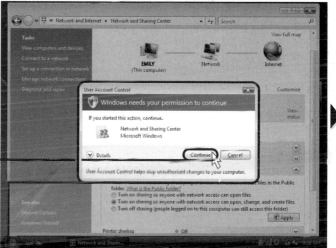

SHARE YOUR PUBLIC FOLDER

4 Click ∨ beside **Public folder sharing** (∨ changes to ∧).

5 Click an option to specify how you want to share your files on the network (○ changes to ●).

Note: You can allow people to only view your files or to view and make changes to the files.

6 Click **Apply** to save your changes.

■ The User Account Control dialog box appears, stating that Windows needs your permission to continue to prevent unauthorized changes to your computer.

7 Click **Continue** to continue.

*Note: If you are not using an administrator account, you must type an administrator password and then click **OK** to be able to continue. For information on administrator accounts and passwords, see pages 184 and 188.*

 CONTINUED

253

TURN ON FILE AND PRINTER SHARING

When you turn on file and printer sharing for your computer, you should also turn off the password protection feature.

Turning off the password protection feature allows other people on the network to access your files and printer without having to type a password.

TURN ON FILE AND PRINTER SHARING (CONTINUED)

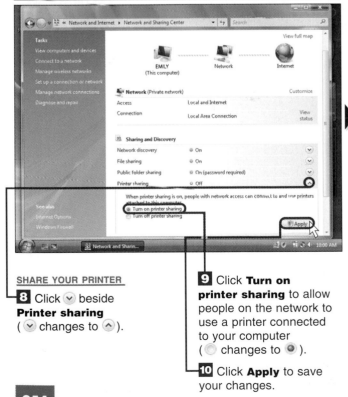

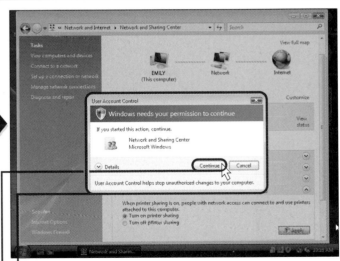

SHARE YOUR PRINTER

8 Click ⌄ beside **Printer sharing** (⌄ changes to ⌃).

9 Click **Turn on printer sharing** to allow people on the network to use a printer connected to your computer (◯ changes to ◉).

10 Click **Apply** to save your changes.

■ The User Account Control dialog box appears, stating that Windows needs your permission to continue to prevent unauthorized changes to your computer.

11 Click **Continue** to continue.

Note: If you are not using an administrator account, you must type an administrator password and then click OK to be able to continue. For information on administrator accounts and passwords, see pages 184 and 188.

Tip

How can I tell if my printer is shared?

To view the printers available to your computer, click to display the Start menu and then click **Control Panel**. In the Control Panel window, click **Printer** to display the Printers window. A network symbol (22) appears under the icon for your shared printer. You should make sure your computer and the printer are turned on and accessible when other people want to use the printer.

Tip

Do I have to turn off password protection when I turn on sharing?

You do not have to turn off the password protection feature when sharing files and printers. If you do not turn off the feature, other people will have to enter the user name and password for a user account set up on your computer before they can access your files and printer.

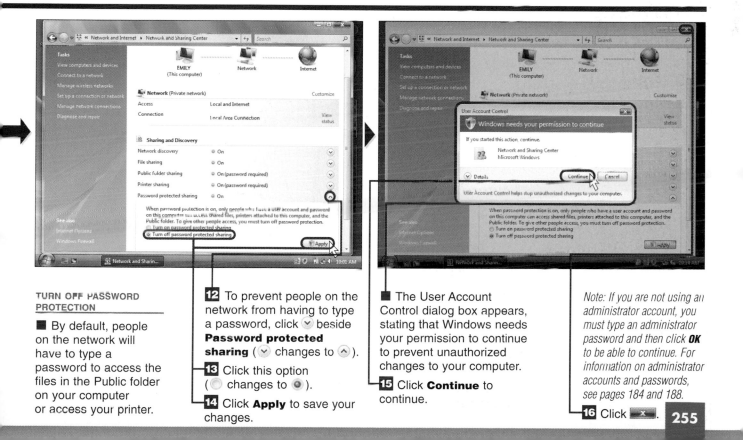

TURN OFF PASSWORD PROTECTION

■ By default, people on the network will have to type a password to access the files in the Public folder on your computer or access your printer.

12 To prevent people on the network from having to type a password, click ⌄ beside **Password protected sharing** (⌄ changes to ⌃).

13 Click this option (◉ changes to ◉).

14 Click **Apply** to save your changes.

■ The User Account Control dialog box appears, stating that Windows needs your permission to continue to prevent unauthorized changes to your computer.

15 Click **Continue** to continue.

*Note: If you are not using an administrator account, you must type an administrator password and then click **OK** to be able to continue. For information on administrator accounts and passwords, see pages 184 and 188.*

16 Click ___ .

SHARE FILES ON A NETWORK

You can share files with other people on your network by adding the files to the Public folder on your computer. Everyone on the network can access files stored in the Public folder.

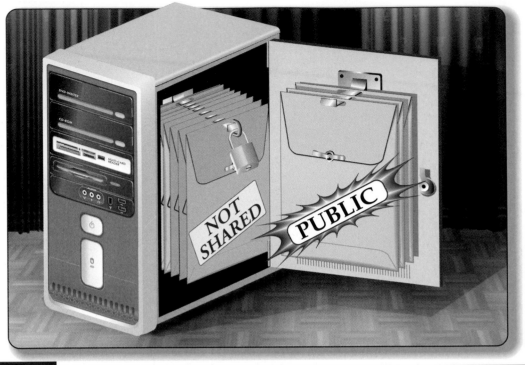

Every person with a user account set up on your computer can also access the files in the Public folder.

SHARE FILES ON A NETWORK

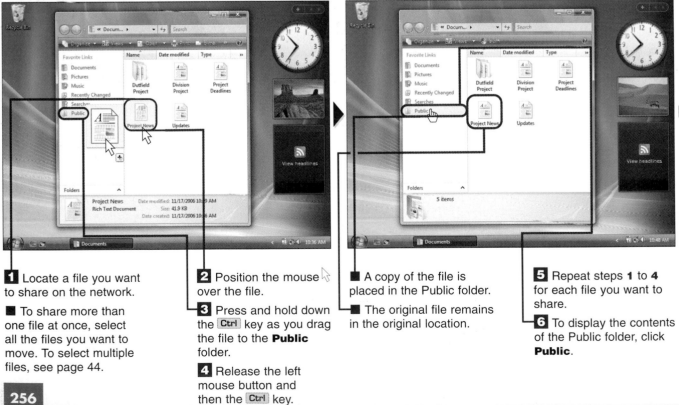

1 Locate a file you want to share on the network.

■ To share more than one file at once, select all the files you want to move. To select multiple files, see page 44.

2 Position the mouse over the file.

3 Press and hold down the **Ctrl** key as you drag the file to the **Public** folder.

4 Release the left mouse button and then the **Ctrl** key.

■ A copy of the file is placed in the Public folder.

■ The original file remains in the original location.

5 Repeat steps **1** to **4** for each file you want to share.

6 To display the contents of the Public folder, click **Public**.

Tip

Can people on the network make changes to the files I share?

Depending on the access type you select when you turn on Public folder sharing, people on the network may be able to only read the files you have shared or they may be able to read, change and create files in the Public folder. For information on turning on Public folder sharing, see page 252.

Tip

How can I stop sharing a file?

To stop sharing a file on the network, you must remove the file from the Public folder. To display the contents of the Public folder, display the contents of your Documents folder (see page 38) and then click **Public**. Double-click the folder that contains the file you want to stop sharing. Click the file you no longer want to share and then press the Delete key. In the confirmation dialog box that appears, click **Yes**.

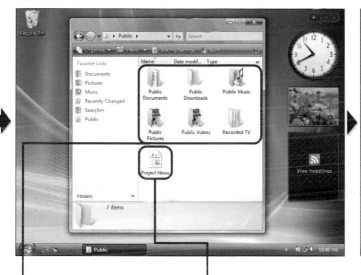

■ The Public folder contains folders for sharing documents, downloaded files, music, pictures, videos and recorded TV programs.

■ You can now position the mouse over the file you shared and then drag the file into the appropriate folder to help organize your shared files.

7 Click to close the Public window.

■ Before people on the network can access files you selected to share, you must turn on Public folder sharing. To turn on Public folder sharing, see page 252.

CONNECT TO A WIRELESS NETWORK

You can easily connect to a wireless network at home or at the office to access the information and equipment available on the network.

If a wireless network is connected to the Internet, connecting to the network will also allow you to access the Internet.

CONNECT TO A WIRELESS NETWORK

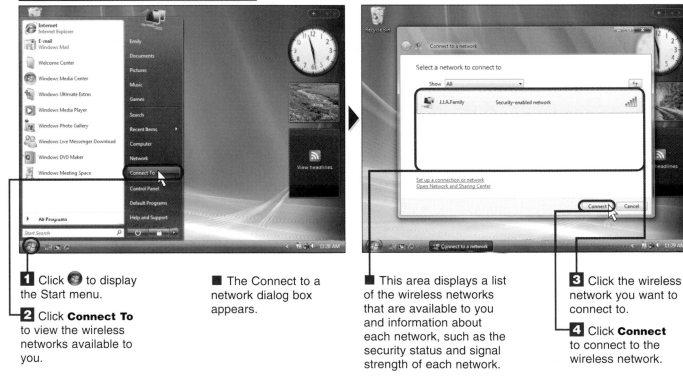

1 Click ⊕ to display the Start menu.

2 Click **Connect To** to view the wireless networks available to you.

■ The Connect to a network dialog box appears.

■ This area displays a list of the wireless networks that are available to you and information about each network, such as the security status and signal strength of each network.

3 Click the wireless network you want to connect to.

4 Click **Connect** to connect to the wireless network.

Tip **Can I connect to a wireless network when I am away from home or the office?**

Increasing numbers of public places, such as coffee shops, hotels and airports, are allowing people to connect to the Internet through wireless networks set up on their premises. These locations are called wi-fi hotspots, or wireless hotspots, and provide a convenient way of accessing the Internet while you are away from home or the office.

Tip **Can I connect to an unsecured network?**

Yes. When you perform steps **1** to **4** below to connect to an unsecured network, a warning screen appears, stating that information sent over the network may be visible to other people. Click **Connect Anyway** to connect to the unsecured network. When using an unsecured network, you should never transfer any sensitive or personal information, such as passwords or banking information.

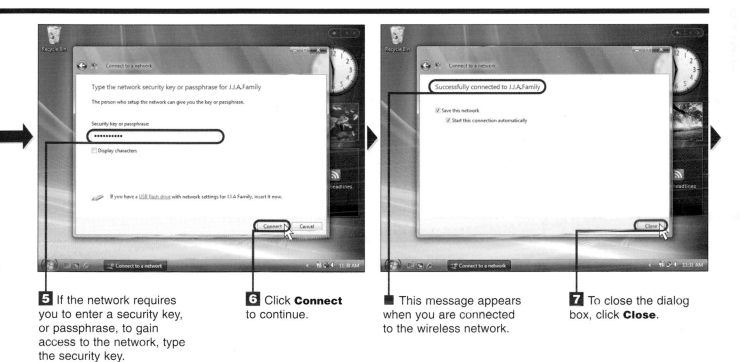

5 If the network requires you to enter a security key, or passphrase, to gain access to the network, type the security key.

Note: A security key helps protect a network by preventing unauthorized people from accessing the network.

6 Click **Connect** to continue.

■ This message appears when you are connected to the wireless network.

7 To close the dialog box, click **Close**.

CONTINUED

CONNECT TO A WIRELESS NETWORK

The first time you connect to a wireless network, you can specify whether you want to set up the network as a home, work or public network.

The option you choose determines the security settings for the computer on the network.

CONNECT TO A WIRELESS NETWORK (CONTINUED)

■ The Set Network Location dialog box appears, allowing you to select the type of location for the network. The type of location you choose will determine the security settings for the computer while you work on the network.

8 Click an option to specify the type of location for the wireless network.

Note: For information on the types of locations you can choose, see the top of page 261.

■ The User Account Control dialog box appears, stating that Windows needs your permission to continue to prevent unauthorized changes to your computer.

9 Click **Continue** to continue.

*Note: If you are not using an administrator account, you must type an administrator password and then click **OK** to be able to continue. For information on administrator accounts and passwords, see pages 184 and 188.*

Tip

How can I ensure a good connection to a wireless network?

When connecting to a wireless network, the strength of the radio signal used to connect to the network is very important. For the best signal, try to avoid obstacles between your computer and the wireless router or wireless access point. Also try to avoid using devices that use the same frequency as your wireless network, such as a cordless phone, near the network.

Tip

What type of location should I choose for working on a wireless network?

Home—Choose the Home location when you are connecting to a wireless network set up in your home. Windows will set up your computer so you can see other computers and devices on the network.

Work—Choose the Work location when you are connecting to a wireless network at your office. Windows will set up your computer so you can see other computers and devices on the network.

Public location—Choose the Public location when you are connecting to a wireless network in a public location, such as an airport. Windows will limit access to other computers and devices on the network.

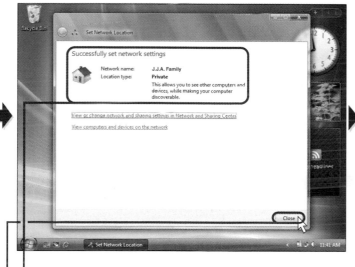

■ This message appears when the wireless network settings have been set for the location you selected.

10 Click **Close** to close the Set Network Location dialog box.

■ You can now access information on the network. If the network is connected to the Internet, you can also access the Internet.

■ The Network icon indicates if you are connected to a network (	), connected to the Internet (	) or not connected to a network (	).

■ You only need to perform steps **1** to **10** once to connect to a wireless network. The next time you are within range of the wireless network, Windows will automatically connect you to the network.

MAKE A WIRELESS NETWORK MORE SECURE

Improving the security of a wireless network helps protect the network and your information from unauthorized access.

You should give your wireless network a name and set up password-protection and other security settings for the network.

When securing a wireless network, a password may be called a passphrase or a security key. Security settings are called encryption.

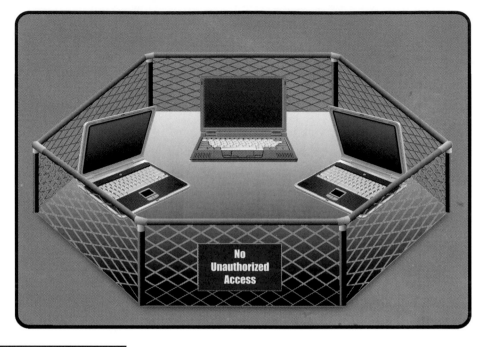

MAKE A WIRELESS NETWORK MORE SECURE

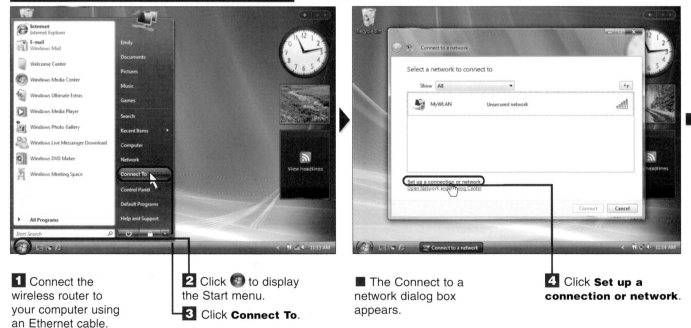

1 Connect the wireless router to your computer using an Ethernet cable.

2 Click ⊕ to display the Start menu.

3 Click **Connect To**.

■ The Connect to a network dialog box appears.

4 Click **Set up a connection or network**.

Tip **Why do I need to make my wireless network secure?**

Using a passphrase and encryption makes it difficult for unauthorized people to access your network. If you do not set up a passphrase and encryption for your wireless network, other people nearby may be able to view and access any information that is transferring on your network. If your wireless network is connected to the Internet, other people may also be able to use your Internet connection to access the Internet.

 Tip **Can Windows help protect my network?**

Yes. Windows comes with firewall software that helps protect computers on a network. Firewall software prevents unauthorized people or unwanted programs, such as viruses, from accessing computers on a network through the Internet or through other computers on the network.

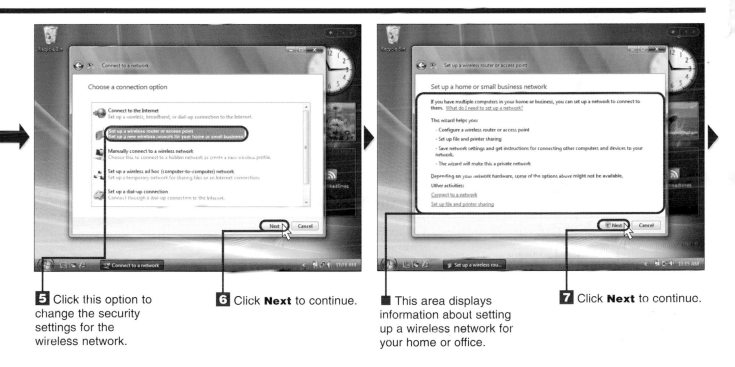

5 Click this option to change the security settings for the wireless network.

6 Click **Next** to continue.

■ This area displays information about setting up a wireless network for your home or office.

7 Click **Next** to continue.

CONTINUED ▶

MAKE A WIRELESS NETWORK MORE SECURE

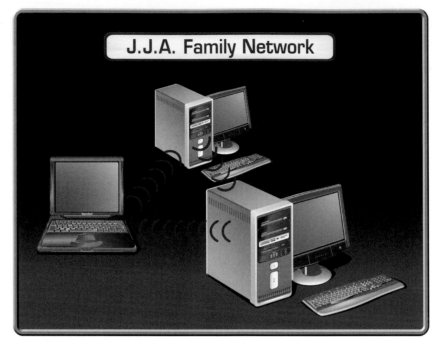

J.J.A. Family Network

To increase the security of your wireless network, you can specify a name for the network.

Keep in mind that other people using wireless networks nearby will be able to see the name of your wireless network. You should choose a name that is meaningful to you, but avoid choosing a name that other people can easily identify with you, such as your name or address.

MAKE A WIRELESS NETWORK MORE SECURE (CONTINUED)

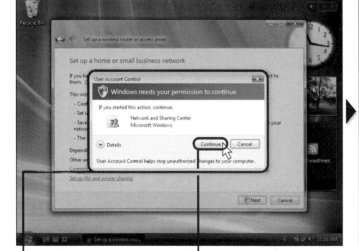

■ The User Account Control dialog box appears, stating that Windows needs your permission to continue to prevent unauthorized changes to your computer.

8 Click **Continue** to continue.

*Note: If you are not using an administrator account, you must type an administrator password and then click **OK** to be able to continue. For information on administrator accounts and passwords, see pages 184 and 188.*

■ The Network discovery dialog box may appear, asking if you want to turn on network discovery for all public networks.

9 Click **No** to continue.

Tip

What type of passphrase should I create for my wireless network?

Your passphrase should be at least eight characters long and should contain both uppercase and lowercase letters as well as numbers and special characters. The longer your passphrase is, the more difficult it will be for an unauthorized person to access your wireless network.

After you set up a passphrase for your wireless network, you will need to type the passphrase the next time you connect to the wireless network.

Tip

What types of encryption are available for wireless networks?

Encryption encodes the information that is transferred between computers on a network to protect the information from being viewed by unauthorized people. There are usually three types of encryption available for wireless networks.

• **WEP** (Wired Equivalent Privacy) does not provide strong security. WEP is only used by older wireless devices.

• **WPA** (Wi-Fi Protected Access) provides strong security and is compatible with most wireless devices. WPA is recommended for most wireless networks.

• **WPA2** is a new type of encryption that provides very strong security. WPA2 may not be compatible with all the wireless devices on a network.

■ A dialog box appears, describing the information Windows needs to finish setting up the wireless network.

Note: In this example, Windows needs a name, also called an SSID, a security type and a passphrase for the wireless network.

10 Click this option to enter the information for the wireless network.

■ An Internet Explorer window opens, displaying a Web page for your wireless router.

Note: The appearance of the Web page depends on your wireless router.

11 Specify a name, passphrase and encryption type for your wireless network.

12 Click ☒ to close the Internet Explorer window and the dialog box. Then disconnect the Ethernet cable from your computer.

■ You can now connect to the wireless network, as shown on page 258.

CHAPTER 13

Optimize Computer Performance

VIEW AMOUNT OF DISK SPACE

You can view the amount of used and free space on your hard disk.

Your hard disk stores all the programs and files on your computer.

Checking the available free space on your hard disk allows you to ensure that your computer is not running out of space.

VIEW AMOUNT OF DISK SPACE

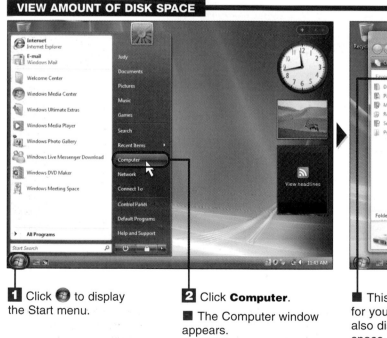

1 Click 🟦 to display the Start menu.

2 Click **Computer**.

■ The Computer window appears.

■ This area displays an icon for your hard disk. Windows also displays the amount of free space and the total amount of space that is available on your hard disk, in gigabytes (GB).

Note: Some computers may display an icon for more than one hard disk.

3 To see additional information about your hard disk, click the icon for the hard disk.

4 Click **Properties**.

Tip

How can I increase the amount of free space on my hard disk?

You can delete files you no longer need and programs you no longer use from your computer. You can also use the Disk Cleanup feature to remove unnecessary files from your computer. For more information, see page 51 to delete files, page 270 to remove programs and page 272 to use the Disk Cleanup feature.

Tip

How often should I check the amount of free space on my hard disk?

You should check the amount of free space on your computer's hard disk (C:) about once a month. Your computer will operate most effectively when at least 20% of your total hard disk space is free.

You may also want to check the amount of free space on your computer's hard disk before installing a program that requires a lot of disk space.

■ The Properties dialog box appears.

■ This area displays the amount of used and free space on your hard disk, in both bytes and gigabytes (GB).

■ This area displays the total hard disk storage space, in both bytes and gigabytes (GB).

■ The pie chart graphically displays the amount of used (■) and free space (■) on your hard disk.

5 When you finish reviewing the information, click **OK** to close the Properties dialog box.

6 Click x to close the Computer window.

REMOVE A PROGRAM

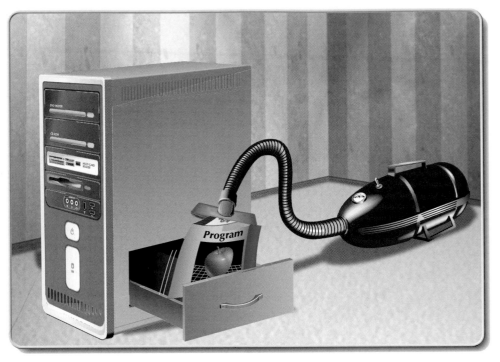

You can remove a program you no longer use from your computer. Removing a program will free up space on your computer.

REMOVE A PROGRAM

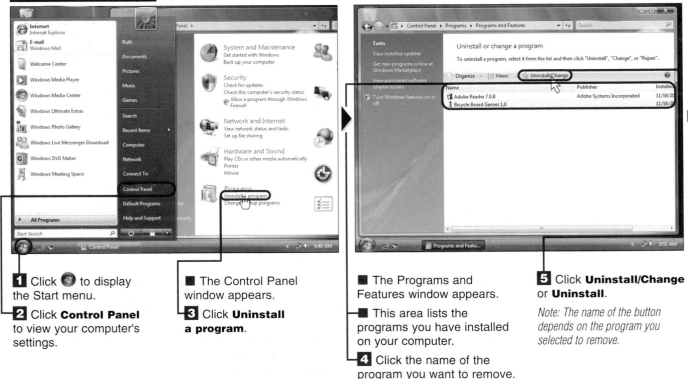

1 Click 🏵 to display the Start menu.

2 Click **Control Panel** to view your computer's settings.

■ The Control Panel window appears.

3 Click **Uninstall a program**.

■ The Programs and Features window appears.

■ This area lists the programs you have installed on your computer.

4 Click the name of the program you want to remove.

5 Click **Uninstall/Change** or **Uninstall**.

Note: The name of the button depends on the program you selected to remove.

Tip **Why doesn't the program I want to remove appear in the Programs and Features window?**

You may not be able to use the Programs and Features window to remove programs designed for an earlier version of Windows. You can check the documentation supplied with the program to determine how to remove the program from your computer.

Tip **What should I do after I remove a program?**

When you finish removing a program, you should restart your computer. Restarting your computer will often delete any remaining files that were used by the program. To restart your computer, see page 288.

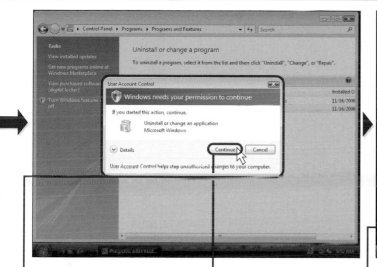

■ The User Account Control dialog box appears, stating that Windows needs your permission to continue to prevent unauthorized changes to your computer.

6 Click **Continue** to continue.

Note: If you are not using an administrator account, you must type an administrator password and then click ***OK*** *to be able to continue. For information on administrator accounts and passwords, see pages 184 and 188.*

■ Windows begins the process of removing the program from your computer.

7 Follow the instructions on your screen. Each program will take you through different steps to remove the program.

8 When Windows has successfully removed the program, click ▬▬ to close the Programs and Features window.

USING DISK CLEANUP

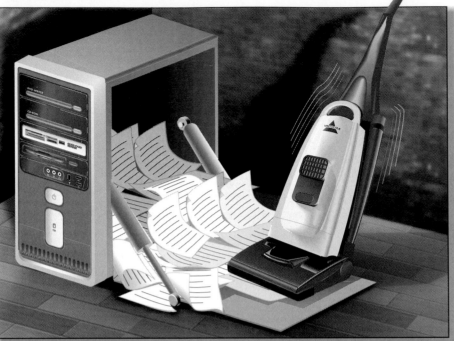

You can use Disk Cleanup to remove unnecessary files from your computer to free up disk space.

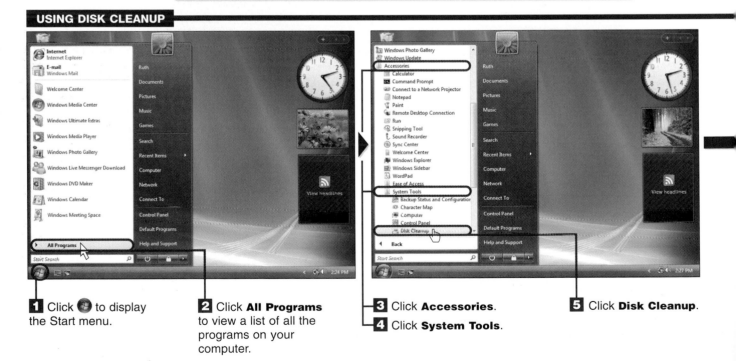

1 Click 🪟 to display the Start menu.

2 Click **All Programs** to view a list of all the programs on your computer.

3 Click **Accessories**.

4 Click **System Tools**.

5 Click **Disk Cleanup**.

Tip **Can I use Disk Cleanup to remove unnecessary files from all the user accounts on my computer?**

You can remove files from all the user accounts on your computer at once, but be aware that you may remove files that other users wanted to keep. Perform the steps below, except click **Files from all users on this computer** in step **6**. The User Account Control dialog box appears, stating that Windows needs your permission to continue to prevent unauthorized changes to your computer. Click **Continue** and then perform steps **7** to **10** starting below.

*Note: If you are not using an administrator account, you must type an administrator password and then click **OK** to continue.*

Tip **Can I see exactly which files will be removed from my computer?**

Before allowing Disk Cleanup to remove files from your computer, you can see which files will be removed. Perform steps **1** to **8** below to display the Disk Cleanup dialog box. Then select a file type of interest and click the **View Files** button. A window appears, displaying the files that will be removed. The View Files button is not available for some file types.

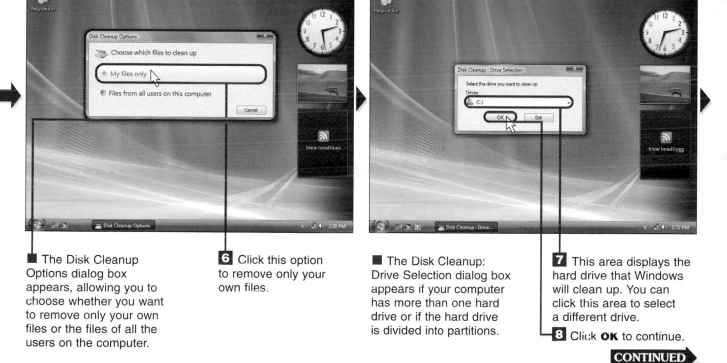

■ The Disk Cleanup Options dialog box appears, allowing you to choose whether you want to remove only your own files or the files of all the users on the computer.

6 Click this option to remove only your own files.

■ The Disk Cleanup: Drive Selection dialog box appears if your computer has more than one hard drive or if the hard drive is divided into partitions.

7 This area displays the hard drive that Windows will clean up. You can click this area to select a different drive.

8 Click **OK** to continue.

CONTINUED

USING DISK CLEANUP

Disk Cleanup can show you exactly how much space you can free up on your computer by removing unnecessary files.

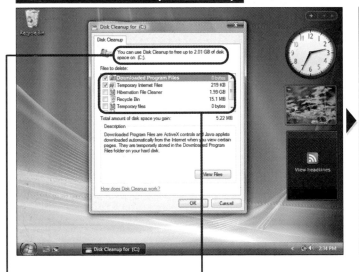

■ The Disk Cleanup dialog box appears.

■ This area displays the total amount of disk space you can free up.

■ This area displays the types of files Windows can delete and the amount of disk space each file type uses.

■ This area displays a description of the highlighted file type.

■ To display a description for a different file type, click the file type.

Note: For information on the file types, see the top of page 275.

Tip

What are some types of files that Disk Cleanup can remove?

	File Type	Description
	Downloaded Program Files	Program files transferred automatically from the Internet and stored on your computer when you view certain Web pages.
	Temporary Internet Files	Web pages stored on your computer for quick viewing.
	Hibernation File Cleaner	Information about your computer used for the hibernation power setting. If you use the hibernation power setting, do not remove this information.
	Recycle Bin	Files you have deleted from your computer.
	Temporary Files	Files created by programs to store temporary information.
	Thumbnails	Small copies of your pictures, videos and documents that can be displayed quickly when you open a folder.

Note: Other file types may also appear, depending on the way your computer is set up.

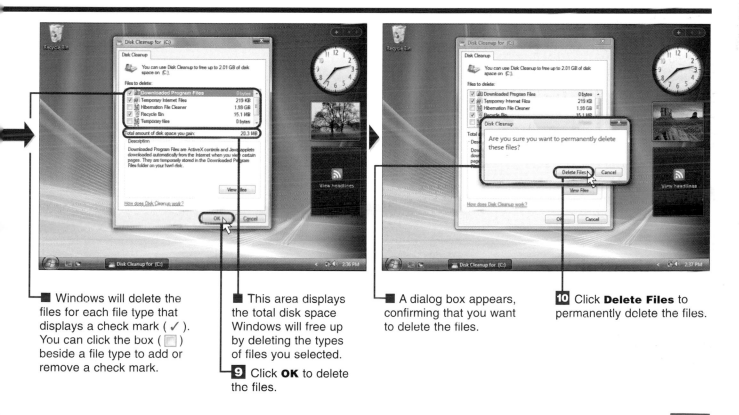

■ Windows will delete the files for each file type that displays a check mark (✓). You can click the box (▢) beside a file type to add or remove a check mark.

■ This area displays the total disk space Windows will free up by deleting the types of files you selected.

9 Click **OK** to delete the files.

■ A dialog box appears, confirming that you want to delete the files.

10 Click **Delete Files** to permanently delete the files.

CHECK YOUR COMPUTER'S SECURITY STATUS

You can check the status of your computer's security settings to make sure your computer is well protected.

CHECK YOUR COMPUTER'S SECURITY STATUS

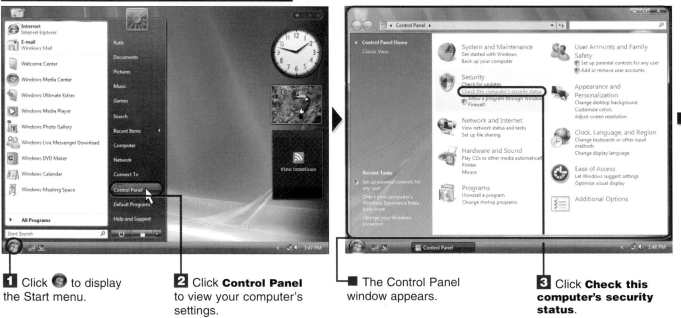

1 Click ⊕ to display the Start menu.

2 Click **Control Panel** to view your computer's settings.

■ The Control Panel window appears.

3 Click **Check this computer's security status**.

Tip

Why does the Malware protection security setting state "Check settings?"

Windows does not come with an antivirus program. To help keep your computer secure, you should install an antivirus program on your computer. To obtain an antivirus program, click **Find a program** below the Malware protection heading in the Windows Security Center window. A Microsoft Web page will appear, displaying companies that offer antivirus programs. You can select the company that provides the antivirus program you want to use and then follow the instructions on your screen to install the program on your computer. For information on antivirus programs, see page 279.

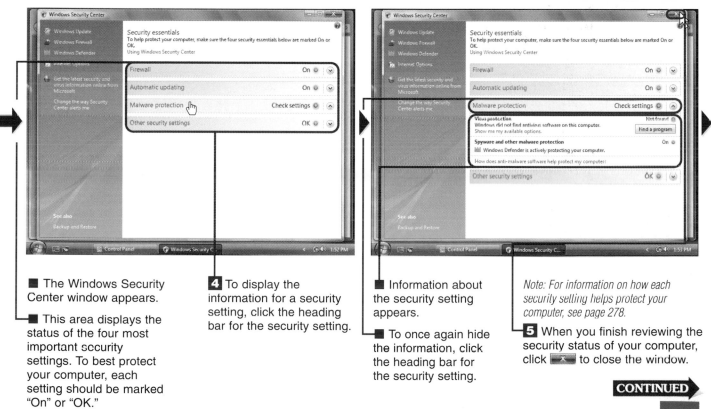

■ The Windows Security Center window appears.

■ This area displays the status of the four most important security settings. To best protect your computer, each setting should be marked "On" or "OK."

4 To display the information for a security setting, click the heading bar for the security setting.

■ Information about the security setting appears.

■ To once again hide the information, click the heading bar for the security setting.

Note: For information on how each security setting helps protect your computer, see page 278.

5 When you finish reviewing the security status of your computer, click ▬✗▬ to close the window.

CONTINUED

CHECK YOUR COMPUTER'S SECURITY STATUS

FIREWALL

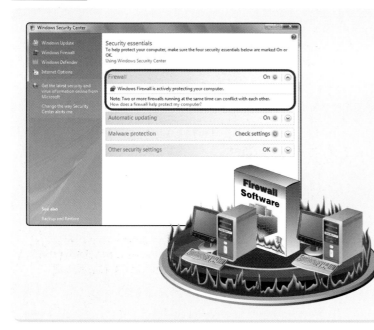

Windows comes with firewall software to help prevent unauthorized people and harmful programs, such as viruses, from accessing your computer through the Internet or a network. When information arrives from the Internet or a network, firewall software either blocks the information or allows the information to carry on to your computer.

The firewall software included with Windows is turned on automatically. This software actively protects your computer.

AUTOMATIC UPDATING

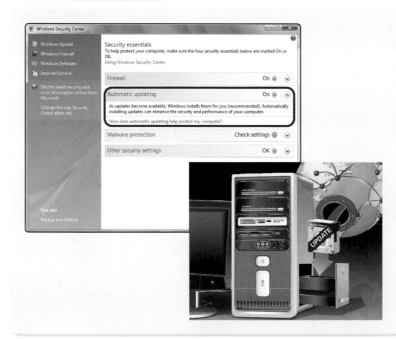

As Windows updates become available on the Internet, your computer automatically downloads and installs the updates for you free of charge. Automatically installing updates can enhance the security of your computer, improve your computer's performance and prevent and fix computer problems. You need an Internet connection for Windows to be able to update your computer automatically.

The Automatic updating feature included with Windows is turned on automatically. Windows automatically downloads updates for your computer when you are connected to the Internet and installs the updates at 3:00 a.m. If you turn off your computer before 3:00 a.m, Windows can install the updates before you shut down your computer.

MALWARE PROTECTION

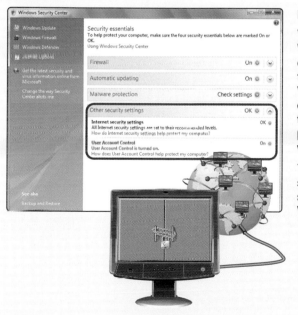

Virus protection

Windows checks to see if your computer is using an antivirus program and whether the program is up to date. An antivirus program helps protect your computer against viruses, which can result in a range of problems, including the loss of information to the slowing down of a computer.

Windows does not come with an antivirus program. To help keep your computer secure, you should install an antivirus program on your computer.

Spyware and other malware protection

Windows comes with an antispyware program, known as Windows Defender, which actively protects your computer from spyware and other potentially harmful programs. Spyware is software that can collect information about you, change your computer's settings or display annoying pop-up advertisements.

The antispyware program included with Windows is turned on automatically.

OTHER SECURITY SETTINGS

Internet security settings

When you browse the Web, Windows helps protect your computer from security threats. For example, Windows will protect your computer from a Web site that tries to install a program on your computer without your knowledge.

Your Internet security settings are automatically set to the levels that Windows recommends.

User Account Control

Windows comes with the User Account Control feature, which helps protect your computer from unauthorized changes, such as the installation of a new program or a setting change that will affect other users on your computer.

The User Account Control feature is turned on automatically. When you try to perform an administrative task on your computer, Windows will ask for your permission or an administrator password before you can continue.

RATE YOUR COMPUTER'S PERFORMANCE

You can view a score that indicates the overall performance of your computer. This score is known as the Windows Experience Index base score, or the base score.

The base score is based on the capabilities of five different parts of your computer, including your processor, memory (RAM), graphics, 3D gaming graphics and hard disk.

A computer with a higher base score usually performs better and faster than a computer with a lower base score.

RATE YOUR COMPUTER'S PERFORMANCE

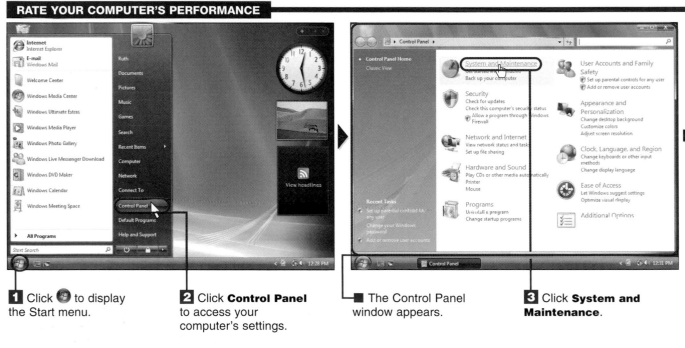

1 Click to display the Start menu.

2 Click **Control Panel** to access your computer's settings.

■ The Control Panel window appears.

3 Click **System and Maintenance**.

Tip

Can knowing my computer's base score help me buy programs?

You can use your computer's base score to help you buy programs that are suitable for your computer. For example, if your computer's base score is 4.2, you can confidently buy programs designed for Windows Vista that require a computer with a base score of 4 or lower.

Tip

How can I improve my computer's base score?

You can upgrade your computer's hardware to improve your computer's base score.

✓ Increasing the amount of memory (RAM) in your computer is one of the easiest and most inexpensive ways to improve your computer's performance. Adding memory will increase the score of your memory (RAM) component.

✓ Many computers are sold with basic graphic capabilities. Buying a good-quality video card designed for Windows Vista will increase the scores of your graphics and gaming graphics components, allowing you to enjoy all the new features of Windows Vista as well as high-end multimedia experiences.

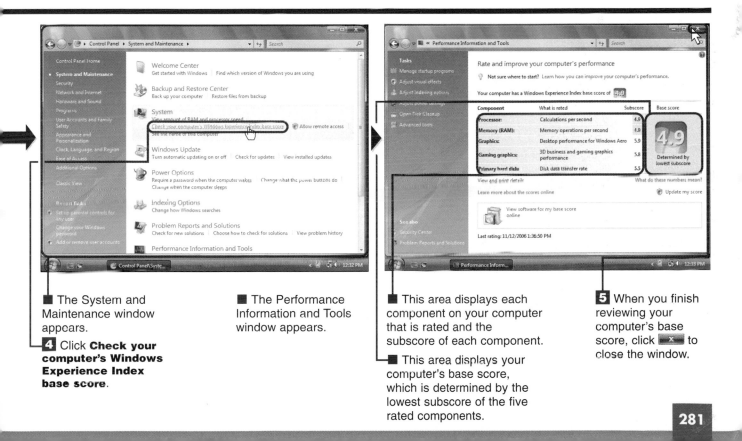

■ The System and Maintenance window appears.

4 Click **Check your computer's Windows Experience Index base score**.

■ The Performance Information and Tools window appears.

■ This area displays each component on your computer that is rated and the subscore of each component.

■ This area displays your computer's base score, which is determined by the lowest subscore of the five rated components.

5 When you finish reviewing your computer's base score, click [×] to close the window.

SPEED UP YOUR COMPUTER

Your computer can use storage space on a removable flash memory device, such as a USB flash drive, to speed up the computer. This feature is called Windows ReadyBoost.

A removable flash memory device stores information on flash memory. Unlike random access memory (RAM), flash memory can store information even when the power is turned off.

A USB flash drive is a small, lightweight storage device that plugs into a USB port on your computer. A USB flash drive is also known as a memory key, pen drive, thumb drive or key drive.

SPEED UP YOUR COMPUTER

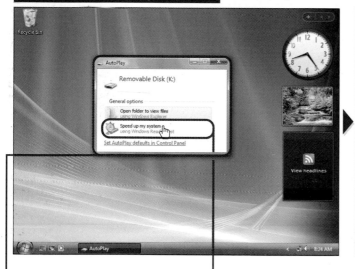

1 Insert a removable flash memory device, such as a USB flash drive, into your computer.

■ The AutoPlay window appears, listing options that you can select.

2 Click **Speed up my system**.

■ The Properties dialog box appears.

3 Click this option to use the available space on the device to speed up your computer (○ changes to ◉).

4 Click **OK** to save your changes.

■ If you want the computer to always use the device to speed up your computer, leave the device plugged into your computer at all times.

Tip

What size of removable device do I need to speed up my computer?

For the best results, you need a removable flash memory device with at least the same amount of memory as your computer's memory. For example, if your computer has 1 GB of memory, you should use a device with at least 1 GB of available memory. To find out how much memory your computer has, click ⊙ to display the Start menu and then click **Welcome Center**. At the top of the window that appears, you will see how much memory, or RAM, your computer has.

Tip

How does Windows use the removable device to speed up my computer?

Windows uses the storage space on the removable flash memory device to add memory to the computer. Your computer will store frequently accessed information on the device so it can quickly access the information at any time.

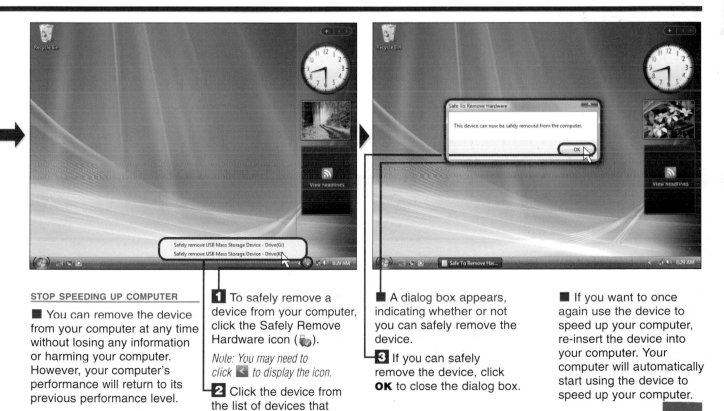

STOP SPEEDING UP COMPUTER

■ You can remove the device from your computer at any time without losing any information or harming your computer. However, your computer's performance will return to its previous performance level.

1 To safely remove a device from your computer, click the Safely Remove Hardware icon ( ).

Note: You may need to click ◄ to display the icon.

2 Click the device from the list of devices that appears.

■ A dialog box appears, indicating whether or not you can safely remove the device.

3 If you can safely remove the device, click **OK** to close the dialog box.

■ If you want to once again use the device to speed up your computer, re-insert the device into your computer. Your computer will automatically start using the device to speed up your computer.

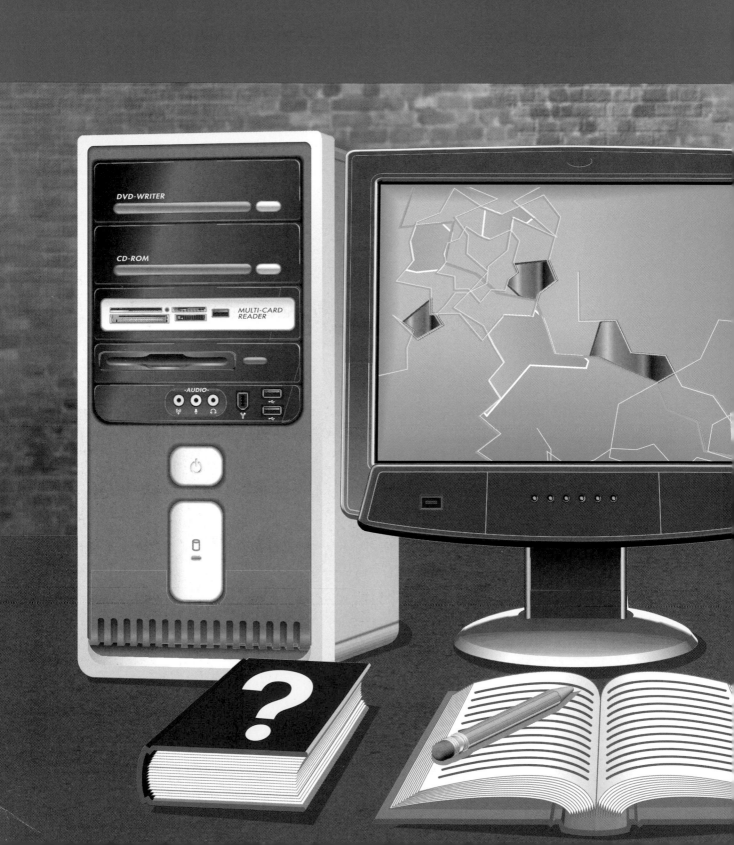

Get Help and Fix Problems

GET HELP

If you do not know how to perform a task in Windows, you can use the Help feature to get help information on the task.

You can also use the Help feature to get answers to common questions and troubleshoot computer problems.

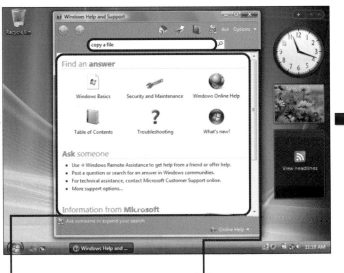

1 Click to display the Start menu.

2 Click **Help and Support**.

*Note: The first time you get help, a dialog box appears, asking if you want to get the latest help information from the Internet. Click **Yes** to access the latest help information.*

■ The Windows Help and Support window appears, displaying the main help window. You can instantly access help information and services by clicking an item of interest in the window.

3 To quickly get help information, click this area and then type a word or phrase that describes the topic of interest. Then press the Enter key.

Tip

Why do some help topics display colored text?

You can click a word or phrase that appears in green to display a definition of the word or phrase. To hide the definition, click outside the definition.

You can click a word or phrase that appears in blue to display information of interest in the current help topic or display a related help topic. If you click blue text preceded by an arrow (→), Windows will open the window that allows you to perform the task.

Tip

Does Windows Help provide video demonstrations?

Yes. Windows provides several video demonstrations that you can view to learn more about performing tasks in Windows. For example, you can view a demonstration about printing documents, working with user accounts and keeping your computer secure. In step **3** below, type "demo" to view a list of the available video demonstrations.

Note: For information on viewing videos, see page 102.

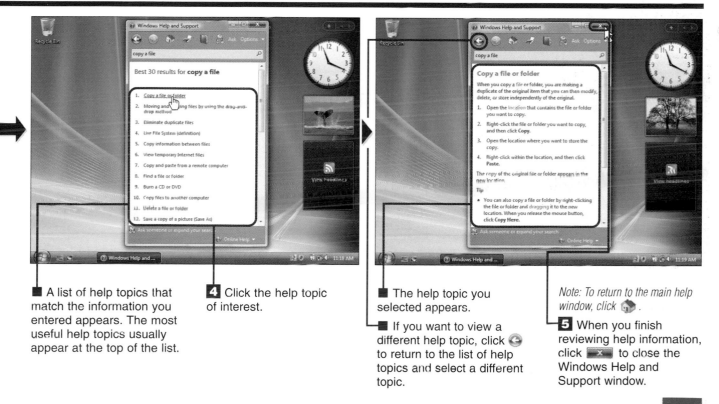

■ A list of help topics that match the information you entered appears. The most useful help topics usually appear at the top of the list.

4 Click the help topic of interest.

■ The help topic you selected appears.

■ If you want to view a different help topic, click ⬅ to return to the list of help topics and select a different topic.

Note: To return to the main help window, click 🏠 .

5 When you finish reviewing help information, click ❌ to close the Windows Help and Support window.

RESTART YOUR COMPUTER

If your computer is not operating properly, you can restart your computer to try to fix the problem.

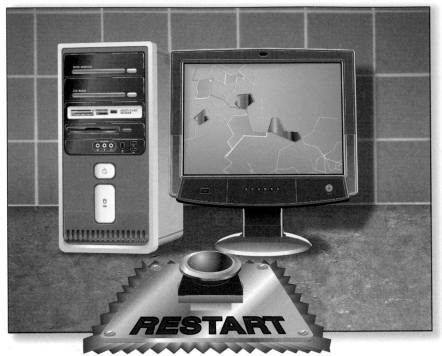

Before restarting your computer, make sure you close all the programs you have open.

RESTART YOUR COMPUTER

1 Click ⊞ to display the Start menu.

2 Click ▶ to display a list of options.

■ A list of options appears.

3 Click **Restart** to restart your computer.

■ Windows shuts down and then immediately starts again.

You can close
a program that
is no longer
responding
without having
to shut down
Windows.

When a program is not
responding, you can
wait a few minutes to
see if Windows can
fix the problem. If you
choose not to wait and
close the program
yourself, you will lose
any information you did
not save in the program.

CLOSE A MISBEHAVING PROGRAM

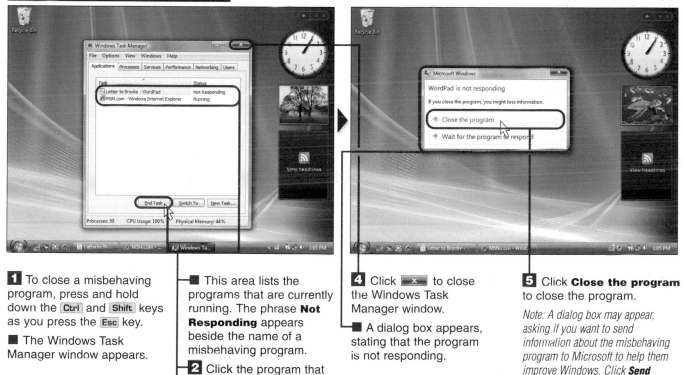

1 To close a misbehaving
program, press and hold
down the `Ctrl` and `Shift` keys
as you press the `Esc` key.

■ The Windows Task
Manager window appears.

■ This area lists the
programs that are currently
running. The phrase **Not
Responding** appears
beside the name of a
misbehaving program.

2 Click the program that
is misbehaving.

3 Click **End Task**.

4 Click ☒ to close
the Windows Task
Manager window.

■ A dialog box appears,
stating that the program
is not responding.

5 Click **Close the program**
to close the program.

*Note: A dialog box may appear,
asking if you want to send
information about the misbehaving
program to Microsoft to help them
improve Windows. Click **Send
information** or **Cancel**.*

RESTORE A PREVIOUS VERSION OF A FILE

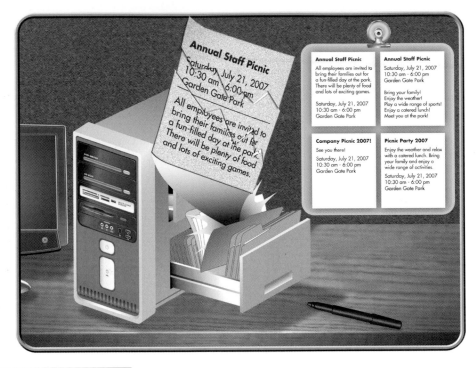

If you accidentally made changes to a file or a file you need is damaged, you can have Windows restore a previous version of the file on your computer.

Even though Windows can restore previous versions of files on your computer, you should still regularly back up your files in case of theft, fire or computer failure. To back up files on your computer, see page 296.

RESTORE A PREVIOUS VERSION OF A FILE

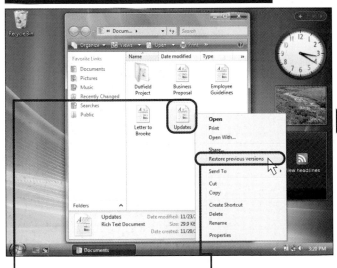

1 Right-click the file you want to restore to an earlier version. A menu appears.

2 Click **Restore previous versions**.

■ The Properties dialog box appears.

■ This area shows the previous versions of the file that you can restore.

■ To open a previous version of the file to determine if it is the version that you want to restore, double-click the file.

Note: You can open shadow copies of files, but not backup copies of files.

3 Click the previous version of the file you want to restore.

4 Click **Restore** to restore the file.

Tip

How are previous versions of files created?

Previous versions of files are either shadow copies or backup copies of files stored on your computer. Shadow copies are copies of files that Windows automatically saves as part of a restore point. Windows creates restore points every day and just before an important change is made to your computer. Backup copies are copies of files that you have backed up. For more information on restore points, see the top of page 293. To back up files on your computer, see page 296.

Tip

How do I restore a file I accidentally deleted?

If you cannot find the file you want to restore in the Recycle Bin (see page 52), right-click the folder that once contained the file and then click **Restore previous versions** from the menu that appears. In the dialog box that appears, double-click the most recent version of the folder that contained the file. A window appears, displaying the contents of the folder. Drag the file you want to restore to your desktop to restore a copy of the file.

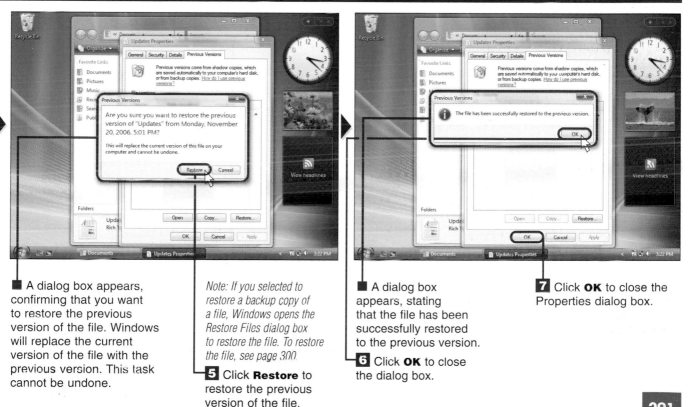

■ A dialog box appears, confirming that you want to restore the previous version of the file. Windows will replace the current version of the file with the previous version. This task cannot be undone.

Note: If you selected to restore a backup copy of a file, Windows opens the Restore Files dialog box to restore the file. To restore the file, see page 300.

5 Click **Restore** to restore the previous version of the file.

■ A dialog box appears, stating that the file has been successfully restored to the previous version.

6 Click **OK** to close the dialog box.

7 Click **OK** to close the Properties dialog box.

RESTORE YOUR COMPUTER

If you are experiencing problems with your computer, you can use the System Restore feature to return your computer to a time before the problems occurred.

For example, if your computer does not work properly after you install a program, you can restore your computer to a time before you installed the program.

RESTORE YOUR COMPUTER

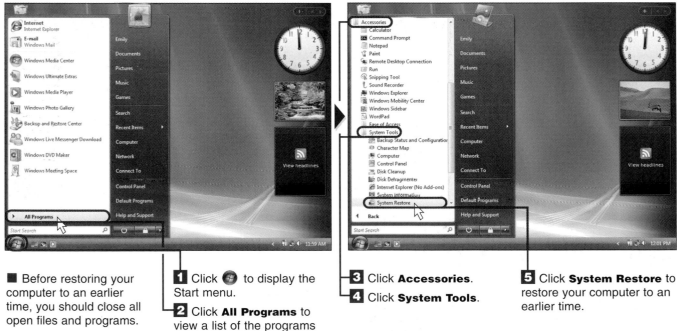

■ Before restoring your computer to an earlier time, you should close all open files and programs.

1 Click 🟠 to display the Start menu.

2 Click **All Programs** to view a list of the programs on your computer.

3 Click **Accessories**.

4 Click **System Tools**.

5 Click **System Restore** to restore your computer to an earlier time.

Tip

How does System Restore work?

System Restore uses restore points to return your computer to a time before any problems occurred. A restore point is an earlier time that you can return your computer to. Windows automatically creates restore points every day and just before an important change is made to your computer, such as before you install a new program.

Tip

Can I choose which date and time I want to restore my computer to?

Yes. To choose the date and time you want to restore your computer to, perform steps **1** to **6** below to display the System Restore wizard. Click **Choose a different restore point** and then click **Next** to continue. Click the restore point created just before the date and time you started experiencing computer problems and then click **Next** to continue. Click **Finish** to start the restore process.

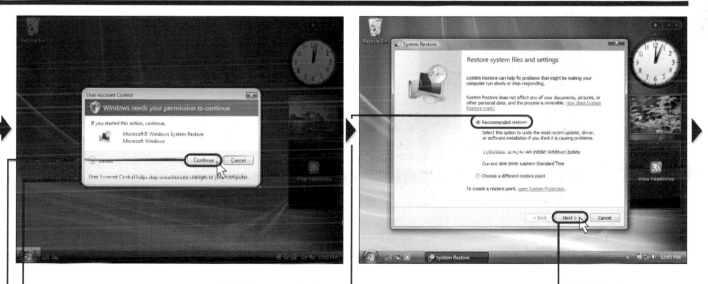

■ The User Account Control dialog box appears, stating that Windows needs your permission to continue to prevent unauthorized changes to your computer.

6 Click **Continue** to continue.

*Note: If you are not using an administrator account, you must type an administrator password and then click **OK** to be able to continue. For information on administrator accounts and passwords, see pages 184 and 188.*

■ The System Restore wizard appears.

7 Click this option to restore your computer to a date and time just before the most recent important change was made to your computer (⊙ changes to ⊙). Windows recommends this option.

Note: To restore your computer to a different date and time, see the top of this page.

8 Click **Next** to continue.

CONTINUED

RESTORE YOUR COMPUTER

When you restore your computer to an earlier time, you will not lose any of your personal files, such as your documents, photos or e-mail messages.

Since System Restore does not affect your personal files, System Restore cannot help you recover lost, deleted or damaged files.

RESTORE YOUR COMPUTER (CONTINUED)

■ This area displays the date and time your computer will be restored to.

9 Click **Finish** to restore your computer.

■ A dialog box appears, stating that once Windows starts restoring your computer, the task cannot be interrupted and cannot be undone until after the restoration is complete.

10 Click **Yes** to continue.

*Note: If you do not want to continue, click **No**.*

Will I need to re-install any programs after restoring my computer?

When you restore your computer to an earlier time, any programs you installed after that date are typically uninstalled. Files you created using the program will not be deleted, but you may need to re-install the program to work with the files again.

Can I reverse the changes made when I restored my computer to an earlier time?

Yes. Any changes that the System Restore feature makes to your computer are completely reversible. To undo your last restoration, perform steps **1** to **6** starting on page 292 to display the System Restore wizard. Click **Choose a different restore point** and then click **Next** to continue. Click the **Undo: Restore Operation** restore point and then click **Next** to continue. Click **Finish** to start the restore process.

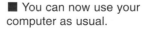

■ When the restoration is complete, a dialog box appears, indicating that the restoration was completed successfully.

11 Click **Close** to close the dialog box.

■ You can now use your computer as usual.

BACK UP YOUR FILES

Backing up important information from your computer to a storage device, such as an external hard drive, CD or DVD, allows you to rest easy, knowing your information is safe.

If your computer's hard drive fails, you may lose valuable information stored on your computer. If you have backed up the information, you can use the backup copy to restore the information to your computer.

BACK UP YOUR FILES

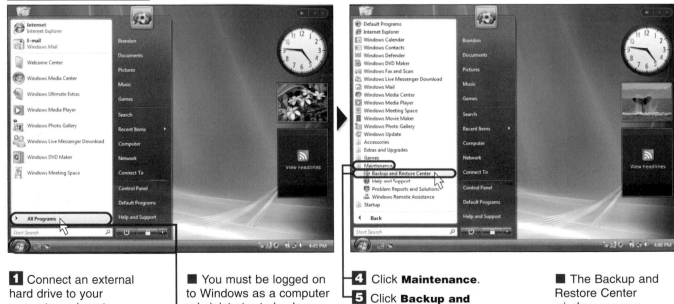

1 Connect an external hard drive to your computer or insert a CD or DVD into your computer's drive.

Note: If a dialog box appears, click ▬✗▬ *to continue.*

■ You must be logged on to Windows as a computer administrator to back up your files. See page 191 to log on to Windows.

2 Click 🔵 to display the Start menu.

3 Click **All Programs**.

4 Click **Maintenance**.

5 Click **Backup and Restore Center**.

■ The Backup and Restore Center window appears.

Tip

How can I back up the entire contents of my computer?

Backing up your entire computer is useful in case your computer is stolen or damaged. You can use the backup to recreate all your files and settings. Perform steps **1** to **7** below, except click **Back up computer** in step **6**. Then click **Start backup** and follow the instructions on your screen to back up your entire computer.

Note: You cannot back up your entire computer if you use the Windows Vista Home Basic or Home Premium edition.

Tip

Can I run another backup at any time?

Yes. After the first time you back up your files, you no longer need to perform all the steps described below. Perform steps **1** to **7** below to open the Backup and Restore Center window and back up your files using the same settings as your last backup.

6 To back up files on your computer, click **Back up files**.

■ The User Account Control dialog box appears, stating that Windows needs your permission to continue to prevent unauthorized changes to your computer.

7 Click **Continue** to continue.

■ The Back Up Files wizard appears.

■ This area displays the location where you will store your backup. You can click this area to select a different storage location for your backup.

8 Click **Next** to continue.

CONTINUED

BACK UP YOUR FILES

You can choose the types of files you want Windows to back up, such as pictures, music, videos and more.

You should back up any files that would be difficult to replace, such as digital photos, music, e-mail messages and important documents.

BACK UP YOUR FILES (CONTINUED)

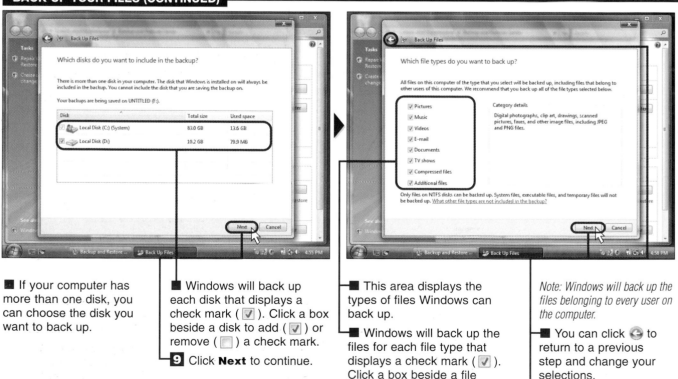

■ If your computer has more than one disk, you can choose the disk you want to back up.

■ Windows will back up each disk that displays a check mark (✓). Click a box beside a disk to add (✓) or remove (☐) a check mark.

9 Click **Next** to continue.

■ This area displays the types of files Windows can back up.

■ Windows will back up the files for each file type that displays a check mark (✓). Click a box beside a file type to add (✓) or remove (☐) a check mark.

Note: Windows will back up the files belonging to every user on the computer.

■ You can click ◉ to return to a previous step and change your selections.

10 Click **Next** to continue.

Tip

Can I change the settings used for backing up my files?

Yes. If you want to change the location where you will store the backup, the type of files that will be backed up or the backup schedule, perform steps **1** to **5** on page 296 to open the Backup and Restore Center window. Click **Change settings** and then click **Change backup settings** in the dialog box that appears. Click **Continue** and then follow the instructions on your screen to change your backup settings.

Tip

How can I keep my backups safe?

You should store the device on which your backup is stored, such as an external hard drive, CD or DVD, in a safe, fireproof location away from your computer. Storing your backups away from your computer helps to ensure that the backups will be useful in the event of a fire or the theft of your computer. You may also want to have more than one device on which you store your backups, in case something happens to one backup device.

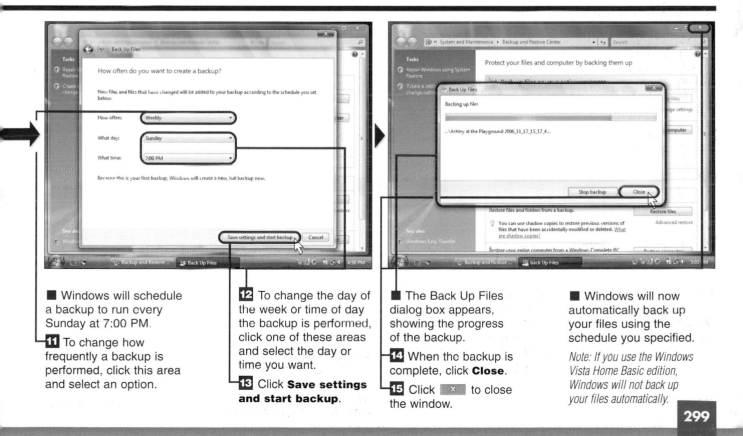

■ Windows will schedule a backup to run every Sunday at 7:00 PM.

11 To change how frequently a backup is performed, click this area and select an option.

12 To change the day of the week or time of day the backup is performed, click one of these areas and select the day or time you want.

13 Click **Save settings and start backup**.

■ The Back Up Files dialog box appears, showing the progress of the backup.

14 When the backup is complete, click **Close**.

15 Click ✕ to close the window.

■ Windows will now automatically back up your files using the schedule you specified.

Note: If you use the Windows Vista Home Basic edition, Windows will not back up your files automatically.

RESTORE BACKED UP FILES

If files on your computer are lost or damaged, you can use a backup you created to restore the files to your computer.

For information on backing up files on your computer, see page 296.

RESTORE BACKED UP FILES

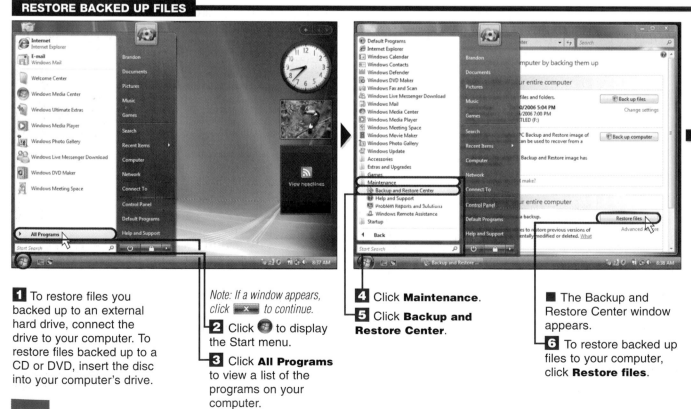

1 To restore files you backed up to an external hard drive, connect the drive to your computer. To restore files backed up to a CD or DVD, insert the disc into your computer's drive.

Note: If a window appears, click [×] *to continue.*

2 Click 🟦 to display the Start menu.

3 Click **All Programs** to view a list of the programs on your computer.

4 Click **Maintenance**.

5 Click **Backup and Restore Center**.

■ The Backup and Restore Center window appears.

6 To restore backed up files to your computer, click **Restore files**.

Tip

Can I restore files from an older backup?

Yes, you can restore files that were backed up at any time. Perform steps **1** to **8** below, except click **Files from an older backup** in step **7**. A list of available backups appears. Click the backup you want to restore files from. Click **Next** and then continue performing steps **9** to **16** starting below.

Tip

Can I restore an entire folder that I have backed up?

You can restore entire folders that you previously backed up. This is useful if you accidentally deleted a folder that you still need. Restoring a folder automatically restores all the files within the folder. Perform the steps starting below, except select **Add folders** in step **9**.

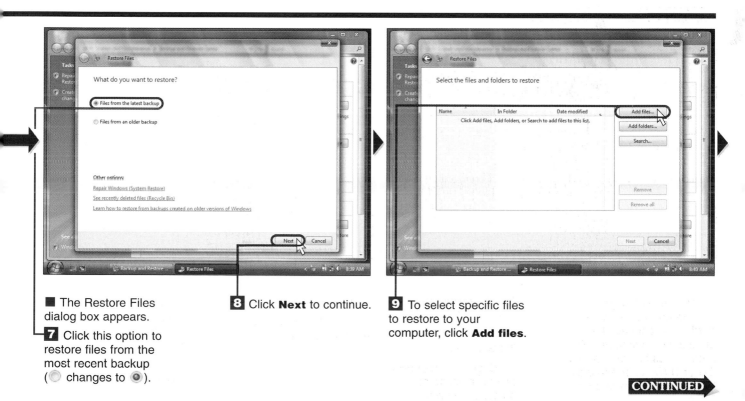

■ The Restore Files dialog box appears.

7 Click this option to restore files from the most recent backup (○ changes to ◉).

8 Click **Next** to continue.

9 To select specific files to restore to your computer, click **Add files**.

CONTINUED

RESTORE BACKED UP FILES

When restoring files from a backup, you can choose the files you want to copy to your computer. You can also choose the location where you want to copy the files on your computer.

You may want to save the files you are restoring in a new location so that you do not accidentally overwrite any files that you wanted to keep.

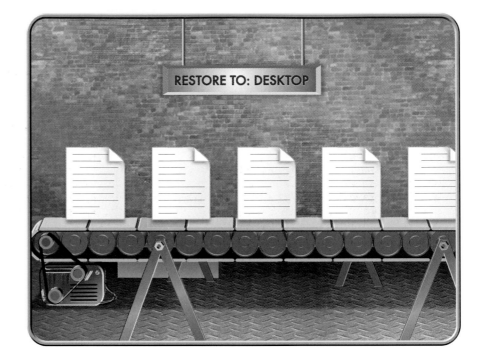

RESTORE TO: DESKTOP

RESTORE BACKED UP FILES (CONTINUED)

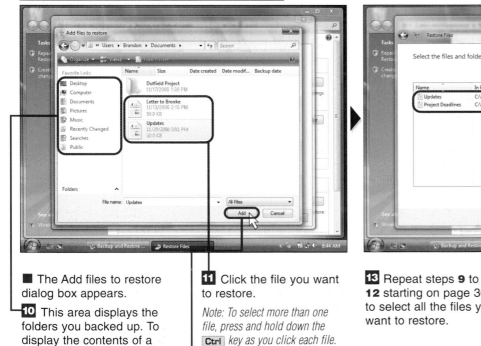

■ The Add files to restore dialog box appears.

10 This area displays the folders you backed up. To display the contents of a folder, click the folder.

11 Click the file you want to restore.

Note: To select more than one file, press and hold down the Ctrl *key as you click each file.*

12 Click **Add** to continue.

13 Repeat steps **9** to **12** starting on page 301 to select all the files you want to restore.

■ This area displays all the files you will restore to your computer.

14 Click **Next** to continue.

Tip

When restoring files, do I have to overwrite the existing files on my computer with the backed up versions?

No. If Windows finds a file in the location where you chose to restore your files with the same name as a file you are restoring, a dialog box appears asking what you want Windows to do. You can choose to replace the file on your computer with the one you are copying, leave the file on your computer as it is and not copy the new file or rename the file you are copying and keep both files.

Tip

Can I restore my entire computer?

If you have backed up the entire contents of your computer (see the top of page 297), you can use the backup to restore your entire computer in the event of a hard drive failure. You will need your Windows installation CD to perform the restore. Before performing a complete restore on your computer, you should seek the advice and guidance of a computer professional.

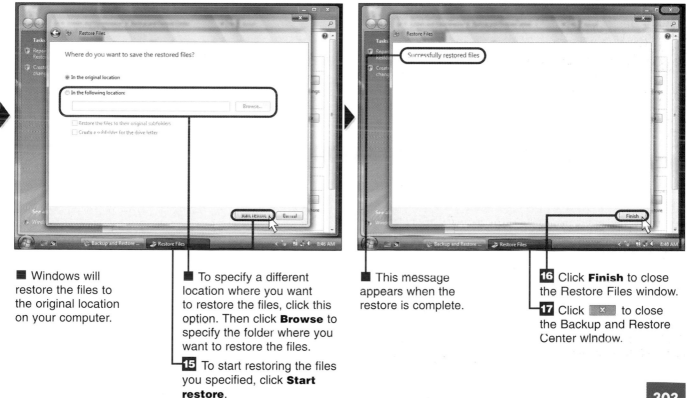

■ Windows will restore the files to the original location on your computer.

■ To specify a different location where you want to restore the files, click this option. Then click **Browse** to specify the folder where you want to restore the files.

15 To start restoring the files you specified, click **Start restore**.

■ This message appears when the restore is complete.

16 Click **Finish** to close the Restore Files window.

17 Click ⊠ to close the Backup and Restore Center window.

303

INDEX

INDEX

INDEX

INDEX

INDEX

Did you like this book? MARAN ILLUSTRATED™ also offers books on the most popular computer topics, using the same easy-to-use format of this book. We always say that if you like one of our books, you'll love the rest of our books too!

Here's a list of some of our best-selling computer titles:

Guided Tour Series - 240 pages, Full Color

MARAN ILLUSTRATED's Guided Tour series features a friendly disk character that walks you through each task step by step. The full-color screen shots are larger than in any of our other series and are accompanied by clear, concise instructions.

	ISBN	Price
MARAN ILLUSTRATED™ Computers Guided Tour	1-59200-880-1	$24.99 US/$33.95 CDN
MARAN ILLUSTRATED™ Windows XP Guided Tour	1-59200-886-0	$24.99 US/$33.95 CDN

MARAN ILLUSTRATED™ Series - 320 pages, Full Color

This series covers 30% more content than our Guided Tour series. Learn new software fast using our step-by-step approach and easy-to-understand text. Learning programs has never been this easy!

	ISBN	Price
MARAN ILLUSTRATED™ Access 2003	1-59200-872-0	$24.99 US/$33.95 CDN
MARAN ILLUSTRATED™ Computers	1-59200-874-7	$24.99 US/$33.95 CDN
MARAN ILLUSTRATED™ Excel 2003	1-59200-876-3	$24.99 US/$33.95 CDN
MARAN ILLUSTRATED™ Mac OS® X v.10.4 Tiger™	1-59200-878-X	$24.99 US/$33.95 CDN
MARAN ILLUSTRATED™ Office 2003	1-59200-890-9	$29.99 US/$39.95 CDN
MARAN ILLUSTRATED™ Windows XP	1-59200-870-4	$24.99 US/$33.95 CDN

101 Hot Tips Series - 240 pages, Full Color

Progress beyond the basics with MARAN ILLUSTRATED's 101 Hot Tips series. This series features 101 of the coolest shortcuts, tricks and tips that will help you work faster and easier.

	ISBN	Price
MARAN ILLUSTRATED™ Windows XP 101 Hot Tips	1-59200-882-8	$19.99 US/$26.95 CDN

MARAN ILLUSTRATED™ **Piano** is an information-packed resource for people who want to learn to play the piano, as well as current musicians looking to hone their skills. Combining full-color photographs and easy-to-follow instructions, this guide covers everything from the basics of piano playing to more advanced techniques. Not only does MARAN ILLUSTRATED™ Piano show you how to read music, play scales and chords and improvise while playing with other musicians, it also provides you with helpful information for purchasing and caring for your piano.

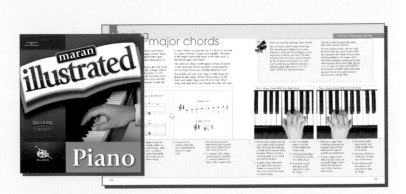

ISBN: 1-59200-864-X

Price: $24.99 US; $33.95 CDN

Page count: 304

MARAN ILLUSTRATED™ **Dog Training** is an excellent guide for both current dog owners and people considering making a dog part of their family. Using clear, step-by-step instructions accompanied by over 400 full-color photographs, MARAN ILLUSTRATED™ Dog Training is perfect for any visual learner who prefers seeing what to do rather than reading lengthy explanations.

Beginning with insights into popular dog breeds and puppy development, this book emphasizes positive training methods to guide you through socializing, housetraining and teaching your dog many commands. You will also learn how to work with problem behaviors, such as destructive chewing.

ISBN: 1-59200-858-5

Price: $19.99 US; $26.95 CDN

Page count: 256

MARAN ILLUSTRATED™ **Knitting & Crocheting** contains a wealth of information about these two increasingly popular crafts. Whether you are just starting out or you are an experienced knitter or crocheter interested in picking up new tips and techniques, this information-packed resource will take you from the basics, such as how to hold the knitting needles or crochet hook, to more advanced skills, such as how to add decorative touches to your projects. The easy-to-follow information is communicated through clear, step-by-step instructions and accompanied by over 600 full-color photographs—perfect for any visual learner.

ISBN: 1-59200-862-3

Price: $24.99 US; $33.95 CDN

Page count: 304

MARAN ILLUSTRATED™ **Yoga** provides a wealth of simplified, easy-to-follow information about the increasingly popular practice of Yoga. This easy-to-use guide is a must for visual learners who prefer to see and do without having to read lengthy explanations.

Using clear, step-by-step instructions accompanied by over 500 full-color photographs, this book includes all the information you need to get started with yoga or to enhance your technique if you have already made yoga a part of your life. MARAN ILLUSTRATED™ Yoga shows you how to safely and effectively perform a variety of yoga poses at various skill levels, how to breathe more efficiently and much more.

ISBN: 1-59200-868-2

Price: $24.99 US; $33.95 CDN

Page count: 320

MARAN ILLUSTRATED™ Weight Training is an information-packed guide that covers all the basics of weight training, as well as more advanced techniques and exercises.

MARAN ILLUSTRATED™ Weight Training contains more than 500 full-color photographs of exercises for every major muscle group, along with clear, step-by-step instructions for performing the exercises. Useful tips provide additional information and advice to help enhance your weight training experience.

MARAN ILLUSTRATED™ Weight Training provides all the information you need to start weight training or to refresh your technique if you have been weight training for some time.

ISBN: 1-59200-866-6
Price: $24.99 US; $33.95 CDN
Page count: 320

MARAN ILLUSTRATED™ Cooking Basics is an information-packed resource that covers all the basics of cooking. Novices and experienced cooks alike will find useful information about setting up and stocking your kitchen as well as food preparation and cooking techniques. With over 500 full-color photographs illustrating the easy-to-follow, step-by-step instructions, this book is a must-have for anyone who prefers seeing what to do rather than reading long explanations.

MARAN ILLUSTRATED™ Cooking Basics also provides over 40 recipes from starters, salads and side-dishes to main course dishes and baked goods. Each recipe uses only 10 ingredients or less, and is complete with nutritional information and tips covering tasty variations and commonly asked questions.

ISBN: 1-59863-234-5
Price: $19.99 US; $26.95 CDN
Page count: 240

MARAN ILLUSTRATED™ Puppies is a valuable resource to a wide range of readers—from individuals picking out their first puppy to those who are looking to correct their new puppy's most challenging behaviors.

This full-color guide, containing over 400 photographs, walks you step by step through finding a breeder and choosing your puppy from the litter. You will then learn how to use positive training methods to work with your puppy on housetraining, socialization and many obedience commands. MARAN ILLUSTRATED™ Puppies will also show you how to use tricks and games to teach your puppy good manners and prevent problem behaviors before they start.

ISBN: 1-59863-283-3
Price: $19.99 US; $26.95 CDN
Page count: 240

MARAN ILLUSTRATED™ Guitar is an excellent resource for people who want to learn to play the guitar, as well as for current musicians who want to fine tune their technique. This full-color guide includes over 500 photographs, accompanied by step-by-step instructions that teach you the basics of playing the guitar and reading music, as well as advanced guitar techniques. You will also learn what to look for when purchasing a guitar or accessories, how to maintain and repair your guitar, and much more.

Whether you want to learn to strum your favorite tunes or play professionally, MARAN ILLUSTRATED™ Guitar provides all the information you need to become a proficient guitarist.

ISBN: 1-59200-860-7
Price: $24.99 US; $33.95 CDN
Page count: 320

MARAN ILLUSTRATED™ Effortless Algebra
is an indispensable resource packed
with crucial concepts and step-by-step
instructions that make learning algebra
simple. This guide is perfect for those who
wish to gain a thorough understanding of
algebra's concepts, from the most basic
calculations to more complex operations.

Clear instructions thoroughly explain every
topic and each concept is accompanied by
helpful illustrations. This book provides all
of the information you will need to fully
grasp algebra. MARAN ILLUSTRATED™
Effortless Algebra also provides an
abundance of practice examples and
tests to put your knowledge into practice.

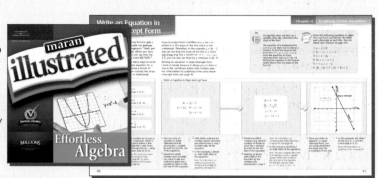

ISBN: 1-59200-942-5
Price: $24.99 US; $33.95 CDN
Page count: 304

MARAN ILLUSTRATED™ Wine is an
indispensable guide for your journey
into the world of wine. The information-
packed resource is ideal for people who
are just beginning to explore wine as
well as for wine enthusiasts who want
to expand their knowledge.

This full-color guide, containing
hundreds of photographs, walks you step
by step through tasting and serving wine,
reading a wine label and creating a wine
collection. You will also find in-depth
information about the wines of the world.
MARAN ILLUSTRATED™ Wine will also
introduce you to sparkling wines and
Champagne as well as fortified and sweet
wines. You will learn the basics of how
wine is made, how to pair the right wine
with your meal and much more.

ISBN: 1-59863-318-X
Price: $24.99 US; $33.95 CDN
Page count: 288

MARAN ILLUSTRATED™ Bartending
is the perfect book for those who want to
impress their guests with cocktails that are
both eye-catching and delicious. This
indispensable guide explains everything
you need to know about bartending in
the most simple and easy-to-follow terms.
Maran Illustrated™ Bartending has recipes,
step-by-step instructions and over 400
full-color photographs of all the hottest
martinis, shooters, blended drinks and
warmers. This guide also includes a
section on wine, beer and alcohol-free
cocktails as well as information on all
of the tools, liquor and other supplies
you will need to start creating drinks
right away!

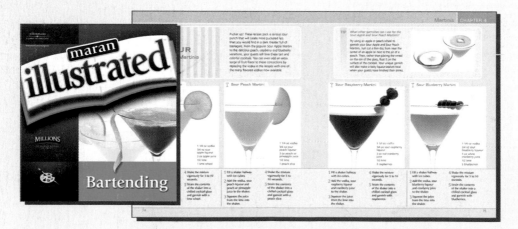

ISBN: 1-59200-944-1
Price: $19.99 US; $26.95 CDN
Page count: 256